THE BRITISH SEAMAN

The
British Seaman

1200-1860

A SOCIAL SURVEY

By

CHRISTOPHER LLOYD

Late Professor of History
Royal Naval College
Greenwich

RUTHERFORD • MADISON • TEANECK

FAIRLEIGH DICKINSON UNIVERSITY PRESS

ISBN: 0-8386-7708-8

Printed in the United States of America

Contents

Illustrations

For Michael Lewis

Introduction

ON THE EVE of the battle of Waterloo the Duke of Wellington said to Creevey, pointing to a soldier, "There, it all depends on that article whether we do the business or not. Give me enough of it and I am sure." Every admiral for the past five hundred years would agree with him.

It is strange that in spite of innumerable books about battles and ships and tactics, the biographies of admirals and histories of sea-power, even more recently the valuable studies of the naval profession and of naval administration, there has been so little written about the British seaman himself. The "people," as the ship's company came to be called, remain an anonymous mass, too often neglected by those in authority because of the gulf between the lower deck and the quarter-deck. Of all sections of the community, seafaring men and agricultural labourers have been the most ignored and therefore the worst treated.

This book aims at giving an account of those who "used the sea" in the days of sail from the earliest times to the eighteen-sixties, when the establishment of continuous service and of a naval reserve, together with the introduction of steam, fundamentally altered conditions in both the naval and merchant services. Only occasionally is it possible to discern through the mists of the past the identity of an individual seaman, to say what he looked like, who was his father, where he came from, because (like the farm labourer) he was usually illiterate and inarticulate. On the other hand, it is possible, though not always easy, to discover a good deal about how he lived. Hence in this book I have tried to find out how many of them there were, how they were recruited for the naval service, why such service was so unpopular, how they were fed, paid and treated. The modern distinction between the merchant seaman and the naval rating is virtually meaningless during the period with which we are concerned. It only emerged about the time of the Crimean War with the establishment of continuous service, in other words of a regular standing navy.

Anyone who has studied social history of this sort knows to his cost that the two principal difficulties are the paucity of reliable statistics and the fact that more survives of what may be called the bad side of history than the good. Hells afloat occupy more space in the records than happy ships simply because of the mistakes, crimes and mutinies which occurred on board them. Sailors have always been grumblers, usually with good reason. As fighting men they have written some of the most glorious pages in our history, but such services do not appear in the files of administrators. In their petitions or their few surviving journals and letters it is the darker side of life at sea which is usually painted. To redress the balance it is well to bear in mind Nelson's saying: "Aft the more honour: for'ard the better man." Not the least of Nelson's legacies to the nation was that by his victories he enhanced the prestige of hitherto despised members of society. It is significant that they are still called "hands."

More has been written about life in the navy than on board merchant ships because naval records are so much fuller, though even these are incomplete and often contradictory. My intention has been to impose some sort of form and image on this amorphous mass of "hands" by expressing, whenever possible, the voice of the lower deck. It is a book about mariners and seamen, not about officers or operations.

Much of it is therefore about impressment and its consequences. The press gang has become part of the folklore of

English history, so that it is usually regarded as a typical example of eighteenth century brutality. In fact, it goes back to remote medieval times and forward into the twentieth century, when it is called conscription or national service, and the methods of implementing it are both more polite and more effective. The only book on the subject, which was published in 1913, draws a false picture of its incidence because it was written to oppose compulsory service. It ends with a pathetic sentence: "A people who for a hundred years patiently endured conscription in its most cruel form will never again suffer it to be lightly inflicted upon them." Three years later it was introduced once more, in a modern form but on the same principle on which five hundred years ago feudal service was required.

To explain the necessity of impressment it is necessary to describe conditions afloat, which made the navy so unpopular with professional seamen from the earliest times. As the mutineers complained in the first recorded court martial— that on board the *Golden Lion* in 1587—"We were pressed by her Majesty to have her allowance and not to be thus dealt withal: you make no men of us, but beasts." Almost the same words may be found in lower deck writers of Nelson's generation: "they look upon us like dogs, though not so good," complains a correspondent whose letter is here printed for the first time.

It was only when the navy became smaller and manners changed in early Victorian times that life at sea improved, because there was no longer any need to have recourse to pressing. It required a series of stringent Merchant Shipping Acts before things changed for the better in the merchant service, owing to the avarice of owners. If it took the Admiralty fifty years to introduce lemon juice to combat scurvy, it took the merchant navy twice as long. Perhaps the most relevant lesson to be drawn from our story is the obvious one, though so often neglected in the past for reasons of false economy, that recruiting is only possible when conditions are made attractive.

Something should be said about the plan on which this book is written. For the earlier centuries, where records are sparse, I have tried to give a general picture of the mariner (as he was usually called), together with the sort of detail which alone makes social history valid as well as interesting. Facts rather than trends are the stuff of such history, however selective one is compelled to be, and however much one must crave the indulgence of the reader for the inadequacy of the statistics. Thenceforward, when records become more abundant and the demands on the nation's manpower increase with the expansion of trade together with the extension of wars at sea, the chapters are devoted to more specific topics such as the nature of the manning problem, the legality of the means taken to solve it, the wastage due to disease and desertion on account of conditions prevailing on board, and the reasons why impressment fell into abeyance in the nineteenth century, only to be revived in a different form in modern times.

I

The Medieval Mariner

"NO FREEMAN shall be taken or imprisoned or diseised or exiled or in any way destroyed, nor will we go upon him nor will we send upon him, except by the lawful judgement of his peers or the law of the land."

Centuries later lawyers quoted Magna Carta in protests against the incidence of impressment for the navy. But in the feudal context of his society the medieval mariner was not a free man. He was as much a part of the ship owned by his master or his lord as the standing rigging. His employment in the service of the Crown was a feudal obligation based on military tenure dating back to Anglo-Saxon times and lasting, at least in theory, until those of the Stuarts.

On the first page of Domesday Book it is written that the town of Dover, in return for the privileges of sac and soc, owes the King ship service for twenty ships for fifteen days, as in the time of Edward the Confessor. The same holds for Sandwich, and five ships were due from the other towns which became the confederation of the Cinque Ports. By the thirteenth century these towns were liable for upwards of fifty ships. Just as the barons supplied the knights, and the knights provided the soldiers for the army, so the Barons of the Cinque Ports (until they became boroughs) were responsible for the ships and crews engaged in fighting in the Narrow Seas.

At one time or another various monarchs possessed ships

or galleys of their own Navy Royal, as distinct from all the ships in the country which formed the Navy of Britain. But there is no continuity in medieval naval history, no administrative structure and no consistency in policy. The most permanent collection of ships and men belonged to the Cinque Ports of Dover, Hastings, Sandwich, Hythe and Romney, to which were added the "ancient towns" of Rye and Winchelsea. Early in John's reign charters conferring privileges and exemptions from tolls and taxes were granted to these ports, so that something in the nature of a confederation began to develop. The Lord Warden was held responsible for enforcing writs and mandates, each ward of a port provided a ship and each landlord contributed a crew, the port paying each man's wages. An ordinance of 1229 lists the services due from Hastings as six ships, each containing twenty-one men and a gromet (someone between a man and a boy, from the Dutch word meaning youth), ten from Winchelsea, five from Rye, five from Romney, five from Hythe, twenty-one from Dover, five from Sandwich, totalling fifty-seven ships with 1,167 men for fifteen days' service at the cost of the Ports: if retained longer, at that of the Crown.[1] As late as the year of the Armada the Ports sent out five ships at their own cost.

Since the population of these places consisted of fishermen or pirates (or both), it was easy for the King to "arrest" the ships likely to be of service in his interminable wars with France. The words used are either *arrêter* or *ordonner* and it is this element of compulsion which lies at the root of the word *impressment*. Derived from the Old French *empresser*, it meant commandeering or arresting ships and men for the public service. But it became confused with the word *imprest* (or *emprest*), meaning money lent in advance called *imprest money*. When this took the form of a *prest* or token payment on enlistment, such as the King's shilling, any man accepting it was *pressed* and henceforward liable to service, though it remained doubtful if this included service overseas. The suggestion that he was thereby made ready for service (implying another root for impressment as a derivation from *prêt*, i.e. ready) cannot be supported in a semantic sense. In a sociological sense, the King's right to arrest men and shipping to implement service due was accepted as the military basis of feudalism.

Anglo-Saxon rulers frequently pressed men into their service, but they usually built their own ships. The Normans preferred to employ the ships of their subjects with their Anglo-Saxon crews. When naval activity became more frequent after the crusade of Richard I in 1189, or after John's loss of Normandy in 1204, the privilege to arrest ships and men was more commonly exercised.

Some have regarded John as the founder of the Royal Navy because of the naval activity which marks his reign, though it did him little good. He was certainly the first monarch to demand the salute in the Narrow Seas, thus making a bid for the Sovereignty of the Seas. He was the first to appreciate the value of a standing navy of his own, and hence the first to appoint a Clerk of the Ships under the title of Keeper of the King's Ports and Galleys in the person of William de Wrotham, Archdeacon of Taunton. This key administrative post later became known as the Clerk of the Acts and in the days of Pepys was virtually amalgamated with that of Secretary of the Admiralty. Nevertheless, on John's death the whole organisation fell to pieces. His ships were sold and a Navy Royal ceased to exist. The same thing happened on the death of Henry V, the only other medieval monarch to possess a sizable navy of his own, who at one time owned thirty-eight royal ships.

The first order to arrest ships and men in John's reign was sent to the bailiffs, reeves and King's representatives at various ports in 1205. Thus Yarmouth, Orford and Beccles were told to send two rectors (shipmasters) and 140 mariners to London to take charge of two of the royal ships lying in the Thames.

A payment of one hundred marks was promised, together with half of the value of any prizes taken. Similar steps were taken the next year, and in 1207 the arrest was extended to all ships at sea, English or foreign, the duty of the king's liege subjects being to assist the Barons of the Cinque Ports if any resistance was offered. In 1208 all seamen on the coast of Wales were ordered to repair to Ilfracombe in Devonshire on pain of hanging or sequestration of goods.[2]

The words used in such writs include *sturmanni* (probably masters, if not pilots), *marinelli*, *nautae* and *galioti*. The latter were clearly galley rowers, who in England, though not in the Mediterranean, were not slaves. *Marinelli* and *nautae* were what we should call sailors, but one cannot discover any difference between them. Usually the men involved were mariners, though occasionally they included shipwrights. In the lawyer's dog Latin of one such writ, in order to man the admiral's barge sheriffs were instructed to arrest *bonos et abiles marinarios pro sufficienti skippagio bargae*.[3]

Until the seventeenth century the most common word in use was "mariner." "Seaman" may have been older, as its Anglo-Saxon form suggests, but it does not appear in written English until the appearance in 1436 of the first treatise on naval policy, *The Libelle of English Policie*. Would that the authors of some modern strategic works might suffer the same fate as its supposed author, Adam de Moleyns, Bishop of Chichester, who was murdered by Portsmouth seamen in a dispute about pay! The word makes an occasional appearance in Tudor times, as in the act of 1540 for "the maintenance of many masters, mariners and seamen," but in Elizabeth's day the word "sailor" was beginning to come into use, though it was not common for another hundred years.

According to Sir Richard Hawkins, writing at the end of her reign, the word "mariner" "ought not to be given but to the man who is able to build his ship, to fit and provide her of all things necessary, and after to carry her about the world;

the residue to be but sailors", that is to say, those that manage the sails.⁴ This distinction was seldom made in practice, though wherever mariners and sailors are mentioned in the same document the writer must have had it in mind. By 1627, according to Captain John Smith's *Sea Grammar*, the sailor is "the older man who hoists the sails and the younker is the younger man called foremast man to take in top sails etc." The word "mariner" is not mentioned, and the early spelling of the word as *sayler* suggests its origin.

Drake's famous sermon in the course of his circumnavigation, distinguishing between the amateur seamen on board and the professionals, uses two words for the same man:

> "Here is such a controversy between the sailors and the gentlemen, and such stomaching between the gentlemen and the sailors, that it doth even make me mad to hear it. But, my masters, I must have it left, for I must have the gentlemen to haul and draw with the mariners, and the mariners with the gentlemen. What, let us show ourselves to be all of one company and let us not give occasion to the enemy to rejoice at our decay and overthrow."

Golden words, which found the tradition of a happy ship and a united ship's company, but unintelligible in the Middle Ages when the soldiers put on board by the king did all the fighting and the mariners attended to the working of the ship. After the introduction of firearms at sea (in 1410 the *Christopher of the Tower* mounted three cannon and a hand gun), the gunner appeared to manage these new devilish weapons of destruction. English ships had not yet developed that hierarchy of officers already known in the Mediterranean, but from an early date there is mention of a rector or master, a constable or boatswain, a lodesman or pilot, a trumpeter and a carpenter; steward, purser and cook appear soon after. In the first document to give the proportion of men to tonnage in 1324 it is stated that a 240-ton ship should carry sixty mariners, one master and two constables.⁵ In addition, there should be a proportion of gromets and boys. In tracing the evolution of the naval profession, it is significant that those who were to become commissioned officers appointed to give orders where to sail and how to fight—admiral, captain, lieutenant—should have Anglo-Norman names, whereas those who worked the ship had Anglo-Saxon names—boat-swain, coxswain (cogswain i.e. the man in charge of a small boat or cog), lodesman (pilot), seaman. The business of fighting was left to the soldiers and archers on board, but from what little we know of the character of the medieval mariner we can imagine that, to say the least, he lent a hand.

Our view of such an anonymous person as the seaman of those days must perforce remain vague. He was already apparently regarded as belonging to a race apart from the landman (or landsman, as the word began to be spelled in the nineteenth century). His rolling gait, his weather-beaten face, the strange jargon he talked about "the mystery of the sea" marked him distinctly, though his voyages were short and his numbers small. A scrap from a primitive shanty suggests his tough, carefree disposition—

> Hale and howe rumbylowe
> Stir well the good ship and let the wind blow.

We know far more about how an army was raised, where the archers, foot-soldiers and men-at-arms came from and how many were shipped abroad for service in the Hundred Years War, than we do about those engaged in what Froissart calls the "very murderous and horrible" naval battles of Sluys or Les Espagnols sur Mer. Thus the army at Agincourt, which was transported from Southampton in 1,400 vessels of all types, is said to have consisted of 6,000 men-at-arms, and 24,000 archers, but the number of seamen is not given. Since each "ship" was supposed to have a crew of forty-eight men and each "balinger" forty, the total must have been in the neighbourhood of 40,000 men. All we have is Henry's order to the captains of the following royal ships ("of the

Tower" signifies H.M.S.) to take up as many mariners as may be necessary:[6]

John Kyngston	*Katherine of the Tower*
William Robinson	*Nicholas of the Tower*
John Piers	*Trinity of the Tower*
John Huterell	*Petite Marie of the Tower*
Stephen Thomas	*Trinity Royal of the Tower*
Hawkins Pitman	*La Rude Cog de la Toure*

In 1346 Edward III provided twenty-five royal ships with 419 mariners out of a total Southern Fleet of 493 ships and 9,650 mariners. The Northern Fleet consisted of 217 ships and 4,521 mariners, giving a grand total of 14,151 men. Eleven years later he commissioned the captains of the following ships to take up specified numbers of mariners and send the refractory to prison:

William Barrett	*Julian*	36 men
John Gobbet	*Margaret*	26 ,,
William Henry	*Nicholas*	24 ,,
William May	*James*	26 ,,
John Burgess	*Gregory*	20 ,,
Stephen Stonyng	*St. Marie Bote*	15 ,,
Simon Stephen	*Michael*	26 ,,
John Lewe	*Joan of Yarmouth*	26 ,,

In 1378 Richard II ordered his Serjeant at Arms to take up one hundred mariners in Essex and conduct them to Sandwich: if any objected their goods were to be seized and the doors of their houses sealed up.[7] Such were the powers of arrest.

It is to this period that Chaucer's Shipman belongs. The description of him in the Prologue to the Canterbury Tales may be dated about 1387 and the poet, as a Customs officer, knew the originals of his composite portrait at Dartmouth— Peter Rishenden, the owner of a vessel called the *Madaleyne*,

and John Hawley, the mayor of the town and a collector of
customs, who was once charged with unlawfully attacking
other ships at sea. When Chaucer calls his Shipman "a good
fellow" he means a "tough customer," and where he says
that he sent his prisoners home by water he refers to the common practice of drowning the enemy. As the master of a ship,
the Shipman is of course much superior to the mariners
impressed by the king, but his ship could also be arrested and
many of the details of his portrait must have been common to
those whom he employed—his sea cloak of falding (a coarse
wool), his experience in the Bordeaux wine trade, his skill in
navigation from Jutland to the coast of Spain, his proclivity
for piracy and smuggling, even his beard shaken by many a
gale, which makes him the prototype of master mariners,
especially those from the West Country who were beginning
to displace those from the Cinque Ports as the backbone of the
navy of England.

> The hoote summer hadde maad his hewe al broun,
> And certainly he was a good felawe.
> Ful many a draughte of wyn had he ydrawe
> Fro Burdeux-ward, whil that the chapman sleep.
> Of nyce conscience took he no keep.
> If that he faught, and hadde the hyer hond,
> By water he sente them hoom, to every lond.
> But of his craft to rekene wel his tydes,
> His stremes, and his daungers hym besides,
> His herbewe, and his moone, his lodemenage,
> Ther has noon swich from Hulle to Cartage.
> Hardy he was, and wys to undertake;
> With many a tempest hadde his berd been shake.

A historian of the medieval navy has said that "the whole
history of the seamen from the thirteenth to the eighteenth
century is one long story of social depression and loss of
privilege."[8] During the Middle Ages a comparatively high
degree of security was guaranteed to the mariner by the adop-

tion of various laws and customs of the sea. As far as this country was concerned, the most important of these were the Laws of Oléron, established here by Eleanor of Aquitaine and confirmed by Richard I on his return from his crusade. This code provided security of tenure and payment, a scale of punishments and a primitive form of welfare. It was inscribed in the book of precedents compiled about 1410 and known by the sinister name of the *Black Book of the Admiralty*, merely on account of the colour of the binding of the earliest version. The amount of food, wine, pay and punishments is minutely specified. If one took such laws at their face value, (and one must recall how easily even in the eighteenth century such Admiralty regulations were circumvented at sea), the mariner was assured of a reasonable status. Every member of the crew had to take an oath to the master of the ship for the voyage. The latter was empowered to retain him until the end of his contract, or pay him his wages and his passage home. Members of the crew were consulted before sailing if the weather was doubtful. They could only be dismissed for theft, brawling or disobedience.

If a man fell sick or was injured, provision must be made for him at a *maison dieu* run by a religious confraternity at most of the bigger ports. The hospital of St. Bartholomew at Sandwich seems to have been the first to be administered by a town on behalf of mariners in 1244. Bart's in London also looked after them. In 1445 a society of mariners at Bristol founded a hospital for twelve men to be maintained by the masters of ships in harbour and a contribution levied from each of the mariners. The reason was said to be that "the crafte off mariners is so aventurous that dayly beying in their viages sore vexed, trobled and deseased and distried, the which by gode menys of prayers and gode werkes might be graciously comforted and better relieved of such trobles."[9]

In 1457 a similar Guild of the Blessed Trinity at Hull established almshouses for thirteen mariners "which by infortune

at sea shall hap to fall in poverty by loss of goods." Since
such charitable institutions received short shrift at the time
of the dissolution of the monasteries and chantries, many had
to be refounded in Elizabethan times.

The rate of pay in John's reign was 2/- a day for an admiral,
1/- for a captain, 7d. for a master and 3d. for a mariner. This
remained constant for a long time. In 1336 it was raised to
3½d. a day and 6d. a week "for consideration" or reward after
the first recorded seamen's strike that year, when impressed
men in Wales refused to sail unless they were paid their wages.
The king said there was no precedent for such a demand, but
graciously granted the "consideration" or bounty, as it came
to be called, provided this was not regarded as regular sea
wages.[10]

In the next year we have the first minutes of the King's
Council relating to the navy, consisting of a commission to
the admiral, Sir John de Roos, to arrest all ships over thirty
tons with their crews. In 1335 a similar commission appointed
the Earl of Arundel admiral, "for no one can chastise and rule
them (the mariners) unless he be a great man." It was precisely for the same reason that Howard of Effingham was
appointed in 1588, the office of Lord Admiral having been a
perquisite of the Howard family for two generations. Prize
money was to be shared between the Crown, the Admiral,
the Owner and the Crew. Pay and reward was the same as
before and a set of Articles of War for disciplinary purposes
was brought up to date. Mariners were to be punished according to the Laws of the Sea, e.g. a fine of £5 or the loss of a
hand for a theft, or a year's imprisonment for refusal to serve
or desertion.[11]

A decline in pay seems to have set in during the fifteenth
century. In 1440 men were paid and victualled at a weekly
rate of 3/- a head. Previously the wage rate had been 1/9
a week, instead of as now 1/6, excluding the sixpenny reward
and the share of prize money. By 1480 weekly wages were

only 1/3 at sea and 1/- in harbour, with a victualling allowance of 1/0½, though there was some provision for clothing in the form of jackets.[12]

Desertion from the King's service by pressed men called for attention from the beginning. In the fleet of Richard I there was a penalty of one year's imprisonment. Under an act passed in the reign of Richard II the penalty remains the same "because that divers mariners after that they be arrested and retained for the King's service upon the sea in defence of the realm, and thereof have received their wages pertaining, do flee out of the said service without licence of the admirals or their lieutenants, to the great danger of the King and his realm, and hindrance of the said voyages."[13]

Most of the provisions of this statute of 1379 were still in force early in the nineteenth century, but the penalty for desertion had increased to that of death, though this was seldom enforced. So were the provisions of the first Navigation Act passed in Richard's reign for the encouragement of that pool of seamen on which the Crown relied for the next four centuries. Other punishments laid down in the Laws of the Sea were more savage. Tarring and feathering, ducking and keel hauling were common for serious crimes. Nailing a man's hand to the mast, or cutting off his right hand for striking an officer or drawing a weapon, or binding a man to the corpse and throwing him overboard in cases of murder were probably less common. For the fourth offence of sleeping on watch, a man "shall be hanged on the bowsprit end of the ship in a basket, with a can of beer, a loaf of bread and a sharp knife, and choose to hang there till he starve, or cut himself into the sea." Such customs were still in force in the time of Henry VIII.

As pressing became more frequent with the sporadic operations of the Hundred Years War, we hear the earliest complaints from the shipping community about interference with trade which are to echo down the centuries. In 1347 the Commons complained that trade was suffering and no compensation had been paid for the arrest of shipping. Subsequent petitions from shipowners and port towns received a dusty answer, usually in the time-honoured governmental phrase that the matter would be looked into—*le roi s'avisera*. But when ships or men on the King's service were interfered with by zealous bailiffs or pressing masters, reprimand was swift.

Protections from impressment originated in this way, because the Crown found it must curb the zeal of its own agents. Passports or certificates of exemption, were therefore issued: "Whereas our beloved merchant Anthony de Pessaing hath sent John le Fraunseys his servant in our ship called the SEYNTEMARIEBOTE laden with victuals, to Scotland, no mariner is to be taken out of the said ship." This was in 1314. In 1337 occurs the first recorded complaint from an individual that he had been unlawfully pressed—on this occasion for the army. Significantly, it is from a lawyer who had been told to equip himself as a man-at-arms and report at Orwell for France. Since he established that he had never borne arms, his summons was dismissed.[14]

Impressment did not become a serious social problem until the seventeenth century because it was accepted as a feudal obligation and the number of men it affected was small. Moreover, much of the fighting that went on at sea had nothing to do with the King. It was either piracy or cross-raiding across the Channel. Sometimes the prey was an English merchant ship, sometimes a Frenchman. During the anarchy of the Hundred Years War the chronicler Walsingham tells how the men of Portsmouth and Dartmouth, "hired by none, bought by none, but spurred only by their own valour," sank enemy vessels in the Seine when the King's ships could do nothing. There must have been a lot of that sort of thing.

By the end of the medieval period, as Hakluyt as well as

many foreign ambassadors complained, the English seaman was regarded throughout Europe as "the most infamous for outrageous, common and daily piracies." In the absence of any consistent naval policy on the part of the state, it was out of this virile and turbulent spirit of piracy and privateering that the Royal Navy was born.

II

The Tudor Mariner

THE NOTION that any people has a natural propensity for the sea, that it has salt in its blood, does not commend itself to the historian. A numerous seafaring population depends on specific geographical advantages and economic necessities. Few men in any age follow the sea of their own accord, or willingly embrace so hard a way of life. In the Middle Ages England was not a seafaring nation, nor can it be said to have become one until the latter part of the sixteenth century.

It is to the Portuguese and the Spaniards of one or at the most two miraculous generations that the credit for opening the ocean routes of the world belongs. They developed the ocean-going ship; they discovered astronomical navigation and drew the charts by which such ships could sail; they were responsible for the geopolitical revolution which brought England and the countries of the western seaboard of Europe into the centre of the world map, instead of being, as heretofore, on the periphery of maritime affairs.

Except for the Cabots, Genoese by birth and Spanish by inclination, English seamen played little part in the first century of exploration. But their voyages were lengthening. Men from Bristol were regularly visiting Iceland. The Newfoundland fishery was fast developing. The Baltic and the Mediterranean were penetrated and by the middle of the century voyages were being made to the coast of West Africa.

As good a date as any for the beginning of the British maritime empire would be 1553, when Willoughby and Chancellor sailed from Greenwich in search of the North West Passage.

The voyage was inspired by Sebastian Cabot, recently returned from a long sojourn in Spain, whither he had been driven by the lack of interest shown in the earlier voyages of himself and his father when the broils of the English Reformation supervened. Until much later, all information about new methods of navigation and gunnery were drawn from Spanish and Italian books. Such notoriously conservative and largely illiterate seamen as the masters of the coasting trade looked askance at new fangled things like charts, quadrants or even the mariner's astrolabe. When William Bourne, a Gravesend innkeeper, printed the first practical manual of navigation, *The Regiment of the Sea*, in 1574, to explain the log-line method of obtaining the longitude and extol the merits of the portolan chart, he complains that the average master preferred to grope his way around the coast "and derided and mocked them that have occupied their cards and plats, and also the observation of the altitude of the Pole, saying that they care not for their sheepskins, for they could keep a better account upon a board," i.e. a traverse board. As late as 1625 Captain Luke Foxe, on his return from a search for the North West Passage which he describes in considerable navigational detail, expresses a similar disdain. In a rare and eccentric little book which he called *North West Fox* he explains that, having been apprenticed to the coastal trade, he has no use for "mathematical seamen . . . for I do not allow any to be a good seaman that hath not undergone the most offices about the ship, and that hath not in his youth been both taught and inured to all labours; for to keep a warm cabin and lie in sheets is the most ignoble part of a seaman; but to endure and suffer, as a hard cabin, cold and salty meat, broken sleeps, mouldy bread, dead beer, wet clothes, want of fire, all these are within board; besides boat, yard, top-yards, anchor-moorings and the like." For such men, and of such were Drake and his company, seamanship, not navigation, was the thing.

Of the many putative fathers of the Royal Navy—Alfred, John, Henry V—Henry VIII has the strongest claim. In his reign the navy began to be regarded for the first time as a principal weapon of defence instead of being a mere transport service. By compelling his Lord Admiral to go to sea instead of enjoying a legal sinecure, he established the executive functions of the Admiralty. By founding the Navy Board at Deptford in 1546, consisting of the Principal Officers— Treasurer, Comptroller, Surveyor and Clerk of the Ships— he gave the service an administrative framework which lasted until 1832. With the appearance of the Victualling Office in the next reign, there was now an administrative structure for the upkeep of the royal ships, building them, maintaining them, manning them, victualling and paying them. Arming them remained the business of the Ordnance Board, which served army and navy alike.

As the first monarch to show a personal interest in ships, Henry's achievement is to be applauded, though his use of the fleet as an instrument of foreign policy met with little success. He built and armed the biggest ships yet seen in this country, and by developing the royal dockyards at Deptford, Woolwich and Portsmouth he provided himself with the best naval establishment in Europe. Naturally he had recourse to impressment to man these ships, because the port towns were still small and men had to be raised from further inland. Thus one Peter Pett was pressed from Essex, to become the founder of the Pett dynasty of Deptford, the leading English ship-wrights for the next century. The king also gave orders to local authorities to press for the Lord Admiral if the latter, as was the case with Lord Lisle, set forth ships at his own charge in order to assist in the war with France. Justices were to furnish not only mariners, but shipwrights, gunners, soldiers and victuals as well.[1]

The first Navy List to give details of the King's ships, their tonnage, armament and complement, is the Anthony Roll at Magdalene College, Cambridge. From this and other manuscripts which Pepys collected for his projected history of the navy, one can gain an idea of the size of the early Tudor navy. In 1511, 3,000 men, of whom 1,600 were mariners or gunners, were required. In 1514, twenty-three royal ships and thirty-six hired ships were manned by 4,429 mariners and gunners. In 1545 it was thought that 5,000 men could be raised, though with difficulty, for the largest fleet yet set forth, consisting of 104 ships. Unfortunately it was stricken by plague, so that out of 12,000 soldiers and sailors, 3,502 were sick or dead within a week and the fleet had to be demobilised.[2]

In the following table the number of soldiers at sea has been included in the totals of men.[3]

Year	Ships	Men
1546	58	8,546
1557	21	2,556
1578	24	6,290
1603	42	8,346

Accurate figures for the critical year of 1588 are difficult to come by, because they depend on the month in question and the large number of merchant vessels which came and went from the royal fleet. In July, 9,500 men were victualled for the Queen's sixteen ships, but the total in pay was only 7,901. One estimate gives the fleets at Plymouth and in the Downs as 195 ships of all types with 14,334 men on board, of whom 6,264 were in the Queen's ships. Another gives 17,000 men. According to the latest writer, the figures were 14,385 seamen and 1,540 soldiers.[4]

An important development is the steady increase in the proportion of seamen to soldiers on board. Thus in the

Henry Grace à Dieu or *Great Harry* of 1514, the first real battle-
ship in the navy, there were 349 soldiers, 301 mariners and
50 gunners. In the *Victory* of 1558 there were 100 soldiers,
268 mariners and 32 gunners. In the *Ark Royal* of 1588
there were 125 soldiers and 300 mariners.

The best account of manning a typical small expedition, a
private venture to the South Seas following the Drake
pattern, is that given by Sir Richard Hawkins when describing
the departure of the *Dainty* from Plymouth in 1593.[5] From
this it may be imagined how much more difficult it must have
been to fit out a large official expedition, including soldiers
as well as mariners, when the motive of private gain was
lacking.

> And so I began to gather my company on board, which occu-
> pied my good friends and the Justices of the town two days, and
> forced us to search all lodgings, taverns and alehouses. For some
> would ever be taking their leave and never depart; some drink
> themselves so drunk that except they were carried aboard, they of
> themselves would not be able to go one step; others knowing the
> necessity of the time, feigned themselves sick; others to be in-
> debted to their hosts, and forced me to ransom them; one his
> chest, another his sword; another his shirts; another his card
> and instruments for sea; and others, to benefit themselves of the
> imprest (money) given them, absented themselves; making a lewd
> living in deceiving all whose money they could lay hold of;
> which is a scandal too rife among our seamen.

Cavendish the circumnavigator told him that such men
were to be seen walking boldly about the streets having
robbed him of £1,500 in cash. Some of Hawkins's own men
boasted how they had cheated former commanders of five or
ten pounds.

Once on board, the seamen were supposed to conduct themselves in accord with the regulations laid down by individual
captains, which were the precedents on which the later
Articles of War and Admiralty Regulations and Instructions

were based. The briefest and best of these is the advice given
by Sir Richard's father, Sir John Hawkins, the true founder
of the Elizabethan navy: "Serve God daily; love one another;
preserve your victuals; beware of fire; and keep good company," i.e. keep station in a fleet. More elaborate are those
drawn up by Willoughby and Chancellor: "that no blasphem-
ing of God, or detestable swearing be used in any ship, nor
communication of ribaldry, filthy tales, or ungodly talk be
suffered, neither carding, dicing, tabling, nor other devilish
games to be frequented." One wonders what the poor
mariner was left to do.

Official *Orders to be used in King's or Queen's Majesties Ships or
Navy being upon the Seas in Fashion of War* appear in 1568.
Most of these repeat the medieval punishments previously
described. Blasphemy and swearing are more savagely
(though evidently ineffectually) punished—by a marlin spike
"clapt into their mouths and tied behind their heads, and then
to stand a whole hour, till their mouths be very bloody; an
excellent cure for swearers." In a fight, the practice recommended by Chaucer's Shipman is officially recommended.
Having seized the enemy ship, sink both ship and crew, but
"first take heed that your own men be retired, take the captain
with certain of the best men with him, the rest commit them
to the bottom of the sea, for else they will turn upon you to
your confusion." Advice on fire control is equally primitive:
chain two hogsheads to the sides of your ship for "the soldiers
and mariners to piss into that they may always be full of urine
to quench fire with and two or three pieces of old sail ready
to wet in the piss." Only in 1596 does more hygienic advice
appear: "You shall give orders that your ship may be kept
clean daily and sometimes washed; which, with God's favour,
shall preserve from sickness and avoid inconvenience."

The real expansion of English shipping, and hence of the
size of the seafaring population, did not occur until after the
first decade of Elizabeth's reign. The following table of totals

of tonnage, which exclude naval ships, show that the country
entered its maritime heritage at the same time as the war with
Spain.[6]

$$1560— \;50,000 \text{ tons}$$
$$1572— \;50,000 \text{ tons}$$
$$1582— \;67,000 \text{ tons}$$
$$1629—118,000 \text{ tons}$$

A detailed survey of resources in 1582 shows which
counties men were chiefly drawn from.[7]

Muster of Ships and Mariners, 1582

	Ships	Mariners
Somerset	37	502
Cheshire	14	113
Lancashire	53	199
Essex	154	693
Cornwall	70	1,923
Lincolnshire	21	549
London	129	3,086
Hampshire	86	470
Yorkshire	54	880
Cinque Ports	220	952
Kent	99	243
Sussex	65	521
Dorset	60	645
Devon	119	2,164
Norfolk	165	1,670
Suffolk	100	1,282
Gloucestershire	29	219
Cumberland	12	195
Northumberland	25	851

Total of all vessels=1,512   Above 80 tons=223
Total of mariners=17,157

This expansion was chiefly due to two incentives given to

the shipping industry. One was a bounty on shipbuilding and the other encouragement to the fisheries by the institution of a fish or meatless day once a week and twice a week in the navy (later called banyan days, from Hindu abstainers from eating flesh). The first of these acts in 1563 is specifically aimed at "the preservation of the navy and the maintenance of convenient numbers of seafaring men." Or, as Cecil declared, "for policy's sake, so the sea-coasts should be strong with men and habitations and the fleet flourish more than ever."

Because of this we find two principal areas of increase, both of which were to be long regarded as nurseries of seamen and at one time or another enjoyed some form of protection against impressment. One was the Newfoundland fishery, chiefly from Bristol and the western ports such as Dartmouth and Weymouth; the other was the colliery trade between Newcastle and London. A Greenland fishery developed from the northern ports, whereas the larger ships, which benefited from the bounty on shipbuilding, came largely from the southern ports as overseas trade on the part of the chartered companies began to expand.

Apprentices in all trades, usually about sixteen years old, were exempt from pressing until they had served out their articles, usually for seven years. A detailed study of apprenticeship at Ipswich between 1596 and 1651 shows that out of 381 apprenticeships, 296 were of a maritime nature and about a third of the boys had a maritime background.[8] In return for their clothing, food and training, they were supposed to receive between 30/- and 60/- a year, though plenty of masters defrauded their apprentices by pocketing their wages. What the figures suggest is the growth of a hereditary seafaring population which press-masters could exploit in pursuit of prime seamen.

The increase in ships and men coincided with, and was partly caused by, the opportunity to partake in the national pastime of baiting the Spaniards at sea. The Elizabethan age was the golden age of privateering, which became a business proposition on a considerable scale. The prospect of making a fortune at sea bred the race of men whose exploits are recorded in our national epic, Hakluyt's *Principal Navigations*. Motives of plunder, trade, religion, patriotism and honour combined to release a formidable offensive spirit. For the courtier and the merchant, to find a good ship with a reliable captain had the attraction of horse racing today. Syndicates, often headed by the Queen or her Treasurer or Secretary, were formed to meet the cost of fitting out privateers, nor was there any lack of volunteers to serve in them. Admiralty Courts were kept busy deducting the prize money due to the Queen and the Lord Admiral, provided the prize had not already been plundered illegally. "As for the business of pillage," wrote a contemporary about the habits of seamen, "there is nothing that more bewitcheth them, nor anything wherein they promise themselves so loudly, nor delight in more mainly."[9]

By pillage was meant anything loose on deck which was not part of the ship or cargo, and this was a legitimate perquisite of the crew; but to "break bulk" or plunder the cargo was forbidden. Under current prize law, one third of the value of this went to the crew, and one third each to the owner and victualler, but only after the Queen had taken her fifth and the Lord Admiral his tenth.

The success of Drake's voyage round the world set the fashion and indeed made the reputation of England as a rising maritime power. To what extent this was a privateering venture, and to what extent it was an official act of war, may be endlessly debated. What mattered was that it paid £47 for every £1 invested. The Queen invested her share of the profits in the Levant Company; Drake bought himself a country house near Plymouth, which is still the shrine of his family.

No wonder that "the sweet trade of privateering," as his

buccaneer descendants called it, began to flourish exceedingly. It is estimated that an average of a hundred voyages a year took place in the last decade of the reign. The names of the "infinite number" of private men-of-war swarming in the Indies breathe the poetry of the age—fierce *Dragons* and *Lions* of every hue, *Panthers, Ferrets, Tigers,* Cumberland's *Malice Scourge,* down to the bingo-like craft called the *Wheel of Fortune, Hazard, Poor Man's Hope* or simply the *Why Not?*

Privateering combined profit with national policy to such a degree that it is difficult to distinguish a naval operation from a financial speculation. The news that Drake was going to the West Indies in 1585 on what proved to be the first act of open war because of the number of Queen's ships involved "inflamed the whole country with a desire to adventure unto the seas, in hope of the like good success, so that a great number prepared ships, mariners and soldiers, and travelled every place where any profit might be had."[10] By the time he "singed the King of Spain's beard," almost every captain he employed was an experienced privateer. When Cadiz was captured in 1596, the leaders—Howard, Essex, Raleigh—were all interested in plunder as well as honour and service. What annoyed the Queen was when such expeditions failed to pay their way, or when her due profits were filched by rapacious seamen. The capture of the *San Felipe* carrack by Drake in 1587 was applauded because the cargo realised £100,000, but when the *Madre de Dios* was brought into Dartmouth in 1592, ropes of pearls and handfuls of precious stones disappeared before her officers could arrive from Exeter. One naval official confessed to buying 1,800 diamonds and 300 rubies from a seaman for £130. Another admitted to pocketing £2,000, but protested that an emerald crucifix found in his lodgings had long been his private property. Various mariners agreed that they had stolen packets of jewels, but who can blame them when the Queen only allowed twenty shillings a man for his share in the great prize?

We are not here concerned whether privateering on the scale favoured by the Elizabethans was of economic benefit to the country or not. For our purpose what matters is that it encouraged seafaring. Even an Admiralty official like Sir William Monson, who complained that its use as an operation of war was exaggerated, admits that "the number of seamen and sailors are increased treble by it, by what they are in the navigations of peacable voyages."[11] What annoyed naval authorities like him was that the popularity of privateering drained away the prime seamen, leaving only the dregs to the press-masters for the navy. Such continued to be the attitude of the Admiralty as long as this mode of warfare continued, as it did until the middle of the nineteenth century.

Privateering may have made the existence of a royal navy unimportant in late Tudor times, but in the long run the nation suffered because war was allowed to deteriorate into a scramble for profits. Under such circumstances a national strategy and a naval profession could scarcely be born. Raleigh was speaking of seamen as well as soldiers when he confessed in the next reign, when corruption reached its lowest depths, "We find it in daily experience that all discourse of magnanimity, of national virtue, of religion, of liberty, and whatsoever else hath wont to move and encourage virtuous men, hath no force at all with the common soldier in comparison of spoil and riches."[12]

So, whenever a big military expedition was fitting out, the Queen had recourse to impressment. Writs and warrants flew from the Privy Council. Falstaffian interviews with justices like Shallow and Silence provided much food for powder of an inferior quality. In 1570 the Lords Lieutenant of Suffolk, Essex, Kent and Sussex were told to take up men at a cost of 3/9 a head. In 1594 the counties of Norfolk and Suffolk were punished for the desertion of their men by being compelled to provide substitutes. For their last voyage in 1595 Hawkins and Drake were empowered to take up enough mariners, soldiers and artificers to man six naval and twelve merchant ships. The next year the government was asked not to discharge seventy West Country seamen from this voyage because only inferior replacements could be found for the Cadiz voyage. Some 5,000 men, 1,700 of them for the Queen's ships, were required and a proclamation was issued for all pressed men to travel to their destinations. However, according to a Venetian observer, "the Queen has every opportunity to muster fleets, for all the ports are full of ships, especially the Thames, where one sees nothing else but ships and seamen."[13]

Nevertheless there is evidence that the quality of men was deteriorating. When in 1597 Shakespeare's Earl of Southampton went down to take command of the *Garland* for the Islands Voyage, he found the fleet "altogether unfurnished with good mariners, and we are almost left destitute of any means to supply it." Thirty sick men had to be discharged immediately, while "those that remain are for the most part unable to perform any labour that belongs to them." Other more experienced commanders such as Essex and Raleigh complained in similar terms that the Weymouth press-masters were letting good men go for a bribe of £1 a head and only retaining "men of all occupations, some of whom did not know a rope and were never at sea."[14]

One reason was clearly that the government did not pay its recruiting officers promptly. Even the Lord Lieutenant of Devon complained that he had not been paid for obtaining "forty tall and very sufficient men" from Penrhyn. The officer at Exmouth says that he was sent to press fifty-five men for the *Felix* and fifty-seven for the *Francis*, but had never been paid for so doing. Such officers were responsible for the outlay of very considerable sums of money, not only cash for imprest money, but conduct money to enable men to reach their assigned ports, and often victualling and stores money as well. In 1600 Fulke Greville, the poet and courtier, now Treasurer of the Navy, received £4,988 for press and conduct money and sea stores to man and victual ten ships for three weeks, as well as £3,290 for the payment of wages on board.[15]

A typical pressing commission of this period reads as follows:—[16]

> Elizabeth, by the Grace of God etc., to all and singular our Justices of the Peace, Mayors, Sheriffs, Bailiffs, Constables, Headboroughs, and to all other our Officers, Ministers and Subjects, to whom these presents shall come, Greeting.
>
> Forasmuch as we have appointed our trusty and well beloved Sir Martin Frobisher, Knight, to have the Rank and Government of such Ship, Shipping or Vessels whatsoever as, by order of our Admiral of England, he shall take with him in his Company for certain our special Service in the South and West sea; that is to say the *Golden Lion, Elizabeth Bonaventure, Advice, Sun, Repentance* and to the intent he may be furnished of all and all manner of such Necessaries as thereunto shall appertain.
>
> We therefore let you wit that we have authorised and appointed and by these Presents do give full Power and Authority unto the said Sir Martin Frobisher and to his sufficient Deputy or Deputies, wheresoever he shall have need to press and take up for service, to the Furniture of such Ships as are committed to his charge, in any place upon the Coasts of England or Ireland, any Mariners, Soldiers, Gunners or other needful Artificers and Workmen . . . and punish by Imprisonment such as shall be found disobedient and shall obstinately impugn such good Orders as are usually observed in our Navies and Armies on the Seas . . . Wherefore We will and command you and every one of you, by these Presents, to be with all care and diligence aiding, helping and assisting to our said Subject and Servant in the execution of this our Commission, as ye and every of you tender our Pleasure herein and will answer for the contrary at your peril.
>
> In witness whereof etc., Westminster, August 30, 1589.

The raising of men during the Armada crisis was easier because of the obvious threat to the homeland. The consequence was that a better type of man than usual was enlisted.

The tragedy was that the primitive administrative machinery for pay, victualling and medical services broke down completely under the strain. With typical procrastination, the Queen postponed all such preparations until the last moment. The months of waiting in harbour and the unprecedented number of men involved was never foreseen. In February it was thought that 2,990 men at home and 2,900 at sea would suffice. In July the figure was over 14,000. Each port had to provide its own quota of men and ships. A Spanish spy writes "In London they are drawing fifty men from each parish at the cost of the City to send on board the ships; 4,000, they say, being obtained in this way. They give to each man a blue coat, whilst those who remain here receive a red coat"—possibly a distinction between seamen for the fleet under Seymour and soldiers for the camp at Tilbury. Southampton had raised 12,000, but "some very rawly furnished, some whereof lack a headpiece, some a sword, some one thing or other that is evil, unfit or unbeseeming about him."[17]

On May 28 Howard wrote to Burghley from Plymouth: "My good Lord, there is here the gallantest company of captains, soldiers and mariners that I think was ever seen in England. It was a pity they should lack meat, when they are so desirous to spend their lives in her Majesty's service." On July 13 he warned Walsingham that the state of the provisions was deteriorating: "God of his mercy keep us from the sickness, for we fear that more than any hurt that the Spaniards will do, if the advertisements be true. Well, Sir, I would her Majesty did know of the care and pains that is taken here of all men for her service. We must now man ourselves again, for we cast many overboard, and a number in great extremity which we discharged. I have sent with all expedition a prest for more men."

It was immediately after the week's fighting up Channel that the consequences of the government's lack of foresight

showed themselves. On August 9 a captain writes that he has
had to give up the chase from lack of powder and meat, his
men being so desperate for water that they are drinking their
urine.

The next day Howard informed Burghley: "My good
Lord—Sickness and mortality begin wonderfully to grow
amongst us; and it is most pitiful to see, here at Margate, how
the men, having no place to receive them into here, die in the
streets. I am driven myself to come aland, to see them be-
stowed in some lodging; and the best I can get is barns and
such outhouses; and the relief is small that I can provide
for them here. It would grieve a man's heart to see them
that have served so valiantly to die so miserably." Half the
crew of the *Elizabeth Jonas* was sick, so that the big galleon
had to be sent into Chatham. Some who had been eight
months in the ship had not a rag to their backs. Unless £1,000
was spent on clothing immediately, he added, "in very short
time I look to see most of the mariners go naked. Good my
Lord, let mariners be pressed and sent down as soon as may
be, and money to discharge those that be sick here."[18]

The cause was evidently virulent food poisoning, dysentery
and possibly typhoid. The ships were overcrowded and the
stores of food turned bad during the summer's wait in
harbour. The men attributed their sickness to sour beer, but
the real cause must have been the low standard of hygiene
on board and the ignorance of any method of preserving food
except by salting. In spite of their most elaborate precautions,
the enemy fared worse because their voyage was longer. Had
the Spanish ships not been damaged at Gravelines and destroyed by the gale encountered as they retreated northabout,
the English would have been in no shape to meet another
attack. Hawkins confessed that without an entire new stock
of food and men, the fleet was "utterly unfitted and unmeet
to follow any enterprise."

The Armada campaign illustrates in dramatic and tragic

fashion one of the principal hazards of Elizabethan life at sea
—the abysmal state of medical knowledge and practice. On
board the flagship was Howard's personal surgeon, William
Clowes, who wrote the first English book on military surgery.
There were other surgeons with the fleet, but such men could
not be pressed directly. It was left to the Company of Barber-
Surgeons by its charter to provide men on request. Every
effort was made by those on whom the choice fell to evade
such service and the minutes of the Company show how
dangerous the practice of providing substitutes could be when
a seaman complained that "an insufficient man" took off his
leg so clumsily that he nearly lost his life.

The College of Physicians did little to help because of their
jealousy of the inferior type of man belonging to the Barber-
Surgeons. This hostility between the two branches of the
medical profession lasted until the nineteenth century and did
incalculable harm at sea, where a ship's surgeon had to be a
physician as well, in practice if not in name. Few physicians
served afloat, nor did the College encourage surgeons to
interest themselves in pathology. Moreover, during the
whole period covered in this volume the dominant aetiology
was climatorial, or miasmatic, as it was usually called, that is
to say that disease was thought to be due primarily to bad air
or a noxious climate. The experiences and clinical observations of those at sea seldom penetrated the obscurantist portals
of the College. In 1572 a merchant captain drew attention to
the association between mosquito bites and malaria, but no
doctor took any notice until the end of the nineteenth century.
Much the same fate befell the seaman's recommendation of
citrus fruit as an antiscorbutic. As a historian of naval
medicine has said, "the medical experience gained during the
Tudor voyages was almost entirely lost."[19]

In 1588 four physicians were sent down to Plymouth.
There is no record that any of them went to sea. The most
distinguished was William Gilbert, famous as the author of the

first book on magnetism, but quite helpless when confronted with epidemics due to bad food and water.

Much will have to be said about the incidence of disease in this book, because it magnified the manning problem. For the next two centuries, if a thousand men were impressed for an expedition overseas it may be taken for granted that half died of disease before it was over. The problem first began to be acute in Elizabethan times for five main reasons. The ships were invariably overcrowded; the standard of hygiene was dangerously low; since nothing was known about antisepsis, any major operation was apt to prove fatal; the longer time spent at sea raised dietetic problems which were insoluble at that date; finally, long voyages into tropical regions brought Englishmen into contact with a variety of diseases from which they had no immunity.

As is well known, bubonic plague carried by rats was endemic in Tudor society. We have seen how it could wreck an expedition such as that of 1545, when the admiral on board the *Great Harry* wrote of "a great disease fallen among the soldiers and mariners almost in every ship, in such sort that if the same should continue, which God forbid, we should have need to be newly refreshed with men."[20]

For some reason we do not hear of the plague affecting ships thereafter, but a new disease, worse than the ague (which was common enough at home,) struck Drake's brilliant 1585 expedition to the Indies, when 300 men died of a more serious type of malaria contracted in the woods of the Cape Verde islands on the way out. Worse occurred in the Lisbon expedition the year after the Armada; indeed, so disastrous was the outcome that even Drake fell into disgrace for a few years. The reason why the casualties were so high was the number of soldiers shipped and the low standard of discipline maintained when they landed. One of their colonels, appalled by the number of those who died or deserted for drink, complained of "our slovenly pressed men, whom the

Justices (who have always thought unworthily of any war) have sent out as the scum and dregs of the country." Once more, inadequate victualling seems to have been the major fault, so that many died either of hunger or dysentery. Under half the original force of 13,500 men returned alive after only ten weeks' absence and nothing achieved.

In the far more successful capture of Cadiz in 1596 the poor quality of the men raised was atoned for by admirable leadership on the part of Essex, Raleigh, Lord Charles and Lord Thomas Howard. A tribute to the latter's care of his men is paid by a physician on board: "His Lordship's honorable care not lesse for the good usage of all his followers of all sorts and degrees, but speciallie for the pour toylinge and continuall labouringe maryners, hymself daylie making inquiries how they did, and cauling to them by name to know in what case they stood, and what they should have in present redresse."[21] In all ages it has been in such ways that good leadership has overcome the deficiencies of man-power.

The most serious disease which began to afflict the European mariner as soon as long voyages became common was scurvy. It was only in the present century that it was found that this is a dietary deficiency disease due to lack of vitamin C. All that was certain in the days of sail was that after five or six weeks at sea on salt provisions pimples appeared on the gums, teeth began to fall out, large dark blotches began to appear on the skin, old sores re-opened, an intolerable lethargy overcame the sufferer and any sudden movement, such as that resulting from a stroke with a rope's end wielded by a boatswain, killed a man outright. Half the shipwrecks in history have been due to crews enfeebled by scurvy, and the navy's manning problem was always exacerbated by the number of seamen rendered unfit for duty because they were suffering from this curse of the sea.

It is significant that the first recognisable description of the disease is on Cartier's voyage up the St. Lawrence in 1534. The first detailed description of it in English is by Sir Richard Hawkins in his account of a voyage to the Pacific in 1593. He reckons that 10,000 men died of it in Elizabeth's reign. Since he first encountered it when his ship crossed the equator, and since he lived in an age when the climatorial theory of pathology prevailed, he put it down to change of air. At the same time he expressed the wish that "some learned man would write of it, for it is the plague of the sea and the spoil of mariners." In the meantime he recorded his opinion that the best cure was sour oranges and lemons: "This is a wonderful secret of the power and wisdom of God, that hath hidden so great and unknown a virtue in this fruit, to be a certain remedy for this infirmity."[22]

Remarkable confirmation of the efficiency of this antiscorbutic was afforded on Sir James Lancaster's voyage to India in 1600. The flagship alone escaped the disease because Lancaster happened to take some bottles of lemon juice on board. One spoonful every morning kept the disease at bay: "The juice worketh much better if the party keep a short diet and wholly refrain salt meat, which salt meat, and long being at sea, is the only cause of the breeding of this disease."

Would that such precious facts had not been lost in the waste of medical theory! Not for a hundred and fifty years was "a learned man," Dr. James Lind, to carry out the first controlled dietetic experiment on record in order to substantiate what he had read in Hawkins's *Observations* and to write a treatise on the subject, which continued to be ignored by the Admiralty and the College of Physicians for another forty years.

In some notes "Concerning the Abuses of our Seamen" which Monson wrote towards the end of the reign to explain the unpopularity of naval service, he points out that "their usage hath been so ill that it is no marvel they show unwillingness to serve the Queen. For if they arrive sick from any voyage, such is the charity of the people ashore that they shall sooner die than find pity, unless they bring money with them."[23]

Anything approximating to a naval hospital or a hospital ship was unknown in England, though the Spaniards had them. Henry VIII having dissolved the charities which cared for the medieval mariner, these had to be re-established for the Elizabethan seaman. Those put ashore after the Armada had, as we have seen, to be paid for out of the Lord Admiral's pocket, or given a licence to beg, thus increasing the number of sturdy beggars, those "caterpillars of the commonwealth" which Elizabethan publicists were always castigating. In 1595 a letter sent to the Mayor of Bristol reminded him that a hospital for seamen once existed in his city and that since a great number of mariners had recently been maimed in the Queen's service, he was to re-establish it with a levy on the Newfoundland fishing vessels.[24]

Perhaps the influence of Sir John Hawkins, Treasurer of the Navy, is discernible here, because the previous year he had obtained permission to found an almshouse for ten poor mariners at Chatham. Earlier still, in 1590, he, together with Howard and Drake, founded the Chatham Chest, a contributory fund for which every seaman in the navy was mulcted sixpence a month out of his wages. In course of time, after having been raided and exploited by unprincipled administrators, the fund was amalgamated with that of the Royal Hospital at Greenwich. A fine silver spoon on the Captain's table at Mess dinners today is engraved with a drawing of a one-legged seaman standing on the Chest, the first contributory medical insurance scheme in the country. The Chest itself, with the slot into which sixpences were dropped, is preserved in the National Maritime Museum.

After the passing of the great Poor Law of 1601 every parish was charged with the responsibility of providing pensions for such disabled mariners, the sum not to exceed

£10 for a mariner or £20 for an officer. Superseding the earlier pension acts, this act laid down that parish officers must apply to the treasurer of the county for the man's ticket from his commander, which certificates must be entered in the ship's books.[25]

When we see what the Tudor mariner ate we are not surprised at the prevalence of intestinal diseases. The victualling of the fleet was done by contract with wholesalers and pursers on board, a type of civilian officer who had a bad reputation from an early date. In 1545 the victualling scale laid down was a pound of biscuit, a gallon of beer and a pound of meat for every man four days a week, cheese and dried fish being provided for the remainder. Attempts to put victualling on a new basis were made early in Elizabeth's reign, when Edward Baeshe was appointed Surveyor of Victuals. He was paid 4½d. a day for each man in harbour, 5d. when at sea. For this Baeshe had to provide the above rations. On active service crews went on short allowance in order to preserve their victuals. Thus on the Islands Voyage of 1597, half the normal allowance of beer was issued and the number of flesh days halved. Even so, at 7½d. a man per day, the fleet cost £8,050 for 28 days.[26]

On the other hand, pay was increased. At the beginning of the reign of Henry VIII it was five shillings a month; at the end of the reign it was 6/8 as a reward for faithful service, but since the shilling was shortly after devalued to sixpence, the rise did the ordinary seaman little good. In 1585 it was raised to ten shillings on the representation of Hawkins, who thought that "by this means her Majesty's ships would be furnished with able men, such as can shift for themselves, keep themselves clean from vermin or noisomeness, which bredeth sickness and mortality." The following table shows the annual harbour pay in 1589, which was slightly lower than sea pay.[27]

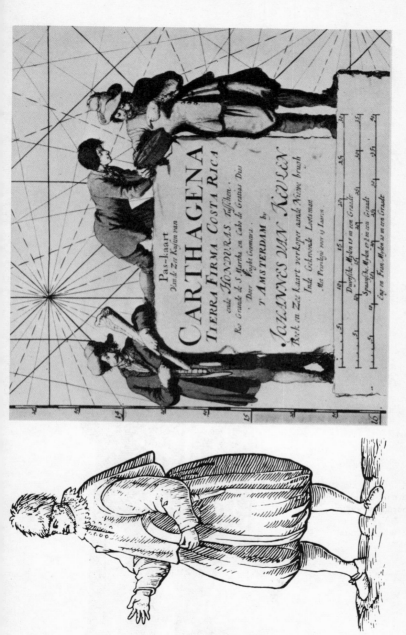

An Elizabethan Seaman, (*left*) with a mariner's astrolabe under his arm. From Cesare Vecelli's *Habiti Antichi e Moderni*, 1600. Dutch Seamen, (*right*) wearing the same sort of clothes as the British, with chart and compass. From Johannes van Keulen's New Great Shining Torch of the Sea, 1682

A wounded Stuart Seaman.
From a coloured wooden
carving in the Great Hall of
St. Bartholomew's Hospital

Master	£26.	1.	8.
Boatswain	10.	17.	3.
Purser	8.	13.	9.
Cook	7.	12.	1.
Carpenter	10.	8.	7.
Gunner	9.	15.	6.
Mariner	6.	10.	0.

These rates do not compare unfavourably with those on land, but the problem was always one of punctual payment. As Hawkins's son observed, "the greatest and most principal robbery of all is the defrauding" men of their pay by withholding it. It is significant that the last allusion to him is after the ill payment of the fleet in 1622 when it was reported that "Sir Richard Hawkins, the vice-admiral, is dead of vexation." No Elizabethan captains did more for the seamen than the Hawkins family.

Drake's name was as prominent in his own day as in ours. It was his brilliant exploits and fine leadership rather than any administrative ability which earned him his rise from a humble boy in a Thames coasting vessel to the office of Vice-Admiral of England. We know that he was a strict disciplinarian, though not a cruel one. He understood everything about the men he commanded and on board his ships he insisted that the captain was in command, not the old-fashioned council of war.

This comes out clearly in his treatment of William Burrough, one of the Principal Officers, who was his vice-admiral on the Cadiz voyage of 1587. When Burrough differed with Drake about the tactics to be adopted, he was peremptorily sent home in the *Golden Lion*. On the way the crew mutinied. The minutes of the court martial are the earliest to have survived and they illuminate the grievances of the Elizabethan seaman, which appear to have been much the same as those of his descendants at the Nore in 1797.[28]

What is interesting is the anxiety of the mutineers not to be sent back to Drake's fleet. They knew what would happen to them there, and indeed Drake sentenced the ringleaders to be hanged in their absence. The causes of the outbreak seem to have been justifiable. The men petitioned the captain "to weigh of us like men, and let us not be spoiled for want of food, for our allowance is so small we are not able to live any longer on it; for whenas three or four men were wont to take a charge in hand, now ten at the least, by reason of our weak victualling and filthy drink, is scarce able to discharge it, and yet groweth weaker and weaker . . . For what is a piece of beef of half a pound among four men to dinner, or half a dried stockfish for four days in the week, and nothing else to help withal—Yea, we have help, a little beveridge (i.e. diluted wine) worse than pump water. We were pressed by her Majesty to have her allowance, and not to be thus dealt withal; you make no men of us, but beasts."

Not for the last time was mutiny due to food rather than pay or hardship. As the navy grew and as its administration tended towards the corruption which became rife in Jacobean times, such complaints and such behaviour became more common. Added to these were complaints about clothing. At the beginning of the century there are references to jackets of white and green cloth for mariners. At the end we find orders for suits, shirts, linen breeches of the baggy type favoured in the days of doublet and hose, and Monmouth caps (flat, round tam o'shanters made of Welsh wool) which were replacing the high, thrum caps shown in the illustration facing page 48.

Howard of Effingham, now Earl of Nottingham, was the only distinguished link between the navy of Tudor and Stuart times, and financial probity was not his strong point. He was too old to take that personal interest in the men which he had certainly shown in the past. In the succeeding era of poor leadership, and corrupt administration, the Elizabethan age shone all the brighter in retrospect. For it was in that age according to the Venetian ambassador, that English seamen "enjoyed the reputation of being, above all Western nations, expert and active in all naval operations, and great sea dogs," by which he probably meant pirates.[29]

III

The Early Stuart Mariner

THE GLORIES of Elizabethan seafaring were dissipated during the short reign of her successor, so that when Charles I tried to use the navy to further a fatuously ambitious foreign policy, a series of unprecedented disasters took place. After such failures, and after the assassination of the Lord High Admiral, the Duke of Buckingham, the remainder of his reign is, from the naval point of view, a blank. The neglect of the navy by the first two Stuarts was therefore the chief reason why the fleet deserted to the Parliamentary side at the beginning of the Civil War.

Warships were certainly built during this depressing period and the size of the navy increased, but the most important of them were built for prestige rather than use. The first three-decker, the *Prince Royal* of 1610, and the first 100-gun three-masted ship, the *Sovereign of the Seas* of 1637, which was the prototype of all first-rate line of battle ships for the next two centuries, were perhaps the most beautiful ships ever built in this country, but their baroque ornamentation, their garlanded ports and elaborately carved sterns made them useless as weapons of war. The *Sovereign of the Seas* was the result of the levy of Ship Money. No doubt the aim of such a tax was sensible in so far as it sought to make the nation as a whole, and not merely the ports, responsible for the upkeep of a naval defence force, but the date and the manner in which it was imposed was extremely unwise. The reputation of the navy was at its lowest, its national importance at its least. Buckinghamshire squires might well be excused for knowing nothing about it and caring less.

The Venetian ambassador reported in James's reign that most of the ships in the fleet were now "old and rotten and barely fit for service," but that the country itself was full of sailors. The reason for this was the rapid increase in the merchant service, which was encouraged by the mercantilist policy of the government and the imposition of restrictions on the number of foreigners permitted to be employed, amounting to only a quarter of the crew. Other prohibitions on the carrying of English cargoes in foreign bottoms continued the old policy of flag discrimination and paved the way for the more famous and stringent Navigation Acts of 1651 and 1660. The whole policy was aimed primarily at the Dutch, whose shipping was increasing faster than that of the English, the inevitable outcome being the three Dutch wars in which a modern navy was born.

The consequences of this mercantilist policy (of which even Adam Smith approved and which continued to hold the field until well into the nineteenth century) was a notable increase in that pool of seamen on which the navy could draw in an emergency. It is significant that the noble formula in the preamble of Cromwell's Navigation Act is repeated with only slight variations in subsequent Naval Discipline Acts up to the present day: "For the increase of shipping and the encouragement of the navigation of the nation, which, under the good providence and protection of God, is so great a means of the welfare and safety of the Commonwealth."

During the period with which we are concerned in this chapter, there continued to be little distinction between the royal and the merchant ship. All vessels trading overseas were heavily armed, because piracy was rife wherever they went. There was no difference between the skills required in a warship and a merchant ship, so that the gunner or the able seaman (that is to say, the seaman able "to hand, reef and steer") was easily transferable. As we shall see, most seamen served indifferently in warships and merchant ships, though they preferred the latter. Trading vessels were hired or requisitioned in large numbers on all expeditions. When a press was called for to man a fleet, it was assumed that all the press-masters had to do was to take up the seamen at the ports, which was easier said than done because professional seamen became adept at avoiding the service of the Crown.

Between 1629 and 1686 national tonnage increased from 118,000 to 340,000.[1] In the Royal Navy the number of ships and men over the century increased as follows:[2]

Year	Ships	Men
1588	34	6,279
1603	42	8,346
1633	50	9,470
1658	157	21,910
1676	148	30,260
1688	173	42,003

Out of a population of England and Wales of about five million, it is doubtful if there were more than 20,000 professional seamen at the beginning of the century. A return of 1628 gives the following numbers at the principal counties and ports:[3]

	Seamen	Fishermen
London	3,422	302
Kent	181	231
Cinque Ports	699	193
Essex	309	357
Suffolk	804	326
Norfolk	600	436
Lincoln	66	126
Devon	453	86

	Seamen	Fishermen
Northumberland	33	260
Cumberland	72	—
S. Cornwall	731	393
N. Cornwall	154	88
S. Wales	753	—
Southampton	321	209
Dorset	958	86
Bristol	823	—

The return is far from complete, because it omits 2,426 Thames watermen, as well as important areas such as Sussex and Cheshire; the small number for Northumberland may be explained if, as seems likely, the Newcastle coal trade is included in the London figure.

Even more than the fisheries, this trade was regarded as the nursery of seamen. A contemporary explanation is that masters of colliers did not worry about apprenticeships, being anxious to ship any hands available: "As it is the chiefest in employment of seamen, so it is the gentlest and most open to landmen; they never grudging in their smaller vessels to entertain some two fresh men or learners; whereas, to the contrary, in the ships that voyage to the southward, or otherwise far out of the kingdom," such unskilled labour was not encouraged.[4]

It must be emphasised that the masters, and even more the owners, of such colliers came from a higher class than the deckhands. But an apprentice, once he had mastered the elements of navigation, which meant in practice the use of the compass, cross staff and quadrant, could aspire to the post of mate and conditions on board were attractive enough to draw many a weaver from his loom or labourer from his plough. Writing in 1670, the political arithmetician Sir William Petty stated that "the husbandmen of England earns but four shillings a week, but the seamen have as good as

twelve shillings in wages, victuals and (as it were) housing."[5]
Long before the appearance of James Cook, the farm
labourer's son who learned his trade in a Whitby collier, the
North Sea bred the best seamen.

Because the merchant seaman was a volunteer, and because
the master of the ship could not resort to the sanctions against
desertion in force in the navy, wages and conditions had to be
of a reasonable standard to attract and retain men. Wages
fluctuated violently, depending on the state of trade, the
length of the voyage, the size of the vessel or her destination,
but they were always a few shillings ahead of those obtaining
in the navy, and in time of war they were double or treble.
They were paid with more certainty at the end of a voyage
for which a man signed on, which was more than could be
said of a warship, and they could be supplemented by small
"ventures" when men traded on their own account. The
standard of victualling was probably slightly higher because
the voyages were shorter, though there was less meat. There
were many drawbacks, such as losing pay if the cargo was
spoiled, but the possibilities of promotion and the prospect of
seeing foreign parts were enough to attract many boys. As we
shall see from the rare comments of a largely inarticulate class
of men, it is far from wise to underrate the hardships of such a
way of life, and there were many who regretted that youthful
curiosity had drawn them to the sea. Once a man had "used
the sea" as a way of life, it was seldom that he could change his
profession.

Men of this stamp must have sung with gusto the most
popular of the sea songs of the time, *Neptune's Raging Fury, or
the Gallant Seaman's Sufferings,* probably written in 1635.[6]

> You gentlemen of England, that live at home at ease,
> Full little do you think upon the dangers of the seas;
> Give ear unto the mariners, and they will plainly show,
> The cares and the fears when the stormy winds do blow.

All you that will be seamen must bear a valiant heart,
For when you come upon the seas you must not think to start,
Nor once to be faint-hearted in hail, rain or snow,
Nor to shrink, nor to shrink when the stormy winds do blow . . .

If enemies oppose us, when England is at wars
With any foreign nations we fear not wounds and scars;
Our roaring guns shall teach 'em our valour for to know,
Whilst they reel in the keel when the stormy winds do blow.

We are no cowardly shrinkers, but Englishmen true bred;
We'll play our parts like valiant hearts, and never fly for dread;
We'll ply our business nimbly, where'er we come or go
With our mates to the Straits when the stormy winds do blow.

When we return in safety with wages for our pains,
The tapster and the vintner will help to share our gains;
We'll call for liquor roundly and pay before we go,
Then we'll roar on the shore when the stormy winds do blow.

If the seafaring population was increasing, why, asks the
Admiral in Nathaniel Boteler's *Dialogues* (written in 1634,
though not printed till 1685) is there "that loathing which of
late days hath so possessed this kind of people against all
service in H.M. ships and fleets?" Captain Boteler, who served
in the navy during its worst years, replies that such has always
been the case because of the lack of liberty entailed, but that it
was worse now because of "some procrastinations which they
have met with in point of pay at the end of the service." Life
on board a privateer was preferable because there was less
discipline and more chance of getting a fair share of prize
money or booty. Recalling his own experiences in the fleet,
he thought that naval victualling—"a foul cosenage and desperate abuse which might have occasioned a general ruin, as
certainly it did a general wrong"—was much to blame. If
only there was more variety of diet in those places where
potatoes, plantains, oranges, lemons and limes ("which are

excellent against the scorbute") were easily come by. But his Admiral's reply anticipates that made by many later innovators, not least James Cook: "Our common seamen are so besotted in their beef and pork that they had rather adventure on all the calentures (fevers) and scurvies in the world than be weened from their customary diet, or the least bit of it."[7] No one is more conservative than the British seaman in matters of food, and it is probable that since most of them rarely tasted meat on land the generous if unhealthy ration in the navy was the more attractive.

The three principal reasons why men were deterred from entering the navy at a time when there was little call on their patriotism to do so were bad food, inadequate clothing and delay in the payment of wages. Two witnesses, one at the beginning of James's reign and one just after the end, use similar language about this lack of volunteers. In some notes on the navy which he wrote for the benefit of Prince Henry, Sir Walter Raleigh says that bad victualling was the chief reason why "they go with great grudging to serve in H.M. ships, as it were to be slaves in the galleys." Sir Henry Mervyn, commanding in the Downs in 1629, echoes Raleigh: "Foul winter weather, naked bodies and empty bellies make the men voice the King's service worse than a galley slavery."[8]

Such reasons suggest a corrupt and inefficient administration. There is ample evidence for this, but it was not entirely the fault of the government. The worst period was that of the ageing Howard, now Earl of Nottingham, and that of the most corrupt Treasurer the navy has ever had, Sir Robert Mansell. The first Commission of Inquiry in 1608 laid bare a sorry state of affairs in the finances of the navy and the state of its ships. Nothing was done until in 1618 a second Commission was established, when Buckingham replaced Nottingham as Lord High Admiral. Buckingham's faults seem to have been strategic rather than administrative, and the Commissioners did their best to check the rampant abuses, but they could do little to put the finances in order as long as the quarrel with the House of Commons continued. A third Commission of 1626 once more failed to solve the problem.

The trouble went deeper than the constant lack of ready cash. Buckingham's secretary declared that the real reason for "the great disorder crept into the ships, with many corruptions, (is) that the commanders and captains almost never come on board."[9] It was a venal and decadent age, when peculation was rife from the rank of Lord Chancellor Bacon downwards. There was every opportunity in the victualling department, with its lack of efficient methods of auditing, to make a private fortune, from which men like Sir James Bagg (commonly known as "Bottomless Bagg") benefited. In John Hollond's *Two Discourses of the Navy* written in 1638 and 1659 he makes the usual excuse for a corrupt administration, namely that the King's officials were so badly paid that they were forced "either to live knaves or die beggars, and sometimes both." He should know, because as a purser he had been charged with charging excessive prices for the sale of slops and he was for a time a naval commissioner himself. His sycophantic royalism led him to level similar charges against the Generals-at-Sea of the Commonwealth, but of this there is little proof. After the Restoration, the old habits crept in again, so that Pepys notes in his diary for 25 July, 1662, that he was "much pleased with them (the *Discourses*), they hitting the very diseases of the Navy which we are troubled with nowadays."

The record of the three futile occasions on which the King, at the instigation of Buckingham, used the inefficient navy which he inherited from his father reveals a truly depressing state of affairs. On all three—Cadiz in 1625, the Isle de Rhé in 1627 and La Rochelle in 1628—the navy was used in the old style of a transport service, there being far more soldiers than sailors involved. Since both had to be pressed, fed and paid, there was no difference in the way they were treated, nor did the consequent outbreaks of disease make any distinction between persons.

The difficulties encountered in raising men is illustrated in a proclamation issued in 1623 and re-issued in 1625:[10]

> We do straightly charge and command that no mariner or seafaring man absent, hide or withdraw himself from our service or prests, and that all such persons having our prest money given or tendered unto them, do dutifully and reverently receive the same and repair on board our ships at the times to them assigned, and thenceforth continue in our service as to the good duty of subjects appertaineth, and do not withdraw themselves or depart therefrom without special licence upon pain to incur the uttermost severity of our laws ... And we do further charge and straightly command that no person or persons that shall be trusted or employed for the pressing of any mariners do at any time, for favour, reward or other similar respect, forbear to prest the ablest and fittest men for such our service, or having prest them to discharge them again, or change them for persons less able and sufficient.

The lack of realism shown in this document, notably the fatuous phrase about pressed men "dutifully and reverently" receiving their money, is shown by the experience of Sir Henry Manwaring at Dover. Having arbitrarily demanded 150 seamen under threat of dire penalties against the Cinque Ports, he was indicted for a street brawl a few weeks later. He defended himself on the grounds that he had raised the finest seamen ever found in the town and refused a bribe of £200 to let them off.[11] Manwaring was a versatile character with interests ranging from piracy to lexicography, but as an admiral he joined in the chorus of complaints about men raised in such a manner: "men of poor and wretched persons, without clothes or ability of body."

Such complaints are common in all ages, but never more frequent than now. It was remarked that "the navy is for the greatest part manned with aged, impotent, vagrant, lewd and disorderly companions; it is become a ragged regiment of common rogues." This in a time of peace. In 1625, when men were being raised for a military expedition, it is said that "the number of lame, impotent and unable men unfit for actual service is very great." Though the numbers pressed were not large—1,000 at Chatham, 2,000 from the West and 2,400 from the North—many were being pressed "rather out of malice than the care of H.M. service," so that all the tinkers, tailors, weavers and such like landmen had to be put on shore again. A letter from the *Anne Royal* (as the famous *Ark Royal* was now called) suggests that better pay was what was required. "Those in this action were the worst that ever were seen, for they are so out of order and command and so stupefied that punish them or beat them they will scarce stir. Their ordinary talk being that his Majesty presseth them and giveth them so little means that it was better to be hanged, or serve the King of Spain or the Turk"—which many of them did, like the notorious Captain Ward and his fellow renegades in the service of the Barbary Pirates, or in later years those that served the Dutch.

In the Ship Money fleet of 1636 Mervyn complains that only a score of the 260 men aboard his flagship could take a turn at the helm, another 220 deserting when they were transferred into another ship. A third of the crew of the *Enterprise* and hardly one on board the *Unicorn* had ever been to sea before.[12]

Mervyn was one of the few officers of the period who took an interest in the welfare of his men. He ascribed their poor quality to "the making of mean men prest masters," that is to say relying on boatswains, crimps and tavern keepers. Such men were easily bribed. Indeed, it was so common an occurrence that there was a saying "that muster masters do carry the best men in their pockets." An attempt to limit the issue of press warrants to reputable officials was made, but there was little control over the conduct of the gangs in implementing them.

Numerous complaints from Weymouth suggest that the men

of Dorset were particularly hostile and the behaviour of the gangs operating there was notoriously outrageous. A warrant having been issued to the Mayor, he ordered all able seamen to assemble the next morning. As no prest master turned up to receive them, he dismissed them after noting that most of them looked more fit for a hospital than a ship. Late that night, after he had gone to bed, the gang burst into his house. One member was so drunk that he fell into the fireplace, another tripped over a stool. They demanded another assembly the next morning, but as soon as they saw the quality of the men they rejected the lot and began to raid private houses in search of young tradesmen or whoever was simple enough to accept the press money they proffered.[13]

Such behaviour was not only beyond the law; it was extremely expensive on account of the law suits which followed and the compensation which had to be paid. Even in the normal way of things it was an expensive way to raise men. If a man lived far from the coast, conduct money to enable him to reach the rendezvous could amount to seven or eight shillings a man, in addition to the shilling prest money. Taking into account wages paid on board, discharge and conduct money for the man's return, payments to prest masters of a pound a day and fourpence a mile, it cost £94,874 to man twelve warships with 3,000 men for six months.[14]

More serious were the losses due to peculation in victualling at a date when the auditing of accounts and the honesty of contractors left much to be desired. The brewers, complains one writer, "have gotten the art to sophisticate beer with broom instead of hops, and ashes instead of malt, and to make it look more lively to pickle it with salt water, so that while it is new it shall seem worthy of praise, but in one month, wax worse than stinking water." The beef issued to the Ship Money fleet was so tainted that "the scent all over the ship is enough to breed contagion."[15]

Captain John Smith, the founder of Virginia, whose *Sea-*

man's Grammar ran through several editions, makes some interesting suggestions how to improve the staple issue of salt
meat and biscuit. In his opinion every ship should carry some
spices, Dutch cheese, wine, bacon, mutton, suet preserved in
earthen pots, marmalade (i.e. jam) and "the juice of lemons
for the scurvy. Some it may be will say I would have men
feast than fight, but I say the want of these necessaries occasions
the loss of more men than in any English fleet hath been slain
since eighty-eight. For when a man is ill, or at the point of
death, I would know whether a dish of buttered rice with a
little cinnamon, ginger and sugar, a little minced meat or
roast beef, a few stewed prunes brewed with a little cinnamon
and sugar, be not better than a little Poor John or salt fish with
oil and mustard, or biscuit, butter and cheese or oatmeal
pottage on fishdays, or on fleshdays salt beef, pork and pease
with six shilling beer, this is your ordinary ship's allowance,
and good for them that are well conditioned, which is not
always, as seamen can too well witness. And after a storm,
when poor men are all wet and some have not so much as a
cloth to shift them, shaking with cold, few of these but will
tell you a little sack or brandy is much better to keep them in
health than a little small beer or cold water, although it be
sweet."

The victualling department was responsible for clothing
and hammocks as well as food, though little of the former was
provided before 1628 because of the typically bureaucratic
proviso that "it is not intended to clothe the men in London
to make them handsome to run away." What the Board overlooked was the fact that pressed men were virtually in such
rags that, as one captain put it, after a few weeks on board
they became "so naked that they are not able to undergo the
duty of their watches and labours at sea." Men reaching
Chatham after a long journey became so "nasty and weak"
that they infected others. After several epidemics had broken
out in the fleet, we find in 1628 the first reference to the pro-

vision of slops, ready-made clothes or "provant clothes," as they were called, to be sold on board—canvas suits, cotton waistcoats and breeches at 2/8 a pair, Monmouth caps, stockings, shirts, shoes and hammocks, all specifically provided "to avoid nasty beastliness which many men are subjected to by continual wearing of one suit of clothes." Only five hundred of the five thousand suits were sold, probably because the price was too high. Up to 1637 two shillings in the pound was deducted for the alehouse keeper where the clothes were stored, and the purser was allowed his shilling in the pound profit on what he sold on board when he opened his pack at the mainmast in the presence of the ship's company, the cost of any purchase being deducted from a man's pay.[16]

The following letter from Mervyn to the Board shows how slight was the improvement:[17]

> May it please your Lordships. The miserable condition of our poor mariners, who in the extremity of this cold tempestuous weather for want of clothing fall down daily into desperate sickness, inasmuch as I am forced to discharge more men by reason of their weakness than we can again supply ourselves withal from ships passing by, make me presume in their behalfs to be an humble suitor to your Lordships that you will be pleased to order £400 or £500 to be sent down for their relief, for on my credit the most part of them are barefooted, without stockings, and scarcely rags to hide their skin. If your Lordships please to have compassion on them in this way, I will, if your lordships please, be accountant for the disbursement thereof ... Some clothes are here, but so unserviceable and deceitful, and the prices so unconscionable by reason of the fees paid to the clerks, pursers and others who send them and stop the moneys at the pay-days due for them little less than four shillings in the pound, which so raiseth the price of the clothes that the poor men had rather starve than buy them.

Just as scurvy was the result of bad victualling, so typhus was the consequence of inadequate clothing. In the history of

Seaman of 1737: A cartoon showing The British Hercules holding a paper 'I wait for orders' attacking Walpole's pacific attitude towards Spain

VOLUNTEERS.

G. R. III.

God Save the King.

LET us, who are Englishmen, protect and defend our good KING and COUNTRY against the Attempts of all *Republicans* and *Levellers*, and against the Designs of our NATURAL ENEMIES, who intend in this Year to invade OLD ENGLAND, *our happy Country*, to murder our gracious KING as they have done *their own*; to make WHORES of our *Wives* and *Daughters*; to rob us of our Property, and teach us nothing but the *damn'd Art of murdering one another*.

ROYAL TARS
Of OLD ENGLAND.

If you love your COUNTRY, and your LIBERTY, now is the Time to shew your Love.

REPAIR,

All who have good Hearts, who love their KING, their COUNTRY, and RELIGION, who hate the FRENCH, and damn the POPE,

TO

Lieut. W. J. Stephens,

At his Rendezvous, SHOREHAM,

Where they will be allowed to Enter for any SHIP of WAR,

AND THE FOLLOWING

BOUNTIES will be given by his MAJESTY, in Addition to Two Months Advance.

To Able Seamen, - - - *Five Pounds.*
To Ordinary Seamen, - - - *Two Pounds Ten Shillings.*
To Landmen, - - - *Thirty Shillings.*

Conduct-Money paid to go by Land, and their Chests and Bedding sent Carriage free.
Those Men who have served as PETTY-OFFICERS, and those who are otherwise qualified, will be recommended accordingly.

LEWES: PRINTED BY W. AND A. LEE.

A poster to attract volunteers at Shoreham, Sussex, with the bounties offered warfare, particularly on land, typhus has killed far more men than any other agency. In the days of sail it was known as ship fever and was distinguished from camp or gaol fever only because it broke out in other overcrowded, unhygienic surroundings. It was the scourge of cold climates among hastily raised ragged regiments of men, whether soldiers or sailors or prisoners. Since it is carried by the human body louse, it flourishes in conditions provided on board a man-of-war, where there was no washing water, no soap (at this time a prized monopoly) and no change of clothes. If an infected man came on board, an epidemic could spread in a matter of days. Before serious official attention was paid to raising the standard of hygiene on board (that is to say virtually before the days of Nelson), typhus was the commonest affliction in the Channel fleet, as Yellow Fever was in the West Indies.

The first major epidemic occurred on the Cadiz expedition of 1625. It is true that plague was raging in England that year, but the symptoms of bubonic plague were so well known that the word would have been used if such had been the sickness complained of. All the evidence suggests typhus, though at the time many ascribed it to "corrupt and stinking" victuals. A quarter of the men succumbed before they reached Cadiz after only twenty-one days at sea. When the ships returned to the western ports, 5,000 casualties were reported. Few ships had sufficient healthy men to man the pumps or trim the sails. In the *Anne Royal* there were 130 dead and 160 sick. One captain complains of a "miserable infection and they die very fast." Another says "they stink as they go, and the poor rags they have are rotten and ready to fall off."[18]

Undeterred, Buckingham urged the setting forth of another expedition. Sir John Pennington was told to collect forty ships at Plymouth. He protested that he could only find four, and those without stores or medical supplies or men. The Mayor would not permit any more sick to be landed in the town in case they infected the inhabitants. In the end he informed one of the Navy Commissioners that he had got together twenty-nine ships, but the men ran away as fast as they were pressed. "I wish you were a spectator a little, to hear their cries and exclamations; here die eight or ten daily." If something is not done immediately, "you will break my heart." He knew that £2,000 was being sent down, but he had already pledged £2,500 on his own credit. "If there be not some speedy course taken for the pay of the men, whereby they may relieve their wants and cover their nakedness, it will be impossible for me to keep them. I pray you to consider what these poor souls have endured for the space of these thirteen or fourteen months by sickness, badness of victuals and nakedness."[19]

Somehow he scraped together 3,800 men and the expedition sailed in 1627. The same tale was repeated on their return. Five hundred men died at Plymouth. The crew of the *Assurance* deserted in a body, though the Mayor tried to prevent their landing. Others roamed the streets, selling weapons filched from the soldiers on board for food. "I vow to God," wrote Mervyn, "I cannot deliver it in words. Unless my Lord (Buckingham) take it speedily into consideration, the King will have more ships than soldiers."[20]

As has been seen, something was now done to relieve the clothing shortage by the provision of slops. The Treasurer was granted £10,500 for the purchase of necessaries. The Surveyor of Victuals ("Bottomless-Bagg," who was widely blamed) was allowed £9,800 for other relief measures.

The cry on all such occasions was for more medical aid. Once more the College of Physicians sent down a few of their members, and as before they were quite ineffective. The Company of Barber-Surgeons provided other unwilling members, but they began to question the legality of such demands. When they expressed their misgivings to the King, the Master and Wardens of the Company received this reply:[21]

Whereas we have lately given you directions and commandments to imprest presently for our service a certain number of chirurgeons to be employed in our fleet, and that we understand you find opposition and hindrance in performing that service by colour of particular protections which they have obtained during this time of parliament and otherwise. And therefore since it is no way fit that the public service should be avoided and prevented by such particular pretences. Our will and pleasure is, and we do hereby authorise and require you, to imprest from time to time such and so many sufficient and experienced chirurgeons for our service as you shall have directions from us, notwithstanding any such protection whatsoever.

The King had ample precedent for adopting such a tone. The Company had been told repeatedly in Elizabeth's time to provide surgeons and surgeon's mates for both land and sea service. He therefore made it plain when renewing the Company's Charter that in the clause "the Master to appoint in any part of England proper surgeons for the King's ships to be sent out to sea," the word "appoint" meant "impress." This seems to have put the matter beyond doubt for the time being, since there are no further complaints.

A letter from the Navy Board to the Admiralty at the time of the setting forth of the Ship Money fleet describes the usual procedure. The Company having been informed that it must press surgeons, those on whom the lot fell were told to appear at Mincing Lane on a Friday afternoon to come before a board of admirals "to be satisfied of their sufficiency." How the admirals could judge this is not clear, but they were doubtless quite satisfied if a sufficient number of persons turned up.

The man in charge of the business, who was at one time medical advisor to the East India Company and Master of the Barber-Surgeons, was John Woodall, author of *The Surgeon's Mate* (1617). At the time of the Cadiz expedition he was asked to take "charge of pressing, furnishing and ordering of his Highness's whole navy and land services with surgeons and surgeon's mates, with all their provisions," that is to say their medicine chests and instruments. He never went to sea himself, but his manual was widely used. It deals chiefly with surgery, though here and there he ventures into pathological mysteries. Since dietetic experiments were still unknown in a scientific sense, and since far too little attention was paid to the experience of men at sea, he is hesitant about trusting to a single cure, preferring a multitude of expedients, the shotgun method well known in cases of medical ignorance. Thus on the question of the use of lemon juice as a cure for scurvy, having written that "the use of the juice of lemons is a precious medicine and well tried, being sound and good, let it have the first place," he proceeds to say that egg flip, barley water with cinnamon, or a few drops of oil of vitriol will do just as well.[22] It was because of such confusion on the part of the learned that expensive fruits such as lemons or oranges fell out of use as the century went on.

Officers who had served in the disastrous expeditions to Spain and France were becoming aware of the necessity of raising the standard of hygiene on board. Boteler was anxious that hammocks should be used instead of the "nasty holes" called cabins, or lying on the bare deck. They had been introduced in the time of Hawkins and were usually called "hammacoes" until the time of Nelson. Raleigh recommended them and they were now in common use, though they often had to be destroyed as infected and loathsome.

Fumigation of ships and the washing of decks were other aspects to which attention was now drawn. The conscientious Mervyn used "my very best cunning to make the *Vanguard* wholesome. I have caused her to be washed all over, fore and aft, every second day to be perfumed with tar burnt and frankincense; to be aired 'twixt decks with pans of charcoal; to be twice a week washed with vinegar."[23] If only his pleas for better clothing had been heeded, such measures might not have been necessary.

It was in the matter of the seaman's pay that most abuses occurred. The grievance was not so much about the amount, but the delay in payment. On paper, the able seaman's pay was reasonably good. Whatever his faults, in other respects, Buckingham showed a real appreciation of the problem and attempted to raise the pay and get it paid more promptly, but in the latter respect he failed from want of ready cash. In 1625 he raised the monthly wage of ten shillings to fourteen and the next year to fifteen. Since there was only £3,000 available, he directed that it should be paid in the first instance to poor mariners only, and when a prize was sold that the cash should be distributed to meet the shortage in wages. But only two-thirds of the wage bill was met until full payment was resumed in 1629, when the number of men in pay was smaller. The Parliamentary authorities took the first opportunity in 1643 to increase pay to nineteen shillings a month and in 1653 to twenty-four for the able seaman, nineteen for the ordinary seaman. At this figure it remained until after the mutinies of 1797. Out of his pay the seaman had, of course, to pay fourpence a month to the preacher (the chaplain's groat of later years), twopence to the surgeon, and sixpence to Chatham Chest.

A wage table of 1626 gives the following monthly rates:[24]

Rank	Ship of over 500 men			Ship of over 50 men		
Captain	£14.	0.	0.	£4.	13.	4.
Boatswain	2.	5.	0.	1.	3.	4.
Surgeon	1.	10.	0.	1.	10.	0.
Gunner	2.	0.	0.	1.	3.	4.
Seaman		15.	0.		15.	0.
Gromet		11.	3.		11.	3.
Boy		7.	6.		7.	6.

In addition to these official rates, the custom continued of paying Dead Shares, that is to say the payment of non-

existent persons for charitable purposes. Later this was regulated as the payment of what were called Widow's Men at the
rate of two per hundred men. A dishonest Clerk of the
Cheque could find many loopholes in this system, and even
more in the practice of false musters. When the men in four
ships were mustered in 1603 it was found that out of a total
complement of 1,350, only 958 were actually borne, so that
the King was being defrauded at a rate of £800 a quarter.[25]

The iniquitous practice of issuing wage tickets instead of
cash began in Charles's reign. A Promissory note of the wages
due was issued by the commanding officer, countersigned by
the local Clerk of the Cheque (or Check) and honoured on
presentation at the Navy Office. The practice originated for
the sensible reason that it was unwise to carry much ready
money on board, but it led to a variety of abuses in the next
hundred years. There was nothing to prevent the Clerk from
issuing tickets for non-existent men. The discount taken when
encashing could be very high: even pursers had to be prevented from taking two shillings in the pound and dishonest
brokers on shore could take much more. Tickets could be
easily forged or lodged with tavern keepers at an extortionate
rate of discount to discharge a debt. In 1656 it was said that
three shillings in the pound was a common figure and ten
years later bumboat women were taking five shillings.

Ships were often kept in harbour for months before the
payment of wages, either to await the arrival of cash from
London, or simply to prevent men deserting. There was a
further distinction between Rigging Wages in harbour and
Sea Pay, the former being considerably lower. From this
had to be deducted the contributions mentioned above and
the cost of everything bought from the purser on board.
According to Hollond, some captains resorted to truck payment of wages by selling clothes and even strong drink on
their own account. The worst sufferers were the widows and
children of those who died abroad. They were legally en-

titled to a man's wages up to the time of his death, but it was hard "for a poor woman with three or four children that hath lost a husband in the service, and to whom there was not due above forty shillings or thereabouts before the ship miscarried, should be forced to spend, besides her time and pains in travel, oftentimes a hundred miles to London, one-third part of the whole to enable her legally to receive her husband's wages."[26]

Captain Sir Ferdinando Gorges, better known as the founder of New Plymouth, summarises the grievances of the early Stuart mariner in these words:[27]

1st. They say they are used like dogs, forced to keep aboard without being suffered to come ashore to refresh themselves.

2nd. That they have not the means to put clothes on their backs to defend themselves from cold or to keep them in health, much less to relieve their poor wives and children.

3rd. That when they happen to fall sick they have not any allowance of fresh victuals to comfort them, or medicine to help recover them.

4th. That some of their sick fellows being put ashore in houses erected for them are suffered to perish for want of being looked unto, their toes and feet rotting from their bodies, and so smelling that none are able to come into the room where they are.

5th. That some provisions put aboard them is neither fit nor wholesome for men to live on.

6th. That therefore they had as lief be hanged as dealt with as they are.

No wonder that recruitment was difficult and desertion frequent. Again and again we hear of the whole ship's company deserting in a body, of men running away as fast as they were raised, of strikes in the dockyards and mutinies on board ships. In 1626 payment of wages was only made after five hundred seamen crying "One and all, one and all! Away, away!" threatened to march on London from Chatham. Two years later the sailing of the La Rochelle fleet was delayed not so much by the assassination of the Lord High Admiral as by

the "contemptuous and sudden running away of their men."
Nor had the officers the heart to discipline such poor wretches,
"for alas! say they, when men have no money nor clothes to
wear, much less to pawn, nor victuals to eat, what would
you have them do? Starve? This is likely to be the condition
of the ships now in the Downs and those at Portsmouth,
having not two days victuals if equally divided."[28]

Throughout the period the tendency to reduce the number
of soldiers on board continued. Action stations on board a
typical ship, the *Speedwell* of thirty guns, were as follows:
18 gunners and 48 men to man the guns, 50 small arms men,
50 sailors to work the ship and man the tops, 4 men in the
powder room, 4 carpenters, 3 trumpeters, 3 surgeons, 4
stewards, 3 cooks and 3 boys, making a ship's company of
190, excluding officers.[29]

The duties of the warrant officers as described by Captain
John Smith remained much the same for the rest of the
century.[30] The Boatswain was responsible for the rigging
and the working of the ship, whereas the Marshal was responsible for the discipline. He is evidently the descendant
of the Constable and the predecessor of the Master-at-Arms.
He is

> to punish all offenders and to see justice executed according to
> directions; as ducking at the yard arm, hauling under the keel,
> bound to the capstern or main mast with a basket of shot about
> his neck, setting in the bilboes, and to pay cobty or the morjoune
> (i.e. cobbing or beating); but the boys the Boatswain is to see
> every Monday morning at the Chest to say their compass and
> receive punishment for all their week's offences, which done, they
> are to have a quarter can of beer and a bisket of bread, but if the
> Boatswain eat or drink before he catch them, they are free . . .
> The Swabber is to wash and clean the ship.
> The Liar is to hold his place for but a week, and he that is first
> taken with a lie every Monday is so proclaimed at the main mast
> by a general cry of a Liar, a Liar, a Liar; he is under the Swabber
> and only to clean the beakhead chains.

The Sailers are the ancient men for hoisting the sails, getting the tacks on board, hauling the bowline and steering the ship.

The Younkers are the young men called Fore Mast Men to take in the top falls, or top and yard, for furling the sails, or slinging the yards, bousing (pulling) or trising (trice up), and take their turns at the helm.

(Having divided the ship's company into the Larboard, or Boatswain's, and Starboard, or Master's, watches, and subdivided these into Squadrons under Mates,) you are to mess them four to a Mess and then give every Mess a quarter can of beer and bisket of bread to stay their stomachs till the kettle be boiled, that they may go first to prayer, then to supper, and at six o'clock sing a psalm, say a prayer, and the Master with his side begins the Watch, then all the rest may do what they will till midnight, and then his Mate with his Larboard men, with a psalm and a prayer, relieve them till four in the morning, and so from eight to twelve each other, except some sudden flaw of wind come, some storm or gust, or some accident that requires the help of all hands, which commonly after such good cheer in most voyages doth happen.

We may conclude this account of the early Stuart mariner, as he was still officially called, with the "character" of such a man. Such generalised sketches of the Theophrastian type were popular at this time, but the common seaman was usually ignored. Those which do include him are excessively literary in style, being written by such people as Thomas Fuller or Sir Thomas Overbury, who were too far removed from what they pretended to describe and too anxious to display their wit to be of much use to the historian. Richard Braithwaite, however, the author of a rare little book entitled *Whimzies* (1631), knew London River well. He was born in the year of the Armada, fought on the Parliamentary side in the Civil War and had a son killed by pirates. He wrote other social satires under such odd titles as *Drunken Barnaby's Journal* or *A Strappado for the Devil*.[31]

The breadth of an inch-board is betwixt him and drowning, yet he swears and drinks as deeply as if he were a fathom from it.

His familiarity with death and danger hath armed him with a kind of dissolute security against any encounter. . . .

He makes small or no choice of his pallet, he can sleep as well on a sack of pumice as on a pillow of down. He was never acquainted with much civility; the sea hath taught him other rhetoric. Compassion himself he could never much, and much less another. He has conditioned with the sea not to make him sick; and it is the best of his conceits to jeer at a queasy stomach. He is more active than contemplative, unless he turn astronomer, and that is only in cases of extremity. He is most constant to his shirt, and other his seldom washed linen. He has been so long acquainted with surge of the sea, as too long a calm disturbs him. He cannot speak low, the sea talks so loud. His advice is seldom taken in naval affairs; though his hand is strong, his headpeace is stupid. He is used therefore as a necessary instrument of action; for he can spin up a rope like a spider and down again like lightning. The rope is his road, and the topmast his beacon. One would think his body were wounded, for he wear pitch-cloth upon it; but that is invulnerable unless a bullet casually finds out a loophole and that quite rips up his sailcloth. He partakes of the chameleon, when he is mounted the topmast, where the air is his diet bread. His visage is an unchangeable varnish; neither can wind pierce it, nor sun parch it . . .

He is of a phlegmatical, watery constitution; very little sanguine, unless it be in a sea-fight, wherein, though he expect no honour, he expresseth some flying sparks of valour, in hope to become shares in a piratical treasure. He hath an invincible stomach, which ostrich-like could well near digest iron.

Associates he hath, and those so constantly cleaving as one voice commands all. Stars cannot be more faithful in their society than these Hans-kins in their fraternity. They will have it valiantly when they are ranked together, and relate their adventures with wonderful terror. Necessary instruments are they, and agents of main importance in that Hydrarchy wherein they live; for the walls of the State could not subsist without them; but least useful they are to themselves, and most needful for others supportance. They taste of all waters and weathers; only the gale of prosperity seldom breathes on their sails; neither are they much for any such companion. . . .

Well: suppose him now drawing towards the port where all mortalities must land. He has tugged long enough upon the main, he must now gather up his vessel within the haven. He has drawn in his sails, and taken adieu of the sea; unless she show him so much kindness as to receive him into her briny bosom, and entomb him dying, whom she entertained living.

IV

The Dutch Wars

THE NAVAL PROFESSION and the administrative basis of the service during the age of sail was forged in the crucible of the three Dutch Wars, 1652-54, 1665-67, 1672-74. The "new model" navy formed during the Commonwealth was institutionalised during the reigns of Charles II and William III so successfully that its administrative structure, the build of its ships, the methods by which it was officered, manned and supplied, continued without fundamental change until half way through the nineteenth century. It was during this period that the warship became, at last, distinct from the merchant ship, and a naval profession, consisting of qualified officers with a hierarchy of rank and pay, began to emerge to provide a career, instead of an occasional occupation, for members of the upper classes.

The same cannot be said of the seamen. As before, they continued to serve either in the naval or in the merchant service, according to the demands of the moment or the exigencies of personal fate rather than choice. The Navigation Act of 1651 aimed at increasing the number of seamen available, but only a small proportion spent the whole of their lives in the navy. Unless a man became a boatswain or a gunner or a master, there was little chance of promotion to make it an attractive career. As long as tarpaulins could become captains or admirals, as so many did in Cromwell's day, there was hope, but such chances became rare as the century drew to a close.

On the outbreak of the Civil War the fleet defected in a body to the Parliamentary cause because the maladministration of the service under the first two Stuarts made such action inevitable. Until the insufferable Colonel Rainborough was appointed commander-in-chief six years later, there was no question where the sympathy of the seamen lay. But when a Leveller was put at their head there was a general mutiny, in the course of which nine ships were taken over to Holland by their crews. Most of them returned to serve under the Protectorate. Discounting the few loyalists who followed Prince Rupert, it is a mistake to suppose that the sentiments of the average seaman were royalist in character. On the other hand, he welcomed the Restoration unreservedly because by that time the zeal and the glory of the great days under the Generals-at-Sea had begun to fade.

During the first three years of the Commonwealth the office of Lord High Admiral was administered by the Admiralty Committee of the Council of State, together with the Commissioners of the Navy Board. From 1652 until the revival of the office under James, Duke of York, these bodies became respectively the Commissioners of the Navy (the equivalent of the Board of Admiralty), including such names as Blake, Monck and Penn at sea, with special commissioners at the major ports, like Peter Pett at Chatham; and the Navy Board, now established at Crutched Friars in Seething Lane, where Pepys joined it after the Restoration. In contrast to the previous lax and corrupt administration of the fleet, when the saints came marching in every effort was made to inject a puritan sense of discipline and efficiency into the service. No captain was permitted to leave his ship for more than six hours without special permission under penalty of a fine amounting to a month's pay. Men absent without leave were subject to a similar fine. Clerks of the Cheque were turned into political commissars to spy on the officers, though such an un-English surveillance seems to have been short lived.[1]

In the creation and use of the fleet, the Commonwealth record is unsurpassed. In eleven years 207 new ships were added and the period witnessed successful wars not only against the Dutch and the Spanish (in which Blake's action at Santa Cruz continued unrivalled till that of Nelson at the Nile) but an extension of naval power into the Mediterranean and the Caribbean, where the first overseas base came into existence after the capture of Jamaica.

Oliver's days shone brighter after the tragedies of the Restoration period—the Plague, the Fire and the Dutch in the Medway. However much the high standards of the early days had in fact declined, the Blake period became more golden as memories lengthened. A pamphleteer writing at the beginning of Anne's reign recalls how well the fleet fared before the appearance of the Gentlemen Captains of the Restoration.[2] According to him (though it is hard to believe) the first time he ever heard a "God damn ye" in a warship was on board the *Naseby* bringing Charles home. "I cannot omit to tell you what I have frequently heard our great and good Admiral Blake say amidst his ship's company. That the meanest of them were free-born Englishmen as well as himself, and that the officers and mariners were all fellow-servants of the Government of this country. This tender and prudent behaviour towards the seamen made them look upon themselves as indispensably obliged to respect their officers like parents."

The historian of naval administration at this date bears him out: "Never before or since, were the combatant branches of the Navy well so supported," writes Oppenheim with somewhat excessive optimism.[3] "As a rule our seamen have had to beat the enemy afloat in spite of the Admiralty ashore, but here they had every assistance that foresight and earnestness could give . . . They had for the Dutch that hatred which their fathers felt for the Spaniards, and for the first time for many years, they found themselves well treated—comparatively punctually paid, properly clothed, well fed, cared for when sick or wounded, and promised advantages in the shape of prize money never previously allowed. What wonder they served the Commonwealth during its earlier years, as the crown had never been served since the days of Elizabeth."

Unfortunately for those who came after the zealots, these things were not paid for. By 1660 the Navy Debt amounted to a million and a half pounds, of which half was due for unpaid wages. Three-quarters of the national income was now devoted to the service, making it by far the most important department of state, but even before the Restoration there are instances of ships going three or four years without payment. No wonder the men welcomed Charles as they had once welcomed Cromwell, and no wonder one of the first entries in Pepys's diary (3 July, 1660) when he took up his duties as Clerk of the Acts is that he found the navy "in a very sad condition, and money must be raised for it." That remained his perennial problem until he resigned at the Revolution, since it affected every side of naval activity—shipbuilding, victualling, manning and even fighting.

Under the burden of this persistent lack of cash, due to Parliament's distrust of the King's expenditure, Pepys struggled heroically to strengthen the sinews of war. Most of his efforts were ruined during the years when he was banished from the Admiralty (and even confined to the Tower) at the time of the Popish Plot disturbances, so that all had to be done over again. In the Second Dutch War naval expenditure jumped from £40,000 to £400,000. In the third the rise was similar. But due to Pepys's efficiency the debt had been reduced by 1686 from well over a million to £171,836. His claim in his memoirs printed in 1690 that the Navy had never been in better condition than when he left it may be accepted. The man whom Monck called "the right hand of the navy" early in his career deserves the title accorded him by his modern biographer, "the saviour of the navy." Of course he welcomed any credit due, for he was that sort of man; but he had the generosity to admit (what many historians forget) that "if it had not pleased God to give us a king and a duke that understood the sea, this nation had ere this been quite beaten out of it."[4]

Among his papers bequeathed to his old college at Cambridge there is a comparison between the size of the navy as he found it and as he left it.[5]

1660   156 ships—19,551 men
1688   173 ships—41,940 men

Both the Dutch and the French navies were larger. The United Provinces at their height could muster 80,000 seamen out of a population of under three million. Colbert's navy, as yet unbaptised by war, is said to have depended on 46,000 seamen, excluding 47,000 coastal fishermen and 10,000 watermen, out of a population of about 16 million. The problem of manning the vastly extended fleet in England and Wales from a population of about five and a half million was obviously much greater. Nor can accurate figures of the seafaring population be obtained: Sir William Petty's guess in 1670 was that the trade needed 48,000, of whom only half would be at sea at any given time.

Instead of relying on rule-of-thumb estimates of manning requirements, Pepys in 1677 drew up an exact computation of the complement of each class of ship, "a solemn and unalterable adjustment of the gunning and manning of the whole fleet," which served the navy for a long time to come. Up till now it had been reckoned that a ratio of one man to four tons was sufficient in a warship. In 1673 a more rational attempt was made to relate the complement to the number of guns carried, now that the rating of warships by the number of guns was accepted. This establishment provides the

following complements, over and above which the Admiral
of the Red (the senior admiral) was allowed fifty men and
other flag officers a retinue in proportion to their seniority.

First Rate	100 guns—800 men
Second Rate	82 guns—530 men
Third Rate	74 guns—460 men
Fourth Rate	54 guns—280 men
Fifth Rate	30 guns—130 men
Sixth Rate	16 guns— 65 men

Pepys breaks down these totals thus when the Establishment was confirmed in 1677:[6]

First Rate	*No. of Men*	*No. of Guns*
Cannon: 8 men to a gun	208	26
Culverin: 5 men to a gun	140	26
Men to govern the guns	8	—
Saker: 3 men to a gun	84	26
Demi-Culverin ditto	12	4
Minion ditto	30	10
Three-pounders: 2 men to a gun	4	2
To carry powder	38	—
To fill and hand powder	16	—
To hand down wounded men	12	—
Chirurgeon and crew	8	—
Carpenter and crew	8	—
Purser and crew	6	—
Boats: 3	30	—
To the tops, if no flag	10	—
For the helm	2	—
To con the ship	2	—
Small shot	80	—
To the sails and rigging	80	—
TOTAL	778	94

One way to meet the needs for manning was to put soldiers

on board, but for the first time these men were specifically allotted to the sea service instead of the land service. They were, in reality, the first marines. By an Order in Council of 1664, 1,200 soldiers were sent to sea as a Regiment under the command of the Duke of York. The next year a second maritime regiment was raised. Though such regiments were disbanded after every war, there is a fairly continuous record of service on the part of the Marines from this date. By 1702 there were six regiments, amounting to 40,000 men. When at sea they were borne on a separate list, paid the same as soldiers on land (30/- a month as compared with the able seaman's 24/-) and raised by a colonel in the same way. When on shore they, like the sailors, were expected to help in the dockyards. When disbanded every man was allowed his uniform (something the sailor had not yet got), his snapsack, three shillings for delivering up his sword, and a passport exempting him from impressment.

The First Dutch War was undoubtedly the most popular, the Second, coinciding as it did with the Plague and the Fire, was less so, and in the Third there was a growing uneasiness that we were fighting the wrong enemy in the United Provinces rather than France. Hence the number of volunteers in the first war was both unusual and significant. It was reported that men were coming in "cheerfully and in great numbers since the publication of the late encouragement to them," that is to say the recent announcement of a pay rise. At Chatham, Commissioner Pett found the "seamen in general to be very tractable and complying, and begin to attend their duties handsomely." On board the *Speaker* there were so many volunteers that the Clerk of the Cheque had "very much trouble to reduce them to their complement." On board the *Sapphire* Captain Heaton reported the same—which is not surprising, since he brought eighty-four prizes into Plymouth in eighteen months.[7]

None the less the government resorted to impressment as

vigorously as any of its predecessors. On 5 April, 1652 an order was issued to press at a shilling a man. When at beat of drum at Sandwich only one person volunteered, fourteen others were promptly pressed and sent to Woolwich. On 22 May four hundred watermen were sent to Chatham. In August local authorities were told to press at one pound a head. The pay increase of January, 1653 (to be described later) brought in many more men, but the government was careful not to interrupt the normal course of trade. Men in the service of the state were already exempt. Presters were told not to take men off outward bound ships in case depleted crews made them vulnerable to enemy privateers. When the master of a collier asked the Council for protection against further recruitment from his vessel. which had already lost two men, he was allowed it. Another master at Ipswich protested that, though given a protection, a boat from the *Amity* came alongside and when the gang could not find the hidden seamen, seized their belongings, declaring they must come on board the warship to fetch them. In an operational area like the Downs such high handed methods were common, fifty men being taken off colliers in a single day in 1657. The constant stream of letters and orders sent to the Generals-at-Sea give innumerable instances of this sort. Some are so detailed that the mayors of coastal towns are even told the names of those who should be taken up.[8]

Such methods form the basis of the system of impressment as practised in this country for the next two hundred years. As Pepys said when he found a navy suddenly expanding from three to thirty thousand men on the outbreak of war, the balance "must be found out of the trade of the nation." A proclamation issued at the beginning of the Second Dutch War resuscitates the prize inducements made in the First, while at the outset of the Third a bounty was offered of a month's wages and a promise that volunteers would not be turned over to other ships without their consent. It is doubt-

ful if such promises were ever honoured, but proclamations of
this sort continue during every succeeding war.

The procedure now becoming standardised was for the
Privy Council to issue an order to the Admiralty for a general
impress. The naval authorities then sent down press warrants
to local authorities, who in turn appointed presters, as they
were still called, to operate either by sea or land. Thus in
1678 James Dunbar, owner of the *Mary*, forty tons, was employed "for the impressing and carrying of seamen for His
Majesty's navy." His tender was allowed twenty-two men,
six guns and small arms. He himself was paid £18 a month
for the hire of his vessel and 2/6 for every man pressed,
"which shall not be under the number of 800 at least."⁹

Pressing tenders such as this not only took men off ships
coming up Channel, they often seized foreigners as well, a
course of action usually followed by diplomatic complaints.
When in 1677 Captain Sir Thomas Allen took men off a
French warship, Pepys was told to demand more discretion
on the part of such fire-eaters: they might send in the names
of Englishmen found on board foreign vessels but not remove them by force. For two centuries this proved a difficulty with neutrals. A partial solution was to issue a proclamation recalling all British subjects. If they disobeyed, they
became rebels or deserters who could be extradited by treaty.
By the thirty-sixth article of a Captain's Instructions he was
thereby empowered to take off any British subject found
serving under a foreign flag, but he was not to touch
foreigners.¹⁰

A press warrant was not necessarily limited to the conscription of men. Timber could be requisitioned for the
dockyards and transported at prices determined by Trinity
House. Carpenters, shipwrights and caulkers were often impressed, as were naval stores such as hemp, or stockfish for
victualling. On 12 May 1677 a hundred shipwrights were
pressed at Deptford and Chatham and other artificers at

Yarmouth. Two years later a hundred watermen were pressed for "the rigging and fetching about of the *Sandwich* to Chatham, where they are to be discharged and left at liberty to return to their ordinary occasions." Pett was told to press twenty carvers, and a general warrant was sent to fifteen captains to press joiners, caulkers and shipwrights for the new building programme.[11]

All this had to be done with one eye on Parliament, where pressing was never popular. Nor was it always with local authorities. On one occasion the Governor of Dover and Warden of the Cinque Ports refused to execute his warrant for fear of political repercussions. But Pepys insisted: "The impresting of men for supply of the King's ships not to be stopped, notwithstanding the inquiries on foot in Parliament, touching that matter." As soon as the war was over, the Navy Board earnestly discussed the matter, but came to the usual conclusion that there was no alternative. The Secretary was always anxious to avoid "offence to the country," particularly in peacetime, when he told the authorities "to invite seamen by beating of drums in the place usual" rather than compel them to come in. As might be expected from a man of his humanity, he intervened time and again in cases of peculiar hardship, for example when two Charterhouse schoolboys were "seduced from Southwark fair and shipped against their wills." As he wrote in his diary on 1 July, 1666, "To see poor, patient labouring men and housekeepers leaving poor wives and families, taken up on a sudden by strangers, was very hard, and that without press money but forced against all law to be gone. It is a great tyranny." None the less in wartime he saw no alternative.

Much of his correspondence consists of reprimands to unscrupulous or over zealous officers, not only because of his humanity but because he was more acutely aware of the legal and political problems involved: "Till this liberty of pressing men without consideration to the safety of the vessels they press out of be once severely corrected, the king's service can never be free from clamour."[12]

An odd list may be made of those exempt for particular reasons: four members of the barge of the Archbishop of Canterbury; five men working a ferry; the lighthouse keeper at Deal; a porter who was "aged, sickly and no seaman"; a baker found to be a Dutchman; the crew of a vessel carrying Portland stone for rebuilding St. Paul's; no Scotsman (this was before the Union). On more than one occasion Pepys had to intervene personally to see that the law was not broken. On 30 June 1666, he was aghast to hear that some of the Lord Mayor's men had been pressed without payment because the gang had run out of cash: "I did there out of my own purse disburse £15 to pay for their pressing and diet last night and this morning, which is a thing worth record of my Lord Mayor (. . . a silly man, I think)."

One of the most moving entries in his diary is that for 13 June, 1666, after the funeral of Admiral Myngs, a popular tarpaulin officer. After the coffin had been lowered into the ground a dozen able, lusty men came forward to speak with him: "We are here a dozen of us that have long known and loved and served our dead commander Sir Christopher Myngs and have now done the last office of laying him in the ground. We should be glad we had any other to offer him, and in revenge of him. All we have is our lives; if you will please to get His Royal Highness to give us a fireship among us all, here is a dozen of us, out of all which choose you one commander, and the rest of us, whoever he is, will serve him; and if possible do that that shall show our memory of our dead commander and our revenge."

It was during this period that the first Articles of War were drawn up for the better maintenance of discipline at sea. They were based on the ancient laws of the sea and on individual methods adopted by previous admirals to impose discipline. The Articles of 1652 codify such heterogeneous lists of crimes and punishments, and they are re-enacted with little change in the Naval Discipline Act of 1661, which lasted until the reign of George II. The first series may well have been due to the bitter criticisms of the behaviour of his subordinates, chiefly commanders of merchant ships, made by Blake after the battle of Dungeness. They have the severity one expects of a General-at-Sea. Twenty-five out of thirty-nine articles carry the death penalty, though this does not seem to have been imposed during the Commonwealth. Only one such sentence is recorded from that period: after six men had been found guilty of incitement to mutiny and condemned to death, their sentence was commuted to thirty lashes in the case of three men, the rest being condemned to stand an hour with their right hands nailed to the mainmast and with a halter about their necks.[13]

The Articles of 1661 empower captains to try a number of offences by court martial and impose death sentences, but in the Narrow Seas such sentences had to be confirmed by the Lord High Admiral. The maximum penalty could be imposed for murder, embezzlement, giving information or supplies to the enemy, desertion, mutiny, striking an officer, setting fire to the ship, robbery, or habitually sleeping on watch. Swearing, drunkenness and "other scandalous actions in derogation of God's honour and corruption of good manners" carried penalties such as flogging or a fine.

Even Commonwealth seamen found the new standards of discipline severe. Their chief complaint (apart from the usual one of delay in the payment of wages) was the prohibition of shore leave.[14] Apparently this was something new and it was due to the danger of desertion. The men pray

"that they may be relieved in those grievances and may reap some fruits of their bloodshed and hardships, and that they may not be imprested to serve, they humbly apprehending it to be inconsistent with the principles of Freedom and Liberty to force men to serve in military employments, either by sea or land; and that your petitioners may be as free as the Dutch seamen, against whom they have been such instruments in the Lord's hands for the good of their country; but that if the Commonwealth have occasion to employ any of your petitioners they may be hired as the Dutch are, and that they, or their lawful attorney, may be paid every six months at the furthest . . . and that all other liberties and privileges due to your petitioners as freemen of England may be granted and secured."

No government, at that or any other time, could afford to listen to such pathetic requests if it was essential to keep the fleet fully manned.

Another petition, which could only have been made during the Rule of the Saints, comes from the men at Chatham. They complain that the chaplain has neglected his preaching, even though he is paid £100 out of their wages. They ask that another be appointed in his place, that they may enjoy the means of salvation; otherwise they are in danger of becoming infidels. To which the chaplain provided a convincing answer: since rowing was prohibited on the Lord's Day, he could not reach the ships.[15]

In matters of discipline Pepys had more trouble with his officers than with the men, on account of the laxness of Restoration morals. Many ascribed this state of affairs to the habits of the new Gentlemen Captains as compared with the Tarpaulins who had risen to command in the more democratic days of the Commonwealth. Such courtiers and amateurs were accused of absenteeism, drunkenness, wasting their time in harbour, bringing undesirable followers on board: "near twenty landmen as his footmen, tailor, barber, fiddlers, decayed kindred, volunteer gentlemen or acquaintances." Such a captain "destroys his breed of seamen by casualties of his own making."[16]

To get rid of these amateurs, to make the tarpaulin something of a gentleman, in fact to produce that amalgam of officer and gentleman which became the qualified naval officer, Pepys in 1677 introduced the most important reform of all in the creation of a professional corps of officers: no one could become a lieutenant unless he passed an examination in seamanship and navigation. To "pass for lieutenant" thus became the first hurdle in an officer's career. That career may be said to have been founded (though it was not realised at the time) by the Duke of York's introduction of the rating of volunteer King's Letter Boy in 1661. This aspirant became in time a midshipman and then, after a stated period of experience, he could pass for lieutenant. The introduction of half pay for a certain number of officers from 1668 onwards meant a retaining fee which guaranteed the existence of a reserve of officers awaiting full pay when actually employed at sea. It took a generation to see the emergence of the naval officer from the chrysalis of the privateer or the short service amateur, but by the end of the century the concepts of rank and seniority and the hallmarks of a professional man— technical qualification and security of service—had become generally accepted.

This development of the naval officer did not improve the chances of promotion from the lower deck. The seaman was seldom literate enough to take the lieutenant's examination, though he could rise as far as midshipman. His social origins prevented him from becoming an officer and a gentleman. He could still become a warrant officer; but whereas early in the century the boatswain and the gunner were treated as officers rather than men, in so far as they were consulted in the appointment of what we should call petty officers and leading seamen, this became increasingly the duty of the lieutenant. As the ladder of rank became more defined, the line hardened between the quarter-deck and the lower deck, between those who emerged from the ship's company to become warrant officers appointed by the Navy Board and those sons of gentlemen who joined as King's Letter Boys or Captain's Servants (i.e. followers) and received their commissions from the Admiralty when they passed the lieutenant's examination. After the age of the Tarpaulin captains, it was only exceptional men who reached quarter-deck status, usually via the post of Master, who, by virtue of his responsibility for the navigation of a ship was better educated than most seamen. Class distinctions were hardening, though it must always be remembered that they were far from reaching the petrifaction which characterised the Victorian navy.

The unpublished comments of Josiah Burchett, Secretary of the Admiralty in 1711, on this point are of interest.[17] After commending the Duke of York's scheme for what we should call cadets, thus encouraging "men of the better rank to breed their younger sons to the sea," and saying that the lieutenant's examination had achieved its purpose, he adds: "Now the Volunteers being grown mighty numerous and very chargeable to the Navy, and all the Commission Officers chosen out of them, there is no room left for the poor Seaman of any sort, Warrant Officers and others (out of which many considerable officers have been produced, as namely Lawson, Harman, Kempthorne, Berry, Narbrough, and Sir Cloudesley Shovell, to name no more) to hope for any preferment, which I take to be a discouragement to them."

"Seamen," said Pepys, "are the most adventurous creatures in the world, and the most free of their money after all their dangers when they come to receive it." That was the point—when they received it. Again, when he said "The King's wages better than merchantmen's yet his service shunned by reason of bad pay," what he meant was the delay or discount in payment. He never succeeded in solving this principal defect in naval administration because of the perennial shortage of ready cash. In peacetime naval pay compared favourably with other wages, though in wartime the state was outbid by shipowners offering three or four times the naval rate. The real trouble was that the nominal rates were seldom honoured in full when a ship was paid off.

Cromwell realised that in the navy, even if not in his more dedicated army, an increase in monetary incentive was the chief solution of the manning problem. In January, 1653, the monthly rate was raised to 24/- for able seamen, 19/- for ordinary, 14/3 for gromets and 9/6 for boys. The good news was announced locally by sound of trumpet. In addition, £10 was to be paid to a seaman's widow (a captain's receiving £1,000) and more generous payments were made from Chatham Chest than its income warranted.

This burst of generosity on the part of the state did not last long. That same year a musket was levelled at the Protector himself when four hundred men burst into Whitehall demanding their arrears of pay, so that it needed four regiments of footguards to repel them. Some of the grievances embodied in their petitions may have been fomented by the dissident Admiral Lawson, as well as by the prospect of an expedition to the West Indies, to which men swore they would prefer hanging. But even Blake's men in the Mediterranean were not paid for twenty months and there was a feeling that the government was reluctant to hand over the prize money due. As for Chatham Chest pensioners, it was said that half the payments for 900 men were in arrears, so that many were "reduced to such extreme misery that I fear many of them have perished of late."[18] Such facts tarnish the accepted picture of the Commonwealth navy.

The government certainly intended a more generous distribution of prize money. Since there was no Lord High Admiral, his share was allocated to the relief of widows and the wounded. In 1653 the ship's company was promised 10/- a ton for every ship taken and £6. 13. 4. a gun if she was a warship. Medals were also awarded for distinguished service, the earliest example being to the officers and crew of the *Adventure* for their gallantry in engaging a superior force off Harwich. In the course of the war, 169 gold medals were awarded, chiefly to officers.[19]

By this date the use of wage tickets had become general. It was inevitable, on account of the size of the navy and the danger of carrying too much ready money on board. With the prevailing shortage of funds after the Restoration, all sorts of abuses crept in, so that it became impossible to honour the nominal rate of pay punctually. At the very start of his diary (3 December, 1660) Pepys complains of insufficient cash to discharge the seamen. Commissioner Hollond (the author of the *Discourses* mentioned earlier) proposed paying half the value of the ticket and half later. Before this could be done, the Second Dutch War broke out, so that in a matter of months the wage bill increased tenfold while Parliamentary grants lagged far behind. On 14 July 1665 an admiral begged the Navy Office for an immediate delivery of cash "to stop the bawlings and impatience of these people, especially of their wives, whose tongues are as foul as the daughters of Billingsgate."[20] Complaints were coming in from every dockyard and reports of riots from every port. The situation in London, where most tickets were due to be paid, became so tense that Pepys and his fellow officials in Seething Lane asked to be provided with "twelve well-fixed firelocks with a supply of powder and bullets for the defence of the said office." It may be added that the fine architectural screen built by Adam across the courtyard of the Admiralty in 1760 was not built for aesthetic reasons but to replace an old wall erected to prevent seamen breaking the windows of Admiralty House.

Pepys's diary is full of heart-rending descriptions of the distress caused by this delay in payment. On 30 September 1665 he says "the great burden we have upon us at this time at the office is the providing for prisoners and sick men that are recovered, they lying before our office doors all night and all day, poor wretches." On 7 October the entry runs "Did business, though not much, at the office, because of the horrible crowd and lamentable moan of the poor seamen that lie starving in the streets for lack of money. Which do trouble and perplex me to the heart; and more at noon when we were to go through them, for then a whole hundred followed us, some cursing, some swearing and some praying to us." On 4 November the windows of his office were broken and they threatened to storm the Treasury, "and if they do once come to that, it will not be long before they come to our's."

A letter from Hull in 1667 illustrates the mood of the country after all the disasters, naval and domestic, in that war. "Some do not stick to say things were better ordered in Cromwell's time, for then the seamen had all their pay, and were not permitted to swear, but were clapped in the bilboes; and if the officers did, they were turned out, and then God gave a blessing to them; but now all men are for making themselves great, and few mind the King and the nation's interest, but mind plays and women, and fling away much money that would serve to pay the seamen. This is the seamen's discourse."[20]

A petition from the officers and crew of H.M. frigate *Harp* off the coast of Ireland that year shows what justification there was for such grumbling. As their wages were fifty-two months in arrears, they humbly request payment, "having neither money nor credit to buy bread for their wives and children, who are now in a starving condition, being forced to lie in the streets by reason their landlords will trust them no longer, and your petitioners going naked for want of clothes, which together are worse ten thousand times than to die by the hands of the enemy."

The obvious course to take was to desert. A captain, having complained that nine of his men had deserted from the *Rupert* at night, asked the Secretary to "send down orders to Ipswich and Yarmouth for the apprehending of them, that they may be brought to trial and some of them made exemplary, else we shall never keep things in order. These towns have been very refractory and backward in sending out men." This was only a week after the bailiffs of Yarmouth had been

warned that "unless you give us better assistance now than
you did lately, you must not blame us if we complain to the
King and Council."[21]

The next summer, when De Ruyter appeared in the Medway, Pepys's sister saw deserters towing out the *Royal Charles*,
firing her guns with joy and crying "We did heretofore fight
for tickets, now we fight for dollars." On 22 August, 1667,
Pepys adds that want of pay "makes them mad, they being as
good men as were ever in the world, and would readily serve
the King, were they but paid." "It can never be well with the
navy till poor seamen can be paid once in a year at furthest,
and tickets answered like bills of exchange; whereas at this
very day ships are kept out two or three years, and four of
them just now ordered forth only for want of money, after
being brought in to be paid off."

Next to bad pay, bad food was the commonest grievance.
A well known minute by Pepys used to hang on the walls of
the modern Supply Officers establishment:[22]

"Englishmen, and more especially seamen, love their bellies
above everything else, and therefore it must always be remembered in the management of the victualling of the navy,
that to make any abatement from them in the quantity or
agreeableness of the victuals, is to discourage and provoke
them in the tenderest point, and will sooner render them dis-
gusted with the King's service than any one other hardship
that can be put upon them."

During the early years of the Commonwealth the old
system of victualling the fleet by contract continued, the
notorious Colonel Pride feeding the men at eightpence a head
per day. But with the enormous demands made on the outbreak of war the task was beyond the resources of any private
person. Orders on such a scale—seven million pounds of
meat, ten thousand butts of beer—required a capital outlay
which no single man could provide. In 1654, therefore, a
Victualling Board of three Commissioners was established.

Even they failed before the Restoration. The Plymouth agent reported that his credit was gone, there were six ships in harbour with starving men on board and six more expected shortly. A captain at Hull complained that, after receiving no reply to his letters, his men were now foraging for themselves on shore.[23]

In 1667 the navy reverted to the system of private contract. Denis Gauden (or Gawden) was appointed Surveyor General of Victuals in a document specifying in minute detail his duties and payment.[24] As before, the daily allowance on four days in the week per man at sea was to be 1 lb. biscuit, 1 gallon beer, 2 lb. beef or pork, 1 pint pease; on Wednesday, Friday and Saturday a man was to have the eighth part of a full sized stockfish, 2 oz. butter and ¼lb. cheese. On voyages south of Lat. 39°N, a different diet was specified, because of the difficulty of preserving victuals for any length of time: a quart of wine or a pint of brandy instead of beer; flour, suet and raisins instead of fresh meat: rice and oil in place of fish and butter. Necessaries such as wood, candles and lanterns were to be provided at a rate of sixpence a month per man through the pursers paid by the contractor and not by the Navy Board. Gawden was to maintain sufficient stores in government storehouses to victual 4,000 men. He was to render his accounts to the Board and be paid monthly by the Treasurer. All this was to be done at a rate of sixpence a day per man in port, eightpence at sea, the contract to be reviewed annually in accordance with the price of food.

Inevitably such a contract broke down with the expansion of the fleet, so that Pepys himself had to intervene. It was resumed later until Gawden went bankrupt, the navy owing him £176,725.[25] Further unsatisfactory contracts were made until another Victualling Board was established in 1683. With all its shortcomings, this at least continued in existence as one of the subsidiary Boards until 1832, with its headquarters at "Old Weevil" at Deptford.

When ships were laid up in "ordinary" during the winter months the skeleton crews were put on Petty Warrant or short commons. An able seaman, Edward Barlow, describes what he calls Petty Warren from a consumer's point of view: "a little brown bread made of the worst of their wheat, a little small beer, which is as bad as water bewitched . . . and a little old, tough beef, when all the best was picked out, leaving us poor seamen the sirlion next the horns; and a little fish."[26]

Just as the experience of the First Dutch War called a Victualling Board into existence, so in the same year of 1653 the Sick and Wounded (or Sick and Hurt) Board was established; this was also responsible for prisoners of war. The history of the two Boards is much the same in as much as they were at first purely wartime bodies, but by the end of the period had attained a permanent status. Of the four Commissioners for Sick and Hurt, the best known is John Evelyn, the diarist, who served throughout the Second and Third Wars. Their duties, once more, were laid down in great and unrealistic detail; to appoint deputies at the ports, to visit the nearest port after an action, to arrange for the care of the wounded by renting sick quarters, to hire nurses and surgeons, to provide for lighting, heating and food for the sick and the prisoners.

The career of a Florence Nightingale of the First War may be recorded here. Her real name was Elizabeth Alkin, commonly known as Parliament Joan, because she nursed the wounded during the Civil War, for which she was given a pension. On the outbreak of the Dutch War she volunteered for service among the sailors at Portsmouth, where she paid for their welfare out of her own pocket until her grant ran out. She was transferred to Harwich, where her health gave way, as did her money after she had spent all she possessed on the Dutch prisoners: "Seeing their wants and miseries so great, I could not but have pity on them, though our enemies." Her last appeal to the government was that she might be sent to a London hospital because she had sold her bed. Two warrants for £10 were made out in her favour in 1654, but as her name does not appear again she must have died that year after a lifetime of self-sacrifice.[27]

The care of the sick by contract proved as unsatisfactory as the feeding of the healthy by the same system. Apart from temporary hospitals at places such as Deal, there were no naval hospitals in the country. Beds were requisitioned at Bart's and St. Thomas's and the derelict Savoy and Ely hospitals in London were reserved for soldiers and sailors. Evelyn pointed out how backward England was in this respect compared with France and Spain. Barlow was amazed to see what was done for the likes of him at Toulon, where there was a hospital "for all poor lame and sick seamen, which are very well taken care of." Only the Chatham Chest existed for similar purposes in England and that was short of funds after being raided and defrauded. One of the duties of the Commissioners was to assess grants and pensions payable by the Chest—£6. 13. 4. for the loss of an eye or a leg, £4. 0. 0. for a hand etc. It was probably the example set by Louis XIV in founding Les Invalides in 1670 which stirred Charles II into establishing Chelsea Hospital for soldiers in 1682. In the same way the much larger Royal Hospital for seamen at Greenwich was founded in 1694, Evelyn being the first Treasurer, though no pensioners were in residence until 1705.

That the earlier troubles with the Company of Barber-Surgeons did not recur was due to the appointment of James Pearse (later Master of the Company and Surgeon-General of H.M. Navy) as surgeon to the Duke of York in the Second War. He acted as what we should call Medical Director General and Pepys got him to draft suitable forms for putting sick men into quarters, for the landlord's charges, the surgeon's attendance fees, for admission and discharge, all to be signed by the persons involved. The discharge form reads:

The bearer—belonging to H.M. ship—was sent to this place on —, and being cured was discharged upon this —, the truth hereof is certified. He hath received clothes to the value of —. In conduct money —. Signed —, agent appointed to take care of the Sick and Hurt seamen at —.

Such were the origins of a more efficient and humane treatment of the sick. The office of Cook on board all ships was reserved for maimed men. From 1652 the sick were allowed to continue in pay when sent ashore—a most important innovation. Every hundred men at sea were allowed £5 worth of medical comforts, such as rice, sugar and oatmeal. This was increased to £10 when, in the Second War, the first two hospital ships were commissioned to attend the fleet. These were well provided with medical stores, including "6 lb. Castle soap," a commodity which did not become a general issue until 1795. It seems to have been at the instance of Pearse and Evelyn that these ships were provided, the latter telling the king of his despair at finding five hundred men dying for lack of food and lodging: "His Majesty's subjects die in our sight and at our thresholds without our being able to relieve them, which, with our barbarous exposure of the prisoners to the utmost sufferings, must needs redound to His Majesty's great dishonour, and to the consequences of losing the hearts of our own people." The reply from Oxford (whither the Court had fled on account of the Plague) was an order for a pound of bread per day for the prisoners, "the straw they themselves must pay for before they be released." They ordered these things better in Holland, where surgeon James Yonge was a prisoner before he returned to take charge of the naval hospital at Plymouth. This was the first specifically naval hospital, though it did not become permanent until 1698.[28]

Naval surgeons now formed part of the complement of all big ships. They were treated as seamen rather than officers. With their mates and loblolly boys, they were called the medical crew, which numbered ten in a first-rate ship of 800 men. There was as yet no sick berth on board, but because of the number of desertions on shore, the sick were sent back for convalescence as soon as possible. As Dr. Whistler pointed out at Portsmouth, "salt meat will not do more hurt than strong drink would here." The chief grievance of the surgeons, which was taken up by their Company, was delay in the payment of their wages and for the medicine chests and instruments which they had to provide. Not that a surgeon's medicaments were much use, however skilful he might be in operating. Barlow complains about their carelessness of the sick on board. After asking how a man felt and feeling his pulse when he was half dead, they gave him "some of their medicines upon the point of a knife, which doeth as much good to him as a blow on the pate with a stick."[29]

The outbreak of the Great Plague in the middle of the Second War does not seem to have affected the fleet seriously. Scurvy, however, continued to be common, five hundred men being landed sick after a few weeks patrolling the Dutch coast before the battle of the Texel. And of course there was always enteritis, dysentery and typhus. Though the association of the latter with dirty clothes was not properly understood, slops or ready-made clothes from the purser's store were now issued on a larger scale. "I think the health of the men is concerned in their clothes," wrote Sir William Coventry, "and men are so hard to get that I should be sorry to lose them so slightly." Hence the orders of 2 March 1663, regulating their sale on board by the purser: Monmouth caps 2/6, blue shirts 3/6, red caps 1/1, yarn stockings 3d., Irish stockings 1½d., cotton waistcoats 3/-, cotton drawers 3/-, neat's leather shoes 3/6, blue neckcloths 5d., canvas suits 5/-, blue suits 5/-.[30] These were to be sold at the mainmast in the presence of the captain and the crew once a week when the purser opened his pack at what was called a fair.

The purser was indeed a very busy man, to judge from the

list of his duties in 1661.[31] He was grocer, draper, salesman and accountant all rolled into one. He was responsible for mustering the ship's company every ten days, for getting the Clerk of the Cheque to issue warrants for victuals once a month, for signing (together with the captain and the boatswain) all pay and discharge tickets, rendering accounts for all slops sold and keeping "counter," i.e. debt books, for all expenses on board. No wonder some of the weaker brethren were found guilty of dishonest practices which gave the branch a bad name with the seamen, for of all the civilian officers he was the one most responsible for their welfare.

The business of the navy was thus put on a modern footing during the period of the three Dutch Wars and up to the time when Pepys was forced out of office on the abdication of his patron, James II. His successor, after an interval, as Secretary of the Admiralty, Josiah Burchett, was generous enough to point out in a letter to the Prince of Denmark, Lord High Admiral in Anne's reign, that "however the reign of Charles II may have been exploded for other things, it cannot be so in relation to the Navy, for His Majesty's care extended no less to the officering the fleet with able seamen than to the maintaining of it with good husbandry."[32]

By putting the office of Lord High Admiral into commission during the Commonwealth and occasionally thereafter, by setting up subsidiary boards for victualling and medical purposes, by maintaining a reasonable standard of efficiency under conditions of desperate financial stringency, those responsible for the administration of the navy (of whom Samuel Pepys was first) put the service on a basis which was to last for the next hundred and fifty years. Only the perennial problems of money and manning remained unsolved.

V

Some Stuart Seamen

A SURPRISING NUMBER of individuals who "used the sea" kept private journals during the latter part of the seventeenth century which illustrate the conditions of life afloat in so far as these affected particular persons. We have a number of journals by admirals and captains, as distinct from the official records which Pepys insisted that such officers should deposit with the Admiralty. These journals are largely of professional interest, dealing with battles and commands rather than life on board or comments on the ship's company, who were regarded as a class apart. More can be gleaned from the private journal of a naval chaplain like Henry Teonge, though his chief interest is in what he ate in the wardroom. There is also the first and only private journal of a naval surgeon, James Yonge, which has recently appeared in print, but again he is more interested in what went on ashore than afloat.[1]

The more adventurous type of journal is that kept by buccaneers and privateers who, exploiting a new interest in travel literature, usually sold their rough diaries to the bookseller James Knapton, who specialised in preparing this type of book for sale. In what has been well called the Age of Observation, such traveller's tales often have a genuine scientific bent which was chiefly due to the success of their prototype, William Dampier's *New Voyage Round the World* in 1697. This, with his later writings, in turn inspired Swift and Defoe to invent the novel about the sea which, as an incentive for boys to follow the sea, is not to be underestimated. Again and again in later autobiographies we come across the formula: "After reading *Robinson Crusoe* I decided to run away to sea."

Dampier's abilities as a travel writer do not concern us here, but a glance at his career illustrates the vicissitudes of many an adventurer who took to the sea from motives of curiosity to visit foreign parts, even if they did not all join the buccaneers. The younger son of a Somerset farmer, he was apprenticed to the master of a Weymouth vessel at the age of eighteen, "complying with the inclinations I had very early of seeing the world." He served out his apprenticeship in the Newfoundland fishery and the East Indies trade before volunteering on board the flagship in the Third Dutch War. After being in two battles, we find him in sick quarters at Harwich, where "I languished a great while," before trying his luck as a planter in Jamaica. By nature a rolling stone, always anxious to see what lay beyond the horizon, he drifted inevitably into the ranks of the Brethren of the Coast, as the buccaneers liked to call themselves, in whose company he made his first voyage round the world in twelve years in as many ships. When he published the precious journal which he had carried with him in a hollow bamboo through all his adventures, he attracted the attention of men like Pepys and Evelyn and even their Lordships, who gave him the command of a naval ship to explore the eastern ocean. He was the first Englishman to visit Australia and in H.M.S. *Roebuck* he might have anticipated Cook's discovery of the more attractive part of that continent had it not been for a rotten ship and a mutinous crew, who resented having an ex-buccaneer as their captain. A quarrel with his lieutenant, a more regular naval officer, resulted in a court martial which wrecked his career by declaring him "not a fit person to be employed as commander of any of Her Majesty's ships."

When the War of the Spanish Succession broke out, Dampier went back to his old trade of privateering, but with no success until he joined the *Duke* and *Duchess* as chief pilot. Captain Woodes Rogers wrote up that voyage round the world in a classic of privateering literature, but he rather obscures the part played by Dampier, now an old man and something of a failure. Before his death in 1715 Dampier had been round the world three times, written some of the best pages in our literature of travel and made a real contribution to the infant sciences of hydrography and meteorology.[2]

For life at sea as experienced by more ordinary seamen we must turn to the two earliest seamen's autobiographies, those by Thomas Lurting and Edward Coxere. Curiously enough, both became Quakers, many of whom were concerned with shipping though none, for obvious reasons, lasted long in a man-of-war. It is worth recalling that the mate who carried Charles II ashore in France when the King escaped in a fishing boat from Brighton was one of the earliest Quakers. After the Restoration this man, Richard Carver, was allowed to do something for his fellow sufferers when they were so cruelly persecuted by Parliament rather than by the easy-going monarch.

Lurting's *The Fighting Sailor turn'd peaceable Christian* is more of a pietistic tract than an autobiography and as such enjoyed great popularity after its publication in 1710. He was pressed in 1646 at the age of fourteen, which was enough to give any man a grievance against the navy. He served throughout the First Dutch War, rising to the rank of boatswain's mate. When he and some of his companions were converted to Quakerism in 1655 and refused to put off their hats to the captain (a Baptist), the latter was "sore troubled and distressed," though confessing that "he cared not if all his men were Quakers, for they were the hardiest men in his ship." Unfortunately, they steadfastly refused to do their duty in action.

The navy had to get rid of such stubborn creatures as soon as possible. Lurting continued as a seaman in merchant vessels until he was pressed on the outbreak of the Second Dutch War. "You must go with us" shouted the pressing officer. " 'I hope not so', said I. Then they swore that I was a lusty man and should go. Then they laid hands on me and lifted me into the boat and carried me on board the ship *Mary*, one Jeremiah Smith, commander, who was a very loose and wicked man." A man of Lurting's principles was not easily coerced. After going on hunger strike for a week and refusing even non-combatant duties, he was put on shore to suffer the persecution which men of his persuasion suffered during that reign.

A more attractive character is his co-religionist, Edward Coxere, whose *Adventures by Sea* was discovered in 1945.[3] Like Lurting, with whom he was shipmate on one voyage, he went to sea at the age of fourteen in 1648, but he was not pressed, only bound apprentice. The next year he somehow transferred himself to the lieutenant of the Admiral commanding in the Downs, "he being willing to have me as his boy," a clear proof that the origins of the followers or servants allowed to every officer in the navy lies in the apprentice system. Thereafter Coxere served in ships of all types, sometimes as a gunner, sometimes as coxswain, sometimes as mate. On some voyages he was a volunteer, on others a pressed man. Once during the Commonwealth, in order to escape the press, he lowered himself down by a rope from the stern, only to find the gangs active on shore. "We got safely into Rotherhithe the backways, and housed ourselves at an alehouse, where we lay perdu, where we refreshed ourselves with fresh meat and drink, but did not dare go into the street." Being anxious about his belongings left on board, he disguised himself as a Billingsgate merchant in a grey hat and red stockings and boldly went on board to collect his gear before taking horse to his home at Dover. Even there, "I was still terrified with the press, for I could not walk the streets without danger, nor sleep in safety. My brother being at home, a seaman also, who was three years older than myself, we keeping our chambers like prisoners, though we knew we could keep any from coming up the stairs to us, yet it was too much like a prisoner's life, so that, we being weary of it, we agreed to ship ourselves volunteers on board of a man-of-war then in harbour."

This was in the First Dutch War, after which he admits to serving many masters—"the Spaniards against the French, the Hollanders against the English; then I was taken by the English out of a Dunkirker; and then I served the English against the Hollander; and last I was taken by the Turks," becoming a slave of the Barbary Corsairs until released by Blake at Porto Farina. Soon afterwards he was captured by the Spaniards and heard of the death of Cromwell, "which was good news to the Spaniards, for he made them cheap."

In 1661 he returned home to Dover, where he was converted to Quakerism and had to give up his trade as a gunner, as had another Friend who, in the middle of an action, suddenly decided not to fire his gun "lest blood might be spilt." Poor Coxere was soon arrested under the Conventicle Act and imprisoned in Dover gaol for many years, suffering "such unkind usage I never had when I was a slave under the hands of the Turks."[4]

Every aspect of life at sea is illustrated in the journal of Edward Barlow, a very ordinary seaman who followed the sea from the age of thirteen to that of sixty-one without ever rising higher than mate. The original of his diary, which was edited by Basil Lubbock in 1934, is now in the National Maritime Museum. It is beautifully illustrated in water colour with drawings of the various ships he sailed in and the countries he visited.

It is interspersed with sad reflections that his native

curiosity had drawn him into a way of life from which there was no escape.

"I was always thinking that beggars had a far better life of it and lived better than I did, for they seldom missed of their bellies full of better victuals than we could get; and also at night to lie quiet and out of danger in a good barn full of straw, nobody disturbing them, and might lie as long as they pleased; but it was quite contrary with us, for we seldom in a month got our bellyful of victuals, and that of such salt that beggars would think scorn to eat; and at night when we went to take our rest, we were not to lie still above four hours; and many times when it blew hard were not sure to lie one hour, yea, often we were called up before we had slept half an hour and forced to go into the maintop or foretop to take in our topsails, half awake and half asleep, with one shoe on and the other off, not having time to put it on; always sleeping in our clothes for readiness; and in stormy weather, when the ship rolled and tumbled, as though some great millstone were rolling up one hill and down another, we had much ado to hold ourselves fast by the small ropes from falling by the board; and being gotten up into the tops, there we must haul and pull to make fast the sail, seeing nothing but air above us and water beneath us, and that so raging as though every wave would make a grave for us; and many times in nights so dark that we could not see one another, and blowing so hard that we could not hear one another speak, being close to one another . . . There are no men under the sun that fare harder and get their living more hard and that are so abused on all sides as we poor seamen, without whom the land would soon be brought under subjection, for when once the naval forces are broken, England's best walls are down. And so I could wish no young man to betake himself to this calling unless he has good friends to put him in place or supply his wants, for he shall find a great deal more to his sorrow than I have writ.[5]

It was curiosity and the love of adventure, not pay, which drew this son of an agricultural labourer living near Manchester to the sea. The parallel with Dampier is very close and the two men even met in the East Indies, where Dampier entrusted Barlow with some journals, but Barlow lost his sea chest in a storm and he never mentions Dampier by name, probably considering him just another penniless adventurer like himself.

In 1659 he signed on as an apprentice, the system operating in the navy in the same way as in the merchant service, to the master's mate of H.M.S. *Naseby* (soon to be renamed *Royal Charles*). The mate clothed him, but never gave him more than the odd sixpence out of his annual wages of £10. 16. o. What makes his career so typical is the way he alternates between the navy and the merchant service, either in the Mediterranean or in the East Indies. Payment seems to have been just as difficult in the one as in the other. He regards £6. 10. o. for a voyage to China as a fair wage for a mate, but he complains about the injustice of deducting the cost of damage done to the cargo when "damnified" by a storm or for some other reason for which the crew was not responsible. In the light of this, naval deductions do not seem so onerous. In 1691 he got two guineas a month as a midshipman in the navy, a post still open to experienced seamen. Many sailors, he says, desert from warships because they think they will get better pay elsewhere, but thereby they forfeit their wages and may well find themselves worse off if the trade voyage is a short one. "Their Majesties ships are better victualled than most merchant ships are, and their pay surer, and there they have no damage to pay; and if they lose an arm or a leg they have a pension for it, and their work is not so hard, neither do they wear out so many clothes; all of which things they find in most merchant ships." A passage like this shows how dangerous it is to generalise when comparing conditions in the merchant or naval services.

If life was not so bad on board a warship, why was it so unpopular? For one thing there was the notorious dishonesty of the ticket system, which was not used on board merchant vessels. Thus Barlow gives an instance of the cynical maxim "Keep the pay, keep the man" when he tells how at Gravesend in 1666 the commissioner came on board, "paying us nine months pay and keeping nine more in hand for fear of our running away from the ship, as they pretended it, but we had no more."

Another was the behaviour of the pursers. We have already quoted his remark on Petty Warrant victuals. Another and more ordinary complaint is the following: "We had but 14 oz. to the pound, the other two being allowed to the purser of the ship for scraping of the cheese and butter and dust in the bread; yet it was always served out to us without scraping, the foul and the clean together, and the rotten with the sound, and mouldy and stinking and all together, and we had Hobson's choice, that or none." But on his own evidence food was no better on a merchantman, and much worse in Dutch East Indiamen: "Our English ships commonly make shorter passages and are better provided with provisions not so old, few of our men dying in our homeward bound voyages; but many of their men die, both going out and coming home in their ships."

It was the custom of pressing men out of homeward bound ships, especially in the Downs, which, more than anything else, gave the King's service a bad name. Returning from a voyage to the Canaries in 1668, Barlow was pressed in this manner. The ship was leaky, so that every man was at the pumps, but on meeting a frigate the captain insisted that the king's ship be manned. Barlow and one other were taken off, so that they could not go ashore for another six months. "It is a very bad thing for a poor seaman when he is pressed in this manner, for if he have a wife and children he is not suffered to go and see them, nor go and look after his wages, nor to take care of his venture, but must leave it to the trust of one whom he knows not whether he will ever see it, and to take up his wages for him." The owner might well defraud him if he was not on board to look after his own interests at the end of a voyage. In Barlow's opinion, this aspect of pressing more than any other "maketh poor men so unwilling to sail in his Majesty's ships, and many to abandon their country, finding better entertainment in another."[6]

Ramblin' Jack: the Journal of Captain John Cremer, which was first printed in 1936, takes us into the next century and the merchant service, but Cremer started in the navy. The son of a naval captain of the tarpaulin breed, he was consigned at the age of eight on his father's death to the care of his uncle, a naval lieutenant. "Soe I was fited out and sent to the Randavoes 'The Black Boy and Trumpet' at St. Katharine's near Tower Hill, wherein he was Pressing." The child was handed over to the care of a "vilenous hard-harted fellow" on board, who robbed him of his pocket money. "Thus I begun my Troubells." The muster-master at least had the heart to discharge him on account of his tender age, but somehow he remained on board to see minor actions in the War of the Spanish Succession and to be beaten with a cat-o'-nine-tails by the boatswain's mate as a mischievous imp, "which at first was five lashes on my poor tender brich, almost like knives cutting me. But by constancy I grew hardened and at nine years of age I had sense enuf to get my vilenous Guardian turned afore the mast," that is to say disrated.

After that he served in merchant vessels, escaping the press in 1721 and again the next year by hiding himself in the house of a relative. It was fortunate for him that no great war broke out before he had risen high enough in his profession to render him exempt. His rumbustious narrative is the only one of its type which has appeared so far. Others of this period may well come to light, since it is unlikely that this habit of journalising should have died out, but it needed a big war, involving the conscription of a more literate type of man, to produce the seamen's autobiographies to be noticed in a later chapter.

We may conclude our picture of the mariners of those days

with the more generalised description of a type which is becoming discernible as standing apart from other members of the community by reason of his idiomatic way of speech, his strange clothes and rolling gait. In 1707 the scurrilous Ned Ward printed his *Wooden World Dissected*. He was a journalist who rivalled Defoe in output, in accuracy of observation and liveliness of style. Like Defoe, he preferred anonymity, on this occasion calling himself "A Lover of the Mathematicks." He is best known for his *London Spy*, but the rarer *Wooden World* is a vivid worm's-eye view of the inhabitants of a man-of-war from the captain down to the cook. However cruel his comments, Ward treats the honest tar with far more respect than he shows towards other members of the seafaring community.

"He looks most formidable when others would appear most drooping; for see him in bad weather in his fur cap and whopping large watch coat and you'd swear the Czar was returned once more from Muscovy; yet he's never in his true figure, but within a pitch'd jacket, and then he's as invulnerable to a cudgel as a hog in armour. Nothing makes him droop like an empty brandy bottle; whilst there's anything in it he sticks by it as close as the lodestone does to cold iron. Plenty of this, and a Mediterranean sun, makes him as dry and duskish in one summer as a roasted bisket . . . His darling liquor is Flip, which makes him as fat as a porpoise and as valiant as Scanderburg. Instigated by this courageous hotch-potch, he shall make a clear stage where'er he comes . . . He's so often used to reeling at sea, that when he is reeling drunk ashore he takes it for granted to be a storm abroad, and falls to throwing everything out of the windows to save the vessel of a bawdy house. His Furlow is commonly but a night or so; and 'tis well for him it's no longer, for he needs but a week to spend a twelve months pay in reversion . . .

He's a rare dog under an honest commander, and will fight everlastingly, if he can but have justice at the end of his labours; but to receive all the knocks and none of the moneys is the devil, and gripes him worse than the Purser's wine-vinegar . . . He loves his honour like roast beef, and is ready to spend his blood upon any fair quarrelsome occasion . . . If his breeding has been north of Yarmouth he's distinguished with the title of Collier's Nag . . .

In fine, take this same plain blunt Sea-Animal, by and large, in his tar jacket and wide-kneed trousers, and you'll find him of more intrinsic value to the nation than the most stuttering Beau in it.

VI

The Manning Problem

THE RECRUITING PROBLEM in the eighteenth century was essentially an arithmetical one. It was a question of what proportion of the nation's population could be made available to meet the requirements of the army, the navy and the merchant service. The fundamental issue in the politics of defence was to find out in what ratio these necessities should or could be met. Would a war ruin commerce by diverting manpower from trade to fighting, or would it benefit the nation in the long run by the conquest of overseas territories and markets which could be protected by the Navigation Acts? Should such a war be conducted by a continental strategy involving, as in Marlborough's day, the raising of a large army to fight in Europe; or should it be of a maritime nature, as in the Seven Years War, necessitating a large fleet and amphibious operations? Was it a war in defence of the homeland, as in 1745 or 1805, or was it war for the conquest of possessions overseas and the prize of maritime empire?

Such were the questions every government had to ask itself. Ministers received little assistance in answering them from Parliament, where commercial interests were strong, hostility to taxation innate, and the fear of a standing army traditional. On the whole, the Navy was treated more generously because its advantages were more obvious and because of the strong Admiralty interest among its members. The subject of impressment, however, raised tempers just as violently as did the fear of military autocracy.

There was little statistical evidence as to the extent of the nation's available manpower. Before the first census of 1801, no one knew the size of the population. Before the establishment of a Register General of Shipping in 1786, the number of ships, their ownership, tonnage and manpower was equally unknown. There were Customs returns and the Port Books (most of them lost), but they were never analysed. The Admiralty records are happily far more continuous as far as naval statistics are concerned, but often inaccurate or conflicting where the numbers of men are involved. Their Lordships were more concerned with recording details about the ships, their stores and their officers, than they were about the men they employed. As soon as a ship paid off, all responsibility for the members of her crew ended. They either had to be pressed all over again, or turned over against their will to other ships. Such was the Hire and Discharge system which was the fundamental weakness in manning the navy in the age of sail.

An attempt is made in the following pages to ascertain the number of men the navy required, the number it actually got, and the number which remained available to the merchant service. The reader's indulgence is craved for the discrepancies in the figures here given, because the subject is still largely unexplored. Even if the evidence is often sparse or conflicting, unless the magnitude of the manning dilemma is appreciated, the brutal and arbitrary methods adopted to solve it cannot be understood. Parliament, on the recommendation of the Admiralty, might grudgingly vote a certain sum of money to pay the wages of the fleet, but it was the business of the press gangs to round up whatever men they could from the highways and taverns to fill the complement of the ships waiting to be manned. The problem itself may be dry and statistical: its solution in practice (as will be seen later) is replete with human interest, sometimes comic, more often tragic.

The first aspect of the problem to be considered must be the size of the population of the British Isles. Before the census of 1801 this cannot be established with any accuracy, but the calculations of Gregory King in 1696, based on the hearth tax, are generally accepted as a reasonable estimate. He reckoned the population of England and Wales was about $5\frac{1}{2}$ million, that of France being 14 and Holland 2. He estimated that there were 20,000 naval officers, 150,000 common seamen and 70,000 common soldiers in the country.[1]

These figures would appear high if we compare them with the estimate made by Sir William Petty a generation earlier. Petty reckoned that the navy needed 36,000 men and trade 48,000, giving a total of 84,000, but he was convinced that there were nothing like enough seamen in existence to satisfy both demands simultaneously.

Captain St. Lo in his *England's Safety* (1693) reckoned that the navy needed 50,000, which almost corresponds with the figure of those in sea pay in 1697. The anonymous author of *An Expedient for Increasing Seamen* (1690) reckoned 44,000, with trade requiring 33,000. In a debate in the House of Commons in 1703 estimates of the size of the seafaring population varied wildly between 50,000 and 80,000. However, all who considered the problem agreed with the author of the 1690 pamphlet—"That there are not seamen sufficient in England and the rest of their Majesties dominions to man the royal fleet and to drive the trade thereof, experience tells us."[2] Such continued to be the problem until the end of the French wars. During the whole of that period the actual number of seamen available remained wrapt in obscurity.

The census of 1801 and that of 1851 provide the following information.[3]

	1801	1851
England and Wales	8,892,536	17,927,609
Scotland	1,608,420	2,888,742
Ireland	5,216,000	6,515,794
Total	15,716,956	27,332,145
Armed Forces	324,630	210,474
Merchant	144,558	124,744

The ratio between the size of the Armed Forces (itemised in 1801 as Army and Militia 198,351, Navy and Marines 126,279) and the population as a whole at the height of the longest war ever fought with France is very remarkable; equally remarkable is the evidence of the increase in the seafaring population due to the expansion of trade during the period 1750-1800.

The problem of manning the Navy became acute in the last decade of the seventeenth century because of the combination of two factors. One was the rapid increase in the size of the merchant marine during the generation preceding the wars of William and Anne. The other was the extended nature of those wars, which were not only fought on a wider scale than hitherto, in the Mediterranean and the Caribbean as well as in northern waters, but required the raising of large armies to fight on the continent of Europe. The increased number of vessels engaged in overseas trade also necessitated more protection in the form of convoy escorts. The slow growth of the population of these islands was being outstripped by that of the shipping industry, which, next to the cloth and building trades, was now the largest in the kingdom. When a war broke out and the needs of the Army and Navy had to be met, competition for manpower became acute. During the first half of the eighteenth century shipping continued to increase, though at a slower rate, but during the second half it expanded with unprecedented rapidity, so that the recruiting problem was intensified when Britain engaged in the longest of her wars.

The difficulties of estimating the growth of the tonnage of merchant shipping have been analysed by Professor Davis in his *Rise of the English Shipping Industry*. Adopting his figures for the century preceding the establishment of a Register General of Shipping, we find the increase in English-owned tonnage shown in Table I (Appendix page 285). Alongside his figures are some which are admittedly less reliable but come from an anonymous compilation in the Liverpool Papers in the British Museum, based on estimates made by the Register General.[4] The compiler thinks them exaggerated, though in 1792, when they were compiled, he thought it probable that there were "upwards of 121,000 seafaring men who are liable to serve the Crown in time of war." He adds an interesting comment on the relation between war and trade which shows that the former was not an unmitigated evil to the shipping industry, which certainly benefited from a successful peace treaty brought about by the wise exercise of naval power:

> "The mind is filled and gratified with the undoubted infor-
> mation that the traders of this island alone possess 1,348,884 tons
> of shipping. It is nearly as satisfactory to know, though it cannot
> be ascertained with equal certainty, that of their commercial
> capital the traders have invested in shipping £11,330,625, calcu-
> lating at 8 guineas for every ton. It is an unquestionable fact that
> Great Britain has constantly enjoyed a greater number of ships at
> the conclusion of every war since 1688 than before each war
> began. And if it be asked to what cause this was owing, it may be
> answered that Government employed during every war many
> transports, whereby the merchants were induced to invest their
> capital in the gainful employment of building ships for that
> purpose. Privateers were also fitted out. All the shipping when
> Peace returned were employed in Traffic or Fishery."

The insoluble problem is to translate tonnage figures into the number of men employed. A Register of Seamen was begun in 1696 but (as we shall see in chapter IX) it was a failure because registration was voluntary. At the same date it was enacted that every seaman, whether in naval or merchant employment, whether registered or not, should pay sixpence a month out of his wages towards the upkeep of the Royal Hospital at Greenwich, just as naval seamen had been doing for a century towards Chatham Chest. The Sixpenny Office records survive, but unfortunately they cannot be related to the number of men employed. Every £1 received represented forty seaman-months employment, but not the number of men employed. Moreover, during the first fifty years of the Office, there were many loopholes through which such seamen as coastal fishermen or American sailors avoided payment. The following selected figures of receipts do, however, reflect the expansion of maritime activity between 1707 and 1827.[5]

1707	£5,481	1797	£12,296
1747	5,985	1807	15,162
1777	10,550	1827	19,681

With the appearance of a Register General of Shipping we are on firmer ground. The tonnage and men employed in the merchant service in 1792 and 1800 are shown in Table II Appendix (p. 285).

The compiler of the 1792 figures adds that of the total number of vessels, 4,039 were under fifty tons and only fifteen over 1,000. Whereas 118,286 men were normally employed in trade, another 127,607 would be needed to fill the complement of the 462 ships in the Navy. Ideally, therefore, there should be a seafaring population of 245,893, whereas in fact only about half that number was available.

Such was the manpower gap on the eve of the Revolutionary and Napoleonic wars. When it is recalled that Britain had to fight almost the whole continent of Europe under Napoleon's domination, and for two years the United States as well, the necessity of having over half a million men under arms in the Army and Navy in 1811, out of a population of about fifteen millions, can be appreciated. It is this that explains the extreme measures adopted to fill the ranks and man the ships in the days of Nelson and Wellington. What is surprising is that the quality of the recruits proved fine enough to win such battles as Trafalgar and Waterloo. The Duke may once, in a moment of irritation, have called his army in the Peninsula "the scum of the earth enlisted for drink"; but, as he said to Creevey on the eve of Waterloo, pointing to a soldier, "There, it all depends on that article whether we do the business or not. Give me enough of it, and I am sure."

Before considering the needs of Nelson and his predecessors for "that article," let us see where it might be found and where recruiting establishments might most usefully be established. The seafaring population was not only increasing, but shifting. Table II (page 285) shows how London was still by far the largest port, but Liverpool has risen to second place and Bristol is falling far behind. There were proportionally more seamen in the north-east than the south-west. The former were normally employed in fishing or coastal traffic, while in the southern ports there was more of a tradition of service in the navy. When the navy had to expand, the obvious recruiting centres lay in the north.

Nor was the increase in the number of seamen due only to the simultaneous growth of the country's population. Various traditional restrictive practices were now regarded as out of date. Earlier objections to the employment of landmen had faded.[6] An Act of 1704 offered landmen exemption from impressment during the first two years of their service at sea and the muster books of warships show that their employment was now regarded as normal in the navy. As regards the employment of foreigners, so severely restricted by the Navigation Acts, these laws were amended in 1708 to permit three-quarters of the crew of a merchantman to be of foreign extraction in wartime, a measure repeated in 1741; hence the large number of foreigners found serving in the navy. The old rules of apprenticeship were also weakening. Instead of being an honourable and privileged state, there were now many pauper apprentices, bound for long periods without wages, receiving only two suits of clothes during the whole time of their servitude. Such youths must have welcomed service in the navy, nor did the press gangs take their indentures as seriously as they did those of genuine apprentices. Marine societies, bounties and other methods of attracting boys to the sea will be considered later. In such ways, together with the more economical use of men on board, the needs of the shipping industry were met; but those of the navy were additional and far more unpopular.

With the increasing scale and length of wars, the balance between the growth of the country's population and that of its shipping industry was upset. The figures in Table III, showing the number of Ships and Men in the Royal Navy between 1701 and 1855 (Appendix, page 286), show the enormous strain on manpower which developed. To understand the figures printed it must first be explained that the number of ships given include all those owned by the Navy, not just those in commission. Even these totals are hard to come by. In 1702 one manuscript list[7] gives 203 ships; Schomberg gives 256 and Derrick 272. In 1792 James gives 411 as a grand total, Schomberg 414, Derrick 498. The figures printed here are those given by Derrick up to 1793; thereafter James's are quoted, in whose tables may also be found the number of those ships which were actually in commission. Thus at the beginning of 1805 there were 570 ships in commission out of a total of 807. The figures from 1826 are from the January monthly lists of ships in commission only.

Of course it was only these ships which required manning, though even those "laid up in ordinary" required skeleton crews. The complements of ships have been omitted, because they were really notional and by no means always attained. At the beginning of 1703 it was stated that the complement of the fleet amounted to 34,940 men, those borne numbered 20,824, those mustered 11,555, that is to say that the fleet was 23,385 short of complement; but later in the year the number borne doubled and the complement requirements fulfilled.[8] The following examples show how complement totals were arrived at. It should be added that flagships were allowed additional men as the retinue of the admiral.

Rate	1762 Complement	1805 Complement
100 guns	850	837
90	750	738
80	650	719
74	600	590
60	420	420
32	220	215
24	160	155

If the figures for complements do not help us to know how many men were actually in the service, those of the number voted annually by Parliament do so still less. In the period 1721-33 there were 6,008 more men borne for wages than voted, and 3,692 less mustered for victuals. The vote figures are interesting as an indication of the general trend of increase or decrease in naval strength, but they do not correspond with the numbers actually in sea pay. They are chiefly valuable for the study of naval finance, because these were the figures which the Admiralty suggested should be provided for in the defence estimates. Whether the number was sufficient, or indeed could be obtained, depended on how events developed: usually they lagged behind the necessities of the fleet during the first months of a war. In 1688, 7,040 men were voted, but 12,714 were borne for pay. In 1697, 40,000 were voted, but only 35,112 were borne for pay in the 179 ships in commission which had a complement of 43,000.

The figures for those borne for wages, that is to say those

actually in sea pay, are the most important. They do not correspond exactly with those mustered for victuals because they exclude those members of the ship's company who happened to be absent on the monthly muster day. Such men would include those sick ashore for less than a month, those deserters marked R (Run) in the muster book, D (Discharged) or DD (Discharged Dead). After the middle of the century total computations of those mustered in the fleet are more difficult to interpret, because they occasionally include prisoners and supernumaries.

Information about the men actually on board a ship in any given month can be obtained from a ship's muster book, but to discover the totals over a century would require a computer; even then they would be found to vary from month to month. Minute instructions were provided for mustermasters (usually the purser); as usual, they were seldom complied with. In 1692 instructions were drawn up for Clerks of the Cheque, the representatives of the Navy Office at the ports, to examine the returns made by the purser and the captain of each ship.[9] Absentees were to be marked with a prick. Those missing muster three times were to be "made a Runaway." Musters were to be held once a fortnight and two signed copies of the books deposited at the Navy Office.

Before long musters were only held once a month and the various columns marked "Whether Prest or Not," "Amount Due for Clothes and Tobacco, Place of Birth, Appearance" etc., were often left blank. The muster-master was only really interested in the man's name, number, pay due and whether he was marked R, D or DD. Even the muster book of such a historic ship as Hawke's *Royal George* in 1759 only tells us that the complement of this first-rate flagship was 880, the number borne 779, mustered 781, sick 2, marines 93, widow's men 59, supernumeraries 48 (of whom the Admiral counted as one).[10]

On the other hand, the muster book of the *Victory* in 1805

is a model of its kind, though some of the columns are left blank.[11] The totals in this case on October 17 were: complement 837, borne 628, mustered 606, sick 3, volunteers and boys first class 31 (boys of the second and third classes being included in the ship's company), marines 144, supernumeraries for wages (Lord Nelson and his retinue) 9, supernumeraries for victuals 112, widow's men 8; 9 are marked Run. Out of this number there are 319 pressed men, the remainder being volunteers, marines, officers and supernumeraries. The ship's company came from every county in the British Isles and there is a scattering of foreigners. There are twenty-three giving America as their birthplace, some of whom must have been negroes, or so one supposes of "Geo. Washington, AB, aged 21, born Providence." Two were discharged on September 4 as American citizens, but Will. Atkins of Charleston remained marked "Prest". Two give Africa as a birthplace, one France, one Switzerland and a fair number from Holland, Sweden, Denmark and Prussia. Altogether there were forty-eight of them. It would be safe to say that the ratio of pressed men to volunteers, and the number of foreigners carried, was fairly typical of ships at this time. The most exceptional thing about both these books is the small number of sick on the eve of a battle. On board the *Warspite* in 1812, out of a complement of 800, there were sixty-four foreigners, twenty-five of whom are marked pressed; there were also thirty-two described as "volunteers from prison ships," such as do not appear on the *Victory's* books.

What conclusion should one draw from the figures printed in Table III (page 286) which shows the number of men voted and actually borne between 1701 and 1855? One striking thing is the rapidity of increase or decrease in naval strength at the beginning or end of a war: from 16,613 men in 1792 to 87,331 in 1794; or during the Peace of Amiens a decrease from 129,340 in 1802 to 49,430 the next year, followed at the resumption of hostilities by an increase to 84,431. Such sudden fluctuations explain the necessity of a hot press at the beginning of a war. Two figures not included here also illustrate this point: the increase from 12,714 men in 1688 to 44,743 in 1692.

The growing size of the Navy is vividly shown. The hundred-thousand figure is first topped in 1783, the last year of the American War of Independence. It may be compared with the 97,000 strength at present (1967). The climax of the war under sail, as far as strength is concerned, is seen to be not 1805 (as is often supposed) but 1809-10, when we get the maximum number of ships in commission—1,061—and of men—142,989. This is an astonishing figure when one remembers that the Peninsular War was just beginning, and it explains the British attitude on the eve of the war with the United States.

The Navy was at its lowest ebb in 1724, with only sixty-seven ships and 6,298 men. A century later it was not much larger in proportion to the population. The 21,141 men and 172 ships of 1835, compared with the 130,127 men and 1,009 ships at the end of the Napoleonic struggle, shows why impressment disappeared when there was no further need for it.

VII

The Methods of Impressment

ALTHOUGH THE METHODS adopted for manning the navy which have been described in previous chapters continued throughout the eighteenth century, impressment began to be organised on a wider and more permanent basis during the wars of William III and Anne. The word was coming to mean recruitment in any form, whether voluntary or conscripted. In this chapter we shall be considering both forms as they were implemented before the outbreak of the wars with the French Revolution and Napoleon, when the impress service was improved to meet unprecedented claims on the nation's manpower. Even then, the basic pattern in the use of incentives or force as developed during previous ages remained, to the astonishment of foreigners and the shame of Englishmen.

Until almost the end of the seventeenth century, pressing was done on a temporary basis to fit out a ship or an expedition, or to man the fleet during the summer months. However, for the winter of 1692-93 it was decided to keep the great ships manned and the first step was thus taken towards continuous service in the navy. The Navy Board warned the Admiralty that the experiment would be a failure, and so it proved at first when the Commissioners read the proclamation at Chatham. The assembled crews promptly left the dockyard in a body to riot in the town. Some drifted back, but in the spring the old methods of recruitment had to be introduced again.[1]

Before studying naval methods, something must be said about how the army faced the same difficulties in recruitment. The chief difference was that the army did not employ press gangs. In their place were recruiting officers acting on behalf of the colonels who raised and owned the regiments. The state was therefore only marginally concerned with military recruiting. Acts such as those of 1703 or 1779 drafted paupers, debtors and those without visible means of livelihood into the ranks of the army, but the main business was left to officers of the type of Captain Plume and Sergeant Kite in Farquhar's play *The Recruiting Officer* (1706). Their methods are familiar: the offer of bounties to those who would volunteer, promises of pillage and prize money, the flattery of simple souls tired of a countryman's life, plenty of drink at the rendezvous and any opportunity to slip the fatal shilling into a man's pocket, on receipt of which he was legally bound to enlist. The distinction between military and naval methods really depends on the degree of force used. On only one occasion did a naval press gang help to fill the ranks of the army. In 1702 such a gang provided men for the Duke's army in Flanders by blindfolding them and transporting them overseas. Normally the two services took care not to poach on each other's preserves.

The reminiscences of General Robert Long describe his instructions when a recruiting subaltern in 1793 on behalf of the 1st Dragoon Guards.[2] He was told to avoid seamen, the disabled, anyone under the height of 5' 7", to pay each recruit a bounty of 14 guineas (a high fee, of which the man was speedily robbed by his fellows), and in return to receive £5 for each man raised. For two months he toured inland counties to avoid competition with naval gangs, accompanied by a sergeant and six troopers. His total bag amounted to eight recruits raised at a cost of £144. Obviously, it was neither a more efficient nor a more economical way of recruiting than those adopted by the navy, but at least it avoided the stigma of force.

The procedure for naval mobilisation became standardised at the beginning of the period of the French wars. The first step invariably taken was to prohibit enlistment in foreign ships and to recall British subjects serving abroad. Since sailoring has always been to a large degree an international profession and communications were then so primitive, nothing much came of this step. More could be achieved by laying an embargo on domestic shipping until the fleet was manned, but this aroused the hostility of the shipping interest, which asserted that trade was thereby impeded, so an embargo was only imposed as a last resort. Even then there was a battle between the merchants, strongly represented in Parliament, and the naval authorities, leaving the Privy Council to decide which demanded priority. If it was war rather than trade, the government ordered steps to be taken to recruit as many seafaring men as possible by means of a "hot press," that is to say by the intensified use of force, or by lavish promises of bounties.

This was done by the issue of proclamations offering such incentives to volunteers and by the issue of press warrants to bring the whole organisation of impressment into force. At the same time quotas of men were demanded from such bodies as the Watermen's Company, though these demands were seldom complied with in full. If a squadron had to be fitted out in haste and seamen were slow to come in, new regiments of marines might be raised. If this took too much time, soldiers were drafted on board, or even (in the infamous case of Anson's voyage round the world) Chelsea pensioners, all of whom died before passing Cape Horn. There was some reluctance on the part of the Admiralty to enlist able bodied landmen except as volunteers because of the legal problems involved, the warrants only empowering officers to take up those who "used the sea." Later the practice became normal and the muster books provide a separate column for landmen and another for whether a man was pressed or not. In the War of the Austrian Succession it was not until 1743 that gangs began to operate inland and captains were ordered to encourage landmen "by mild treatment and all other ways to have a liking to the service."[3]

The establishment of a Rendezvous (or Rondy, as it was popularly called) was the first thing to be done when mobilisation got under way. This was the equivalent of the modern recruiting centre, where both volunteers and pressed men were entered. Having rented a convenient alehouse, which tavern keepers welcomed because the business of recruiting involved a large consumption of liquor, a flag or Jack was hoisted to advertise the nature of the place. Bills and proclamations were stuck up around the town and men hired to form a press gang. Pressing at sea was of course done by trusted sailors, and so was much of the pressing in port towns, but further inland gangs consisted of local volunteers, tough characters who needed a job.

The oldest rendezvous was at St. Katharine's Stairs on Tower Hill, the neighbourhood being frequented by seamen because of the proximity of the Navy Office where pay tickets were cashed. A convenient tavern there was the Two Dutch Skippers. Other well known places in London were the White Swan in King Street, Westminster, and the Cock and Runner in Bow Street. A necessity in such an alehouse was a strong lock-up room, called a press room, where men could be detained until arrangements had been made to send them to the point of embarcation. Such places were foul little dungeons, that at Bristol measuring eight feet square to accommodate sixteen men. Failing a press room, use could be made of the local gaol or pound, though men were not supposed to be kept there for more than twenty-four hours.

Lt. Grant at Yarmouth in 1743 describes the routine duties

of a pressing officer (the word "prester" now falling out of use), who was recruiting at beat of drum without the assistance of a gang. "I beat up yesterday, being market day at Lowestoft, as I have every market day, and stuck my bills in neighbouring villages, but find so little inclination in the people to enter that I can't promise better success. The money advanced being expended on the service, must beg their Lordships will let me have further orders, which shall be complied with punctually by their most obedient humble servant, R. Grant."[4]

Lt. Reddish established his rendezvous at the Red Lion at Godalming on the Portsmouth road in 1782. He was assisted by a midshipman aged forty who had never been to sea, and a gang of eight men, mostly agricultural labourers. He only raised 155 men in three years, besides apprehending nineteen deserters and accepting a vagrant sent him by the magistrates. All this cost £1,618.[5]

Captain Becker was more successful at Shrewsbury that year, raising 279 men in two years at a cost of £5,311, which was high because parties of men had to be sent to Bristol under guard. He employed five gangs covering places as far distant as Welshpool and Bewdley. The justices of Coventry and other Midland towns (Birmingham was a mere village) sent him paupers and undesirables: "By the bearer, Thomas Bird, constable, I send you George Giles, a deserter from the Navy. You will please to pay the conduct money and four shillings in part of his pay to Thomas Bird, P.S. Please to acknowledge the receipt of Giles."[6]

Such a captain was called the Regulating Captain, the word implying his duty to inspect all recruits. They were only appointed to the larger towns, at first in London but after 1745 outside the Thames area. Their duties included examining all men brought in, either volunteers or those pressed by their subordinates. They were empowered to discharge all those unsuitable and those whose protections proved that they had been wrongfully pressed, and to accept substitutes. Since they were paid head money, they often sent men to the fleet who were manifestly useless at sea, for which they were frequently blamed by serving officers. In 1741 the Commander-in-Chief at Portsmouth told the Secretary of the Admiralty that one commander of a pressing tender (admittedly not a regulating captain), "instead of being paid ten shillings a head, deserves to be severely reprimanded for bringing them." [7]

On the whole the record of the regulating captains was good in respect of the zeal, honesty and soundness of judgement exercised in the discharge of their multifarious duties, considering the manifold opportunities of taking bribes or accepting money for the wrong reasons when discharging men. In addition to supervising the rendezvous, he had to make sure that his lieutenants and midshipmen actually went out with the gangs with their warrants and reported accurately on their expenses. If pressing was done afloat, he had to hire, arm and man the tenders and see that recruits were delivered to the ports where they were needed.

Regulating captains were usually elderly naval officers with no prospect of another command at sea. It was a dull but not dishonourable job, at first only temporary but later lasting for many years. In addition to his full pay, he was paid £5 a month, a wage which was later raised to £1 a day, with five shillings' subsistence allowance.

Some, of course (like Falstaff), "misused the king's press damnably" before they were found out, but such knaves were more likely to be needy lieutenants. One, having wrongfully impressed a master's mate, agreed to release him for a bribe of £15 but "having that day been dining with a party of military officers," forgot to do so. When complaints reached the Admiralty, the lieutenant was "broke" and dismissed the service. [8]

The relations between a lieutenant and his captain were

much the same as on board ship. The following candid character sketch might have been written by a man like James Anthony Gardner, whose reminiscences of the navy in the latter part of the eighteenth century are the liveliest we have. In this instance a lieutenant of the Impress Service warns a fellow officer of his new captain's character: "At first you'll think him a fine old fellow, but if it's possible he will make you quarrel with all your acquaintance. Be very careful not to introduce him to any family that you have a regard for, for although he is nearly seventy years of age, he is the greatest debauchee you ever met with—a man of no religion, a man who is capable of any meanness, arbitrary and tyrannical in his disposition. To conclude, there is not a house in Chester that he can go into but his own and the rendezvous, after having been six months in one of the agreeablest cities in England."[9]

As has been said, both volunteers and pressed men attended the rendezvous to enlist. The old King's shilling imprest money fell out of use towards the middle of the century, to be replaced by more reliance on bounty money or wages paid in advance. In order to encourage volunteers, official proclamations were printed and distributed, or private bills advertised peculiar attractions. Such few as have survived make amusing reading. One wonders how many simple men were taken in by such promises. To counteract the dislike of serving in the West Indies, commonly regarded as certain death by disease, one such bill described Jamaica as "that delightful Island abounding in Rum, Sugar and Spanish Dollars, where there is delicious living and plenty of GROG and PUNCH."

Another of the same date, 1780, is more honest and seamanlike in its language.[10]

"All true-blue British hearts of oak, who are able, and no doubt willing, to serve their good King and Country on board his Majesty's ships, are hereby invited to repair to the Roundabout Tavern, near New Crane, Wapping, where they will find

Lieutenant James Ayscough, of the *Bellona* who still keeps open his right real, senior, general and royal Portsmouth Rendezvous for the entertainment and reception of such gallant seamen, who are proud to serve on board the ships now lying at Portsmouth, Plymouth, Chatham and Sheerness, under the command of Vice-Admiral Geary, Rear-Admiral George Lord Edgcumbe, and Commodore Hills.

Lieutenant Ayscough will be damned happy to shake hands with any of his old shipmates in particular, or their jolly friends in general. Keep it up, my Boys! Twenty may play as well as one.

All Seamen will receive three pounds bounty, and Ordinary Seamen two pounds, with conduct money, and their chests, bedding etc. sent carriage free.

N.B. For the encouragement of discovering Seamen that may be impressed a REWARD of two pounds will be given for Able and thirty shillings for Ordinary seamen.

Success to his Majesty's Navy! With health and limbs to the jolly tars of old England.

JAMES AYSCOUGH
GOD SAVE THE KING

Another poster from Shoreham in 1803 offers £5 for an Able Seaman and is addressed to all

> "Englishmen willing to defend their country against the attempts of all Republicans and Levellers, and against the designs of our natural enemies, who intend in this year to invade Old England, to murder our gracious King as they have done their own; to make whores of our wives and daughters; to rob us of our property, and teach us nothing but the damned art of murdering one another."

Bounties inevitably became more generous as the shortage of men increased. In William's day the offer was only three months' wages in advance and not being turned over to another ship without agreement. In 1701 it was 30/- for an Able Seaman, 25/- for an Ordinary Seaman, the total outlay that year being £23,800. Seven years later, following the Cruisers and Convoy Act which made a more generous dis-

tribution of prize money to the captors, thereby making the
naval profession more attractive, a bounty of £5 was offered
to each man serving on board when a prize was taken. The
distribution by this act "for the better and more effectual encouragement of the sea service" was three-eighths to the
captain, one to the lieutenants, one to the warrant and civilian
officers, leaving two-eighths for the crew.[11]

In 1739 two guineas were offered for an Able Seaman by
royal proclamation. This rose to £5 for an Able Seaman, £3
for an Ordinary Seaman, but three weeks later it was said
at Portsmouth that only a dozen seamen had come in. In 1770
the government was offering 30/- and 20/- but various cities
supplemented this by offering their own bounties: Bristol
20/- a man, Edinburgh 42/-, Aberdeen 21/-, London 40/-.[12]

In 1795 the City of London offered ten guineas for an Able
Seaman, eight for an Ordinary, six for a Landsman and one or
two for a Boy, according to height.

It is impossible to estimate with any accuracy the ratio of
volunteers to pressed men. Even if the thousands of monthly
muster books were analysed, so many were carelessly kept
and so many captains entered a volunteer as a pressed man in
order to claim the head money that accuracy is impossible.
A volunteer may have entered the navy with certain financial
benefits, but these were soon dissipated on drink, and on board
he was treated no differently. It might be safe to say that something like half the fleet was manned by volunteers. These
would be chiefly landmen at the start of a war, when professional seamen lay low in the hope of better pay from the
merchants, but even they well knew that in the long run they
would be pressed on a return voyage and might well lose
the "bank" of wages due to them in the process. Vernon's
squadron in 1739 was manned in six weeks by 2,870 men,
chiefly volunteers, but the next year the navy was said to be
taking in "the scum of the world." An analysis of the eleven
ships which did not accompany Vernon to the West Indies

has been attempted, but no meaningful deductions can be made. One ship with a complement of 800 men is manned exactly half by volunteers and half by pressed men; another carries 437 volunteers and one pressed man. During that war it was said that bounties were paid to 4,811 men, giving some indication of the number of volunteers in ten years in a navy averaging 40,000 men.[13]

To implement the pressing service, the government issued in the first instance General Press Warrants to local authorities such as Lords Lieutenant or Mayors, ordering them to depute constables for the service. The Admiralty also sent down Individual Warrants to admirals and captains, telling them to organise their own press gangs. The following examples show how circumscribed such warrants were as regards the type of man who could be legally pressed.[14]

> "*Admiralty to the Captains appointed to regulate the Press in the River Thames*, 16 *March*, 1711
>
> ... You are to direct the aforesaid lieutenants to be very diligent in the impressing of able seamen, or seafaring men, that are fit for her Majesty's service, and no other. And let them know that, as an encouragement for the service which they shall so perform, an allowance of ten shillings will be made to them by the Clerk of the Cheque of her Majesty's yard at Deptford for every such able seaman, seafaring man, or waterman they shall impress by or before the first day of May next, upon their producing to him certificates from you ...
>
> You are further to direct the aforesaid lieutenants to take care not to imprest any man who shall have certificates or tickets signed by flag officers, or who shall otherwise make it appear to them that they do actually belong to any of her Majesty's ships or vessels, which, if they do, they are not to expect any allowance for them. And that they do not disturb or molest the gangs employed in or about this town for procuring men for her Majesty's service."

A more individual type of warrant, dated 28 November, 1745, runs as follows—[15]

"By the Commissions for Executing the Office of Lord High Admiral etc.

In pursuance of His Majesty's Order in Council dated 28 November 1745, We do hereby empower and direct you to impress, or cause to be impressed, so many seamen, seafaring men and persons whose occupations and callings are to work in vessels and boats upon rivers as shall be necessary not only to complete the number of men allowed to H.M. ship under your command, but also to man such others of H.M. ships as may be in want of men, giving unto each man so impressed one shilling for Prest Money. And in the execution hereof, you are to take care that neither yourself, nor any officer authorised by you, do demand or receive any money, gratuity, reward or other consideration whatsoever for the sparing, exchanging or discharging any person or persons impressed, as you will answer it at your peril. You are not to entrust any person with the execution of this warrant but a Commissioned Officer, and to insert his name and office in the deputation on the other side hereof, and set your hand and seal thereto. This Warrant to continue in force till the 31 December 1746. And in the due execution of the same, all Mayors, Sheriffs, Justices of the Peace, Bailiffs, Constables, Headboroughs and all other H.M. Officers and subjects, whom it may concern, are hereby required to be aiding and assisting unto you, and those employed by you, as they tender H.M. Service, and will answer the contrary at their peril.

Given under our hands and this seal of the Office of Admiralty (Date and three signatures).

Overleaf

I do hereby depute Lieutenant — belonging to H.M.S. — under my command to impress seamen, seafaring men and persons whose occupations and callings are to work in vessels and boats upon rivers, according to the tenor of this warrant. In testimony whereof I have hereunto set my hand and seal."
(Date and signature of captain)

Warrants to civil authorities usually included a clause instructing them to get the men to the nearest rendezvous, where they would be paid head or conduct money varying between 2/6 and 10/- a head. Regulating captains produced affidavits for the men brought in, any expenses incurred and whether a man was pressed or volunteered, in which case a bounty was payable.

Lieutenants and midshipmen did most of the actual business of pressing ashore. The latter were "oldsters," that is to say midshipmen who had failed to pass for lieutenant, in contrast to the "youngsters," who were on their way up the naval ladder. The common idea that the brutal and bloody work of the gangs was often entrusted to mere boys is absurd when one considers the nature of the work to be done. The pay of such officers varied: normally it was five shillings a day for a lieutenant in addition to his basic pay, ten shillings a week for the gangers. Officers received threepence a mile travelling expenses, gangers one penny.

Expense accounts were closely scrutinised. When Lt. Atkinson of the *Charming Betsy* tender sent in an account for £128. 3. 4. in 1778 this was regarded as excessive because his total bag was only thirty-eight men, even though he stated that he did thirty-three trips up the Humber and paid all his midshipman's expenses. Lt. Pollard, tired of rolling about the Bristol Channel in a leaky tender, set up a rendez-vous on shore and sent in a bill for £42. 18. 6. for food and small beer for his gang. He was sharply told to go to sea again.[16]

The expense account sent in by Lt. Henry Smith in 1771 shows the kind of scrapes such officers got themselves into. One is glad to note that Lord Sandwich ordered this bill to be paid.[17]

To a surgeon for dressing wounds received by the gangs in frays.   18/9
For bailing himself, two midshipmen and three of the gang for making up a quarrel to prevent a further expense at law.
                                                                                                    £1. 13. 6
Fees of Court at Hicks and Hall on withdrawing his recogni-zance.   10/3

To a Constable for withdrawing an action which he had
brought on account of the Lieutenant, having taken a man
from the said Constable's custody.   £7. 7. 0

Towards the end of a war the number who enlisted could be
remarkably small. A typical quarterly return in 1744 gives
Guildford 5 men, Portsmouth 16, Winchester 9, Southampton
8, Weymouth 6, Petersfield 11, Yarmouth 1, Deal 5. The
next quarter the officer at the last place announces that he had
pressed eleven, three of whom are excellent seamen. Having
heard that they were at Sandwich, he chased them into a barn,
where at first they denied they had ever been to sea, but later
confessed to many voyages.[18]

In the American War of Independence the demand on manpower was more serious. By that date the pressing service
was organised on a national scale, as a glance at the list of
rendezvous on page 291 will show. The table gives 1,019
officers employed on shore, raising 21,367 men at a cost of
£106,591. Far more men were pressed in the Thames area
than anywhere else: 6,514, compared with 1,519 for Dublin
and 1,337 from Dover. The totals do not include the much
larger number pressed at sea.

The number sent in by magistrates is remarkably small.
Some welcomed a hot press to get rid of undesirables who
were a burden on the parish. Men like Francis Juniper of
Cuckfield, "a very drunken, troublesome fellow, without a
coat to his back." Occasionally a man might have his sentence
commuted to service on board one of H.M. Ships. In 1760
Jeremiah Peacock, guilty of the theft of a piece of mahogany,
value half a crown, had a sentence of transportation commuted in this way. In 1775 three young men of Devon,
sentenced to branding and three years in prison for theft,
were similarly treated.[19] It is worth bearing such savage
sentences in mind when considering the rough justice of
pressing and the harsh conditions prevailing on board ship.

The following pathetic letter from a prest-master who does

not seem to have been a naval officer, writing from Hull in 1694, suggests that not even prisoners would go to sea unless they were offered additional bribes:[20]

> My trouble is increased mightily every day for want of a place to secure my men, and my addresses to the magistrate here provided nothing; nor have I had an answer from above. And the people here consisting generally of seamen, neither I nor the prest master can be safe from flaunts and curses; and not a house that I know of that would not receive a fugitive and shut the door on him . . .
>
> A prest master dare scarce carry an impressed man through the streets. The men in hold threaten their lives, and call one such names as you never heard, and curse and damn all before them, and threatened that if I gave not more allowance than the king's I should not see one of them the next day. We capitulated after, and went among them with the gaoler, and I promised if they would keep orderly and quietly, and attempt no escapes, I would give them 2d. per diem apiece to drink more than I gave the gaoler for them, and they promised fair; but I cannot trust them. I am tormented every day, women crying, men complaining, all entreating, the mayor objecting I cannot impress here. I can neither eat nor drink nor sleep without complaints.

However, in 1770 eleven criminals from Newgate and twenty-four at the assizes elected to serve in the navy. Occasionally a lieutenant would visit a gaol to see if there were any volunteers, but in general the Admiralty opposed such a practice. When accepting another nine men from Newgate that year, the Secretary stipulated that they should be washed, purified and clothed before leaving prison, adding "Their Lordships wish that no more convicts may be ordered on board H.M. ships, as such persons may not only bring distempers and immoralities among their companions, but may discourage men of irreproachable character from entering H.M. service, seeing they are to be ranked with common malefactors"[21] Wise words, but written in peacetime. The exigencies of war altered the case.

Captains of ships often complained of the ignorant zeal of simple Justices, but the Justices were too often neither simple nor zealous. In large towns they often refused to co-operate because the business of pressing made them unpopular. Bristol had a peculiar reputation for this, so much so that privateers exalted in their freedom there:

> Here is our chief encouragement, our ship belongs to Bristol,
> Poor Londoners when coming home they surely will be pressed all;
> We've no such fear when home we steer, with prizes under convoy,
> We'll frolic round all Bristol town, sweet liberty we enjoy.[22]

Liverpool was an easier place to recruit in because of the number of poor Irish whom the crimps brought over to sell either to the gangs or to the privateers. So was Chester, but Parkgate further down the river was so hostile that an attempt to establish a rendezvous there failed. The fishermen of Brighton (or Brighthelmstone, as the village was then called) imagined that they enjoyed immunity because they lived under the protection of the Duke of Newcastle. By 1779 he was dead, so it was decided to teach them a lesson. Captain Alms, regulating captain at Shoreham, was told to besiege the place with the assistance of troops from Lewes. On 24 July armed gangs converged on the village from all points of the compass. As the advance party entered the place there were warning shouts of "Press Gang!" For the next ten hours every man kept himself locked up and bolted while the rain poured down on the gangs. Only one man was caught, but on the way home the Newhaven gang ran into a band of smugglers, of whom five were taken. For months afterwards, wrote Alms, the inhabitants were "very shy and cautious of appearing in public."[23]

An early attack on impressment by John Dennis in his *Essay on the Navy* (1702) mentions as "another inconveniency the frequent riots, tumults and quarrels that happen as well among the press gangs (in cutting, heaving and knocking down each other) as with watermen, bargemen, citizens and others, whereby the king's peace hath been frequently broken and several press gangs, with their officers, taken into custody for the same."

"Frays," as they were called, of this type are too numerous to be described. They are commonly instanced as one of the worst consequences of forcible conscription, and the legal problems which they raised will be described in the next chapter. Certainly, impressment was a clumsy business, but equally certainly it was essential for the preservation of the state. As the naval authorities complained on more than one occasion, as long as Parliament did nothing to replace it, and merely made the whole thing more unpopular by giving irresponsible "patriots" an opportunity to inveigh against it without suggesting any alternative, recourse had to be made to forcible methods of recruitment. In this way the activities of the gangs became part of the folklore of Britain. Their reputation for brutality was exaggerated by politicians, pamphleteers and novelists alike. Moralists inveighed against the injustice they inflicted. Lawyers tried to undermine their legality. Shipowners and merchants declared that they ruined trade, while at the same time demanding stronger escorts for their vessels. How such ships could be manned, or how the country was to be defended if they were not, was left unsolved. Because the actual process of impressment did not inflict any hardship on the ruling classes, who were immune by reason of their station in society rather than by any specific protection, because it affected the least desirable parts of a town and the lowest strata of the population, the barbarous business went on. No one could discover an alternative which would be equally acceptable to Parliament and the Navy.

Let us conclude our study of pressing methods on shore

with two stories, one so dramatic that the truth is stranger than fiction, the other, while ostensibly fictitious, is based on personal observation of a hundred such instances in real life.[24]

One night in the year 1723 an apprentice arrived at Deal on his way to Sandwich. Since he had little money, he was allowed to share a bed with a boatswain from an East Indiaman lying in the Downs. At daybreak he thought he would leave the stuffy room to walk about the town before continuing on his journey, but the door would not open. The boatswain lent him his knife to prise it open. Half an hour later he returned to find the boatswain gone. With the man's knife in his pocket, he continued on his road.

When the maid of the inn entered the room and saw bloodstains on the floor and bloody footprints down to the water's edge, a hue and cry was raised and the apprentice speedily apprehended. He could not explain the bloodstains and the knife was still on him. At the Assizes he was soon found guilty of murder and sentenced to hanging. But the executioner bungled his job, so that his friends were able to cut him down alive and hustle him on board a ship bound for the West Indies. There he was transferred to another ship. As he stepped on deck, he was confronted with the man he was supposed to have killed.

The explanation of this remarkable coincidence was that the boatswain had been blooded the night before. When the apprentice left their common bed, the bandage slipped and the blood began to flow again. Failing to staunch it, the man hurried out of the inn to find the barber who had blooded him. Before he reached him, he ran into a press gang, who put him on board a warship destined for the West Indies Station.

Our second story is better known and more in accord with normal experience. Roderick Random is nominally the hero, but Tobias Smollett must have seen something very like it when he joined the fleet of Sir Chaloner Ogle as a surgeon's

mate on the Cartagena expedition of 1740. It is worth recalling that this fleet sailed 1,450 short of complement, in
spite of a hot press.

As I crossed Tower wharf a squat, tawny fellow, with a
hanger by his side and a cudgel in his hand, came up to me,
calling 'Yo, ho! brother, you must come along with me.' As I
did not like his appearance, instead of answering his salutation, I
quickenened my pace, in hope of ridding myself of his company;
upon which he whistled aloud, and immediately another sailor
appeared before me, who laid hold of me by the collar and began
to drag me along.

Not being of a humour to relish such treatment, I disengaged
myself from the assailant, and with one blow of my cudgel laid
him motionless on the ground; and perceiving myself surrounded
in a trice by ten or a dozen more, exerted myself with such dexter-
ity and success, that some of my opponents were fain to attack
me with drawn cutlasses; and after an obstinate engagement, in
which I received a large wound on my head, and another on my
left cheek, I was disarmed, taken prisoner and carried on board a
pressing tender, where, after being pinioned like a malefactor, I
was thrust into the hold among a parcel of miserable wretches,
the sight of whom well nigh distracted me . . .

I complained bitterly to the midshipman on deck, telling him at
the same time that unless my hurts were dressed, I should bleed
to death. But compassion was a weakness of which no man
can justly accuse this person, who, squirting a mouthful of dissolved tobacco upon me through the gratings, told me, 'I was a
mutinous dog, and that I might die and be damned.'

The scene of Roderick Random's incarceration was a
pressing tender, from which he was transferred to a man-of-
war the next day. These tenders varied in size from schooners
and cutters to hulks and guardships, which were virtually
floating prisons providing temporary accommodation for
recruits of all sorts before they could be distributed to ships
needing men to fill their complements.

Apart from the ship's boats, which a captain might employ
when empowered to press men for his own ship, the impress

service hired handy craft to cruise in promising areas in order to intercept ships returning home. They had to be well manned and armed, both to meet the opposition of desperate men on board merchant ships, and to defend themselves against enemy privateers cruising in the Channel. In 1740 the Commander-in-Chief, Portsmouth, told the Secretary of the Admiralty "I must beg leave to offer my opinion that a lieutenant and twenty men will be too few, considering there may be privateers three and four times that force in the Channel, and besides it will not be safe for them to stay out after they have prest twelve or fourteen men, lest they should rise upon them."[25] Moreover, they had to provide the "men-in-lieu" to take vessels from which they had pressed men to their moorings, say from the Downs to the Pool of London.

Outward bound ships were normally exempt, but homeward bound ships were fair game. The consequence was that half the object of the convoy system was ruined. Time and again, in the Chops of the Channel, a convoy would scatter in order to avoid the press known to be waiting for it further up Channel. Vessels thus separated became easy prey for privateers from places like St. Malo or Dunkirk, the protection of escorting frigates being lost. A vicious circle was thereby created: not only were good men taken from the fleet to man the pressing tenders, but the strategic aim of the convoy system which the merchants demanded was imperilled by the activities of the impress service.

In the early part of the century much trouble was caused by pressing from homeward bound Indiamen. Sometimes the best seamen took to the boat, abandoning the vessel to the men-in-lieu; at others they mutinied, overpowered their officers and resisted violently when the boarding party came over the side. A situation which often occurred is thus described by Admiral Wager for Walpole's benefit in 1740:[26]

I suppose you may have heard how the East Indie ships have behaved to our boats, that went on board to press, when they arrived in the Downs . . . We had three men-of-war there, they sent all their boats, but they fired on them from their ships and wounded several men. One was drowned; in the evening the East Indie men got into their boats with arms, and went ashore, but were attacked by our boats who took some, but most of them escaped; so that we got, in the whole, but 156 men when we should have 500; they passed by the Nore and would not bring to there, though several shots were fired at them. I hope you will not give protections to the next that ask for them.

Four years later we have the first-hand evidence of a Liverpool pilot to show how this sort of situation repeated itself. On boarding a vessel he was asked if there was a hot press in the town. He replied that there was not at the moment. Nevertheless he heard the men plotting how to defend themselves if they were boarded. Soon afterwards a boat from H.M.S. *Winchelsea* approached. The lieutenant in charge was told to keep off and muskets were fired on both sides. While this was going on, the master of the merchant-man retired to his cabin, nor did he ever use any "means, threats or persuasions to prevent his crew from taking the ship's arms and firing at the boats, but left them wholly to themselves." The pilot took the ship into dock, where the whole crew escaped on shore. Presumably because the Admiralty wished to avoid publicity, the master was not proceeded against on this charge, but only for failing to strike his colours to a warship.[27]

As the East and West Indies interests grew in political power, some agreement had to be reached between the merchants and the navy. Shipowners demanded protection: the navy demanded men. The only sensible way out of the dilemma was to allow the press gang to take a stated number of men off the vessel. By the end of the century the compromise was working well for everyone except prime young seamen, who knew that they were being sacrificed to the needs of the country.

The worst hardships occurred when the master of a merchant vessel avoided paying a man his due wages when he was taken off the ship. It was laid down by law that all such arrears should be paid, but in the hustle of the moment a man could easily be taken off before he received his due. In such cases he was not only cheated of what might well be a substantial amount of money, but he was prevented from seeing his family after an absence of months, if not years.

In pressing from small vessels in the less organised coastal trades there was often a battle to board, or, having done so, to find the ship already abandoned by her crew. A ballad describes how they plan to get away, "R" standing in the muster books for "Run":

> Cheerily, lads, cheerily! there's a ganger hard to wind'ard;
> Cheerily, lads, cheerily! there's a ganger hard a-lee;
> Cheerily, lads, cheerily! else 'tis farewell home and kindred,
> And the bosun's mate a-raisin' hell in the King's navee.
> Cheerily, lads, cheerily! the warrant's out, the hanger's drawn;
> Cheerily, lads, cheerily! we'll leave 'em an R in pawn!

Uprisings by pressed men on board tenders were less common because the hatches were well guarded and the ports barred. However, in 1755, on board the tender *Tasker*, taking men from Liverpool to Spithead, fourteen men were allowed on deck at a time for exercise. She carried a crew of thirty-eight, two of whom acted as sentries at the ventilating scuttle, two on the fo'c'stle, two on the poop and one at the door of the great cabin. One day while the exercise party was on deck there was a cry of Man Overboard! A sentry rushed to the side, was overpowered from behind, his musket seized, and the ship taken over by the pressed men, who sailed her into the nearest bay and abandoned her.[28]

As has been explained, a tender had to carry extra men to

serve as men-in-lieu to take a vessel to her moorings after her crew had been depleted by the gang. Such men were often very unsuitable and expensive. Local fishermen hired themselves out at exorbitant wages; old men, incapable of work at sea were found employment; or good men might be given protections to return to base, though the temptations to desert on the long road back must have been great.

The following instructions to lieutenants in command of tenders show how the business was organised in the end. It will be seen how well armed, manned and victualled such vessels had to be, and how recruits were shipped in order to transport them to the fleet:[29]

Whereas you are appointed to go on board the —— Tender, in order to be employed in procuring Seamen for the service of H.M. Fleet, you are hereby required and directed to observe the following instructions, in addition to those given you with the Press Warrants.

1. You are to take care to have always a sufficient quantity of provisions on board; and to have at all times a proper number of slops, beds and hammacoes, for the use of the new-raised men; and to apply in time to the proper office when any of the said provisions or stores are wanting.

2. You are to see that the guns, small arms, and ordnance stores are kept always in good order; for which purpose your captain is to let you have an armourer or armourer's mate on board the tender, if he can supply you with either of them. And the Principal Officers of the Ordnance Board having represented that masters of tenders have been very negligent in their care of the small arms, though they are allowed oil to clean them and a chest to keep them in, you are to cause those on board the tender to which you are appointed to be oiled frequently and kept in a chest when not in use, and to let the master of the tender know that the Navy Board are directed to stop his pay till he produces a certificate that he has returned his arms and stores in as good order as the reasonable use thereof will admit.

3. You are to see that the master of the tender does furnish what deals (planks) shall be necessary to make platforms for the men

to be on, according to his contract with the Navy Board, that they are not forced to lie on the casks or ballast to the prejudice of their health; and if he is negligent or refuses to do it, to inform the Navy Board.

4. Your captain being directed to put a surgeon's mate, with some of the surgeon's medicaments, on board the tender, for the relief of such of the seamen sent out with you, or procured afterwards as happen to be sick; you are to take care that the said mate gives a constant attendance on board the tender for that purpose. And you are strictly charged not to send any sick men to quarters ashore, where there are no agents or surgeons appointed to take care of them, unless their distempers are of such a nature as absolutely to require it; and in that case you must put them in quarters fit for people in their condition, at the rate of 12 pence a man per day, and under the care of some skilful apothecary or surgeon for cure at the rate of six shillings and eightpence a man. And in case of death you are to cause them to be as decently buried as ten shillings a man will admit, and to draw upon the Commissioners for taking care of Sick and Wounded Seamen for the money, sending to them at the same time a list of the men's names when you have set the sick on shore, with an account of the times when they were put on shore and when they returned on board again, or died, with receipts from the persons to whom any monies shall have been paid on their account, attested by the master of the tender and the surgeon's mate; and at the foot of the said list and account, yourself, with the said master and surgeon's mate, are to make affidavit to the truth of every article contained therein.

5. You are to repair to the port of — and apply to the Mayor or chief magistrate and let him know that you are sent by us to his place to raise seamen for H.M. Service, and to pray his countenance and assistance therein. And you are strictly charged to behave with that discretion in the exercising of your Press Warrant as not to give any just cause of complaint either to the magistrates or inhabitants.

6. You are diligently to employ yourself accordingly in procuring volunteers or pressing such seamen as will not enter voluntarily, both on shore and from merchant ships, vessels, and boats, which are not protected.

7. You are at liberty to go to any adjacent ports where there may be likelihood of procuring seamen, but if you find that there are but few seamen to be got in port, you are strictly charged not to idle your time away, but to go out and cruise upon the neighbouring coasts in order to meet with merchant's ships and procure seamen from them when you find they are not protected; but you are to return once a week/month to — to enquire for orders that may be lodged there for you, and to send hither the journal and account required by the 11th article of these instructions.

8. Whenever you put any men on board merchant ships in lieu of pressed men, you are to give them tickets of leave for such time as you shall judge reasonable for their return, either to their ship or the tender, as you shall think best to order them.

9. If any seaman [*space for other categories, such as landmen*] fit for H.M. Service shall be sent to you by the civil magistrates, or by the Collector of Customs, you are to receive them and give a receipt to the person who brings them, but you are not to receive any boys or infirm people, or any that are unfit for H.M. Service.

10. You are to take care that every man on board be as well accommodated with lodgings as the vessel will allow, and that they all have H.M. full allowance of provisions daily; and if the copper be so small that one boiling will not suffice, to order a second or more boilings if necessary.

11. You are once a week to send to our Secretary a journal of your proceedings, with an account of the new men procured in that week, and the total number of new-raised men on board, and to be very particular in representing if any men have escaped from the tender, or otherwise, and how the same happened, which journal and account you are to send away so as to arrive at this office on a Monday.

12. You are not to discharge any man, on any pretence whatsoever, without our orders.

13. When you have got such a number of men as the vessel will conveniently stow, you are to return without loss of time to the port where your ship shall be, and apply to the Commander-in-Chief there for his directions how to dispose of the said men.

14. When you deliver any new-raised men to the Commanders of any of H.M. ships, you are to deliver along with them lists of their

names, and to set down against them the times of their coming into the Service in order to their commencing wages accordingly. 15. You are lastly to observe that proper notice will be taken of your diligence or remissness in this service; of the number of men you procure; and whether you pester your vessels with unfit people, or take care to entertain none but good men.

The use of crimps for the naval service was not encouraged. Such rascals existed primarily for the benefit of merchants, to whom they sold men at a high price, particularly in the West Indies, where men were at a premium. Many a man who detested the navy took refuge with a crimp when he deserted, or was hidden by an alehouse keeper for a fee, only to be caught again months later on some return voyage. Poor Irish labourers sold themselves to Liverpool crimps for service in privateers. Altogether, the whole business was too much like the slave trade. No wonder pamphleteers urged Wilberforce and his like to stop worrying about black slaves and take a look at what was happening at home.

Informers were another matter, since every zealous regulating officer made it his business to find out where men might be. There is an amusing case of a jilted girl turned informer in a letter received by a captain in 1771.[30]

"Captain B, Sir, there is a Desarter of yours at the upper water Gate. Lives at the sine of the mantion house. He is an Irishman, gose by the name of Youe Mack Mullins, and is trying to Ruing a Wido and three Children for he has Insenuated into the Old Woman's favor so far that she must Sartingly come to poverty, and you by Sarching the book's will find what I have related to be true and much oblige the hole parish of St. Pickles, Deptford. Nancy of Deptford." [St. Pickle's = St. Nicholas's]

It is impossible to ascertain exactly what the business of impressment cost, but it was certainly very expensive both in men and money. The cost in the year 1703 was estimated at £35,000. When in 1745 the Navy Board was asked to supply figures, no reply was vouchsafed. A pamphleteer guessed that the cost during the Seven Years War amounted to £300,000, but he gives no details.[31]

What must be emphasised is that no one—Admiralty, naval officers, merchants, or Parliament—liked the method or thought it efficient. Once the attempt to register seamen had failed (see below, chapter IX), there was just no alternative. The point is made very clear in correspondence which passed between Admiral Vernon and the Secretary of the Admiralty. The one was a notably humane commander, the other had studied the sad history of impressment more than anyone else. Vernon, like many other reformers, informed the Secretary that he esteemed it "to be highly for his Majesty's honour and service that while Parliament is sitting some humane method should be established for preserving the lives of so valuable a body of men as our seamen, and reconciling their good will to the public service." To which Thomas Corbett, the Secretary, replied on 11 October, 1745: "Their Lordships command me to acquaint you that they are as much averse to the present method of Pressing as any man can be and wish some better method was established to man his Majesty's ships. But till the Legislature has done so, their Lordships think it their duty and also of all his Majesty's officers to exert their utmost diligence to procure men to serve his Majesty at sea, according to the present methods, how disagreeable soever they may be; and not to expose the nation to danger from reasons of private tenderness."[32]

VIII

The Law and the Press

VOLTAIRE DESCRIBES how he found a Thames water-man, who had been boasting about the liberty of Englishmen, confined the next day in a prison cell by the press gang. In our last chapter we were concerned about how he got there: in the present we shall consider the legality of the proceeding.

The embarrassing paradox of the exercise of a seemingly arbitrary and irresponsible power in a country which prided itself on the freedom of its constitution is well expressed by David Hume. After describing the efforts of Parliament to check the privileges of the Crown, he admits that one irregular power remains in existence with tacit permission. "While this power is exercised to no other end than to man the Navy, men willingly submit to it from a sense of its use as a necessity; and the sailors, who are alone affected by it, find no body to support them in claiming the rights and privileges which the law grants without distinction to English subjects. . . . I pretend not by this reasoning to exclude all possibility of contriving a register for seamen, which might man the Navy without being dangerous to liberty. I only observe that no satisfactory scheme of that nature has ever been proposed. Rather than adopt any project hitherto invented, we continue a practice seemingly the most absurd and unaccountable. A continued violence is permitted in the Crown, amidst the greatest jealousy and watchfulness in the People."[1]

In the next chapter we shall consider the only attempt made

to register seamen and the numerous futile projects which were suggested to replace what was admitted on all sides to be an inefficient, costly and brutal method of manning the navy. Here we are concerned with the ambiguities and limitations in the legality of that method.

In the course of a debate on the subject in 1740 Walpole stated: "The hardships of an impress have been long dwelt upon, and displayed with all the powers of eloquence. Nor can it be affirmed this method of raising seamen is either eligible or legal."[2] But he was wrong. "Eligible" impressment might not be, but it was certainly "legal" in principle. What strikes the reader of the four fat packets of the recorded opinions of the Law Officers, which were sought by the Admiralty in order to unravel the legal difficulties with which it was frequently presented, is the absence of any attempt to challenge the principle of impressment in the courts.[3] On the other hand there are innumerable individual cases of alleged unlawful pressing, though not nearly as many as those involving prize money, neutral rights etc. One obvious explanation is that those who suffered were no Hampdens. They had neither the money nor the opportunity to go to law, because they were usually on the high seas before it ever occurred to them to do so.

Except for frothy talk about liberty on the part of politicians in the rare debates on the subject, the exercise of this prerogative of the Crown empowering the Lords Commissioners of the Admiralty to impress seamen was accepted as part of Common Law; but because of the complicated system of protections which grew up as the demand for manpower increased, an officer on the impress service had to be very careful to avoid overstepping the bounds set by his warrant. In every case where the legality of his proceedings was in doubt, the Attorney General or the Solicitor General advised the Admiralty to avoid bringing an action in the courts. Prosecution was only advised when a favourable verdict seemed certain. Even when it was a question of protecting a naval officer in the exercise of his duty, legal advice was never to indict unless an assailant was positively identifiable, or a protection was being patently abused.

Innumerable statutes tacitly recognise the legality of impressment, though none formally enact it. As a modern judge has put it, "On the substantive question of legality, the Common Law, recognised by statutes, was held to supply the answer, founded as it was held to be upon necessity and sanctioned by ages."[4]

For this reason the first reasoned defence of its legality is largely composed of precedents. This was compiled by Thomas Corbett, Secretary of the Admiralty, about 1740 for his own use and was therefore never printed.[5] He explains that he was compelled to undertake the task because of the current hostility to impressment (which was greater in the earlier part of the century than in the later), from "the many outrages and insults and sometimes murders committed upon officers and seamen employed in pressing, the People thinking themselves well justified to oppose and resist men engaged in unlawful acts of violence; from the browbeatings and discouragements the said officers and seamen almost constantly meet with from the Justices of the Peace and Officers of Corporations, when either they complain to them of ill usage, or are complained against for acts of force which may be perhaps necessary or unavoidable in the execution of their warrants; from the notorious prejudice of Juries, who condemn them in almost all trials of law. And lastly what is worse than all the rest, from the discontented impressions it fixes in the minds of our seamen, who instead of esteeming it their duty or honourable to serve their country, are taught to think that they are enslaved into the service by methods unjust and tyrannical and in violation of their lawful rights and liberty."

Since Parliament had never suggested any other method of

manning, the Crown was compelled to use those powers of arrest recorded in the Black Book of Admiralty and going back to the act of 1378 in the reign of Richard II (an act which lasted until 1863). After instancing numerous cases recorded by Rymer, and all the relevant statutes, Corbett concludes that, however many subsequent acts of limitation there might be, no branch of the royal prerogative "appears to be better warranted, or founded on more solid authorities, being established upon the principle of Common Law and virtually confirmed by several statutes."

The only extensive defence of legality to appear in print is the ably written pamphlet *On the Legality of Impressing Seamen* published by Charles Butler in 1778, the third edition of which in 1814 carries on the title page "with additions, partly by Lord Sandwich." It is not clear what these additions are. Since Butler adopts the same method as Corbett, he may well have seen Corbett's manuscript in the Admiralty Library by permission of Sandwich when First Lord. He wisely confines himself to a legalistic defence of the government's right to press seamen, never attempting to argue the case for conscription on wider grounds. He prints the same list of statutes and precedents, adding a curious defence on sociological grounds which could only have been made at that date. In replying to the objection that only one section of the community suffers, he says that "irregularity of rank is inseparable from society, and in the distribution of the duties of society, those that are offensive and disagreeable public duties (among which we reckon personal service in the armies and navies of the state) must fall to the lot of that part of mankind which fills the lower ranks of life . . . In the advanced state of government which the British nation has reached, personal service neither is, nor ought to be, nor can be, the duty of every citizen." So, with refreshing honesty, he dismisses as sentimentality the view that the naval seaman's lot is one of unmitigated hardship: one has only to look at his condition when employed by merchants to see how much better off he is in the Navy.

In 1727 a humane bill which sought to improve conditions in order to encourage volunteers was defeated by the Opposition on the grounds that it contained the word "pressed" which might be thought to give impressment the force of law. This argument is developed in an anonymous pamphlet entitled *The Sailor's Advocate*, which ran through several editions and evidently expresses the popular view that pressing is no better than kidnapping. It was contrary to Magna Carta and the Petition of Right. It ruined trade and cost the state a lot of money. It "sets up numbers of little tyrants in all our seaports, when you shall see droves of these lawless fellows, armed with great sticks, force such as they think proper into the service and knock down any who will not submit to appear before their magistrate, who is sometimes a lieutenant, but oftener an officer of the lowest rank in an ale-house at Wapping or St. Catharine's, a midshipman, a boatswain's mate, or some such like judge of liberty and property."

The alternative proposed was a register; but a register had been tried and failed. Like other writers, the author condemns the current methods of impressment without taking into account the way their exercise was hedged about with limitations. No one liked it, the Admiralty no more than the House of Commons. The point was, how to make it as humane and serviceable as possible.

The most important case in the history of impressment was that of *R. v. Broadfoot* in 1743, because it elicited the opinion of Serjeant Foster which was to be quoted with approval on many subsequent occasions. The lieutenant of a sloop of war had been sent out with a warrant to board a vessel returning to Bristol in order to search for men. As Alexander Broadfoot, one of those on board the vessel, saw the boat approaching he called out "Who are you and why do you come?" "We come for you and your comrades." "Keep back, I have

a blunderbuss loaded with swan shot. Where is your lieutenant?" One of the boat's crew named Calahan replied "He
is not far off" and proceeded to climb on board. Broadfoot
fired and killed him.[6]

Sir Michael Foster, Recorder of Bristol, directed the jury
to bring in a verdict of manslaughter because the lieutenant
was not actually present with his warrant. He then proceeded to give a learned opinion on impressment in general.
"The practice of pressing is one of the mischiefs war bringeth
with it. But it is a maxim of law, and good policy too, that all
private mischiefs must be borne with patience for preventing
a national calamity. And as no greater calamity can befall
us than to be weak and defenceless at sea in time of war, so I
do not know that the wisdom of the nation hath hitherto
found out any method of manning our navy less inconvenient
than pressing . . . According to my present comprehension
(and I have been at some pains to inform myself), the right
of impressing mariners for the public service is a prerogative
inherent in the Crown, grounded upon Common Law, and
recognised by many acts of Parliament."

An equally important judicial opinion was that expressed
by Lord Mansfield in the case of *R. v. Tubbs* in 1776.[7] Tubbs,
a Gravesend waterman, was pressed on board the guard ship
at the Nore. The Watermen's Company sought a writ of
Habeas Corpus on the ground that he was liable to serve as
one of the Lord Mayor's watermen. The Admiralty refused,
because they held that watermen as such were not protected
unless they were specifically engaged on such a duty. Mansfield supported this view, adding

> The power of pressing is founded on immemorial usage,
> allowed for ages. If it be so founded and allowed for ages, it can
> have no ground to stand upon, nor can it be vindicated or
> justified by any reason but the safety of the state. And the practice
> is deduced from that trite maxim of the constitutional law of
> England, that private mischief had better be submitted to, than

that public detriment and inconvenience should ensue. To be sure, there are instances where private men must give way to the public good. In every case of pressing, every man must be very sorry for the act, and for the necessity which gives rise to it. It ought, therefore, to be exercised with the greatest moderation and only upon the most cogent necessity. And though it be a legal power, it may, like many others, be abused in the exercise of it . . . Persons liable must come purely within the description of seamen, seafaring men etc. He therefore who is not within the description, does not come within the usage. The commission to press is not to press landmen, or persons of any other description of life.

The difficulty was to decide who was a seaman, who did in fact "use the sea." Was a ship's carpenter who had for some years plied his trade on land a seaman? The Law Officers said yes, because he had been accustomed to a life at sea. But a glover pressed when looking at a shop window, who swore that he had never seen a ship in his life, or an alderman who was carried off to sea as a common seaman, were clearly not. Landmen were theoretically exempt, though encouraged to enter as volunteers; to be on the safe side it was wise to carry one's apprenticeship credentials with one if a man was young and strong. But since pressing officers were paid by results they were none too careful and frequently took men unsuited to the hard life at sea. Hence the many complaints about the rabble produced by the gangs: "All the ragg-tagg that can be picked up—Men more fit for an hospital than a ship—Sad wretches—A nuisance to the ship—Miserable poor creatures, not a seaman amongst them—Poor ragged souls, and very small—Sad, thievish creatures—Black-guards." When in 1758 the *Bristol* received sixty-eight men, eighteen were found to be seamen and the rest "ragged wretches, bad of the itch, who have not the least pretensions to eat his Majesty's bread," so that forty were sent back on shore. The next year Admiral Mostyn complains; "I don't know where they come from but whoever was the officer who received them, he ought to be ashamed, for I never saw such except in the condemned hole at Newgate. I was three hours and a half mustering this scabby crew, and I should have imagined that the scum of the earth had been picked up for this ship."[8]

The most precious document any man living in a coastal area could possess was his protection or passport, a certificate attesting that the bearer belonged to what we should call a reserved occupation, or had a ticket of leave, of which this is an example from 1691:

> The Bearer (name) hath hereby leave to follow his private occasions on shore from (date) to (date) before which he is at his peril to return on board his Majesty's ship (name) to which he belongs, and until then and no longer to be freed being otherwise imprest. Witness my hand and Seal of the Navy Office (signature)

As the years went by such documents became much more detailed but, as may be seen from the following, they were easy enough to forge before the days of photography.

> *By the Commissioners etc.*
> Whereas by an Act of Parliament passed in the 13th year of the Reign of his late Majesty King George the Second it is enacted That the persons under the Age and Circumstances therein mentioned, shall be freed and exempted from being impressed into H.M. Service, upon due Proof made before us of their respective Ages and Circumstances as the Case shall happen; And whereas we have received Testimony that the Bearer (name) was born the (date) and will not therefore be of the Age of Eighteen Years until the (Date, or "is a Foreigner", or "Apprentice etc.") and he being entitled to a Protection, in pursuance of the said Act of Parliament; We do hereby require and direct all Commanders of H.M. Ships, Press-Masters and others whom it doth concern, not to Impress him into H.M. Service, provided a Description of his Person be inserted in the Margin hereof.
> *By Command of their Lordships*

How seriously the Admiralty took these protections may be

seen from the detailed lists of such documents between 1702
and 1815, preserved in the Public Record Office.[9] Every
variety of person at one time or another obtained one, and
pressing officers were always being warned to take notice of
them if "great trouble and clamour" was to be avoided.

To take some random samples. Trinity House was allowed
200 protected persons employed in laying buoys; the Customs
Office and the Salt Office could reserve large numbers of men;
Smeaton's men building the Eddystone lighthouse (to make
doubly sure he gave them metal badges); crews of privateers;
hoymen and lightermen employed by the East India Company; bargemen and all those employed on official naval
business, such as in the Royal dockyards or on board trans-
ports and victuallers. Occasionally protections were issued
as rewards for gallantry: eight members of the crew of the
transport *Atlas* in 1814 were given exemption for three years
"in consideration of her gallant conduct in action with an
American privateer of superior force." In one unusual case
the Navy Board won a protection for its bargemen when the
Admiralty officers tried to press a man carrying timber to a
dockyard.[10] Men working the Woolwich ferry went free;
but when the Lord of the Manor of Ryde in the Isle of Wight
tried to exercise his ancient privilege of exempting twenty men
on the Gosport ferry, regulating officers were told "to press
every man as soon as possible."

The act of 1739 gives a general list of such protected
persons: all those under eighteen and over fifty-five; foreigners; volunteers after two years' service; harpooners, line
managers, boat steerers engaged in the Greenland fishery, but
not the Newfoundland fishery; herring fishers on the east
coast during the season. It was estimated that there were
14,800 protections in use, of which about 7,000 were in the
coastal trades.[11]

To take the case of the foreigners first. The same act
amends the Navigation Act by allowing masters to ship three-

quarters of the crews with foreigners during wartime. If such a man was employed on board a warship for over two years he could become a naturalised Englishmen, and as such liable to impressment. The same thing happened if he married an Englishwoman.

A great deal of the correspondence of eighteenth-century admirals is occupied with complaints from foreign embassies seeking to free their subjects. One bulky file covering the years 1697-1708 is filled with letters from the Foreign Office to the Admiralty.[12] On 22 November 1697 "The King of Sweden's Minister having represented to Mr. Secretary Trumbull that one John Paterson, a Swede pressed in the river Thames about twenty months ago, and carried on board the *Neptune*, afterwards put on board the *Royal William*, and since turned over to the *Edgar*, where he now is, and desiring he may be discharged, Mr. Secretary desires you will be pleased to move the Lords of the Admiralty to give directions immediately." As might be expected, most complaints came from Sweden. One is happy to hear that Mr. Rosencrantz the Danish Envoy was successful in obtaining the release of eleven of his countrymen.

A class of men who gave endless trouble were the Thames watermen. The ancient jurisdiction of the Lord Admiral was limited to the main stream of rivers near the sea, but later it was extended. By an act passed at the beginning of the reign of Philip and Mary, watermen operating between Gravesend and Windsor were exempt provided the Company provided a quota of men for the Royal Navy on demand. This was re-enacted in 1706, in spite of Pepys's experience that "the Company served the government very slightly after all the noise they have made to the king and the favours received." The next year the new Fire Insurance was allowed to employ thirty watermen for service on the wharves. But as we have seen in the case of Tubbs, all watermen were not allowed to go as free as the acts suggested. Indeed, on one shocking occasion even the crew of the Lord Mayor's barge was pressed while rowing him to the City. What usually happened wherever a trade was sufficiently organised was to compound with the company to provide a certain number of men if the rest were left alone—two hundred by the Watermen's Company, one-tenth of the Tyneside keelmen, one-seventh of the Isle of Man fishermen, one-ninth of the Nantwich salt trade employing 900 men. The trowmen of the Severn and Wye enjoyed protection until in 1798 the passage of the Severn as far up as Gloucester was decided to be "open sea," whereupon they were pressed by scores. Similarly the estuary of the Dee was protected, hence the immunity of sailors living at Parkgate: when a rendezvous was at last established there in 1804 in the face of traditional hostility, the sailors simply disappeared and the trade of Chester declined.[13]

Another favoured class were the crews of the North Country colliers, which were allowed four free men per hundred tons, usually the master, mate, carpenter and one other. On account of vociferous representations on the part of the metropolitan coal trade, recruitment from colliers was avoided as far as possible, because, Corbett says, "the colliery trade is esteemed a nursery for seamen, and therefore enjoys immunities peculiar to itself, and several acts of Parliament have been passed in its favour."[14] It is worth recalling in this connection that James Cook, the finest seaman ever produced in these islands, volunteered at Wapping in 1755 in order to better himself after being employed in the *Freelove* collier of Whitby. Had he not done so, he might well have been pressed, because hostilities were beginning and the immunity of colliers did not last long in time of war.

The same was true of the Greenland fishery, which in 1739 employed 320 men, who took 400,000 cod in a season and paid a special duty on them (as did the coal merchants on chaldrons of coal) for the benefit of Greenwich Hospital. Oyster men and mussel men, as well as herring fishers, enjoyed immunity

A poster issued by Lord Cochrane to recruit men for his frigate, later called *The Golden Pallas,* in 1805

Scene on the Main Deck of a ship in port,
c.1800. From a print by Sutherland

The Middle Deck of the *Hector* in 1782.
From Rowlandson's tour to see the wreck
of the *Royal George*

By the Commissioners for Executing the Office of Lord High Admiral of the United Kingdom of Great Britain and Ireland, &c. and of all His Majesty's Plantations, &c.

WHEREAS by an Act of Parliament passed in the 13th year of the reign of His late Majesty King *George* the Second, it is enacted, that the persons under the age and circumstances therein mentioned, shall be freed and exempted from being impressed into His Majesty's service, upon due proof made before us of their respective ages and circumstances as the case shall happen: And whereas we have received Testimony that the Bearer *Richard Anson* has bound himself Apprentice to *Clerk Harrison of Scarbrough* to serve at sea, by indenture dated the *20 January 1804* and that he never used the sea before that time; and he being therefore intitled to a Protection in pursuance of the said Act of Parliament, to free and exempt him being impressed for the space of Three Years from the aforementioned date of his indenture: We do hereby require and direct all Commanders of His Majesty's Ships, Press-masters, and others whom it doth or may concern, not to impress him into His Majesty's service during the said space of Three Years, provided a description of his person be inserted in the margin hereof. But in case it shall appear, that the person for whom this Protection is granted; or in whose behalf it shall be produced, is not under the aforementioned circumstances, then the Officer, to whom it shall be produced, is hereby strictly charged and required to impress such Person, and immediately to send this Protection to us. Given under our hands, and the seal of the Office of Admiralty, the *Third* Day of *April* One thousand eight hundred and Four

To all Commanders and Officers of His Majesty's Ships, Press-masters, and all others whom it doth or may concern.

St Vincent

T. Troubridge

J Neale

By Command of their Lordships,

W Marsden

A Protection for an apprentice signed by St. Vincent in 1804. The description on the left reads: "Richard Anson, aged 20 years, stout made, middle stature, brown complexion, wearing his own dark brown hair" at times, and in 1801 all those engaged in the taking, curing and selling of fish. This was by far the widest exemption so far. Needless to say, it did not last long.[15]

What usually happened was that a few members of the crew of a merchant vessel, whether a fishing smack, a collier brig or a large homeward (but not outward) bound Indiaman were pressed, but that the officers were exempt. Such was the custom, but not the law. When a case came up in 1780 the Attorney General said "I should not advise a trial of the question, though it would be very difficult to support a legal exemption where the practice is from the favour of indulgence of the Lords of the Admiralty, not from the law."

In 1783 a Quaker shipowner named John Scales sued Captain Richards for the false imprisonment of two of his employees whom he described as masters of herring boats and procured writs of Habeas Corpus. Richards defended himself on the ground that neither man had called himself a master at the time, and anyhow the herring season was now over. The Attorney General supported him by interpreting an act of 1762 to mean shipowners, not masters, but advised that Scales's claim for £78 damages in respect of loss of profit should be paid.

Any disrespect on the part of a master when meeting a man-of-war, such as the failure to lower topsails, met condign punishment. Even unseamanlike behaviour met its deserts. Captain Archer of H.M.S. *Isis* wrote in 1795 "A few days ago a ship called the *Jane* ran on board of us in a most lubberly manner—for which, as is customary on such occasions, I took four of his people." But if he took the master, as Captain Brereton of H.M.S. *Falmouth* did in 1765 at Manila, he might have to pay £400 damages.[16]

Pressing ashore presented far more legal problems than did pressing afloat. Any men taken out of vessels could be construed as seamen, but how to tell a seaman ashore except by his looks and his walk? If he called himself an apprentice, he could be asked to show his credentials. But what if he called himself a freeholder or a freeman of the town? There was some doubt about this, so that in Good's case in 1760 a decision was reserved, but in the later cases of Douglas and Young no exemption was granted. After the Mayor of Dover had broken down the doors of the press room in 1791 to liberate one of his freemen, the regulating officer was reprimanded, leaving him so incensed that he swore to "impress every seafaring man in Dover and make them repent of their impudence." A few months later the Mayor again objected to a man being pressed, adding that a man-of-war was a bad place to send such a man to. Captain Hills, the regulating officer, replied that he was ashamed to hear a man in his position say so and that he was obstructing him in the prosecution of his duty. According to the Law Officers, the Mayor might be prosecuted, but not until it was certain that the man in question was not a freeman.[17]

To buy oneself a small freehold property seemed an easy way to escape the attentions of the gang. In 1777 George Duncan, having been pressed at North Shields, got his lawyer to claim that he was a freeholder in the county of Middlesex. It was pointed out that the man was a known smuggler. Lord Thurlow called his purchase of the property "a mean trick" and went on: "I see no reason why men using the sea, and being otherwise fit objects to be impressed into H.M. service, should be exempted only because they are freeholders. Nor did I ever read or hear of such an exemption. Therefore, unless some use or practice which I am ignorant of, gives occasion to doubt, I see no reason for a mariner being discharged, seriously, because he is a freeholder. It is a qualification easily attained: a single house at Wapping would ship a first rate man-of-war. If a freeholder is exempt, *eo nomine*, it will be impossible to go on with the pressing service."

Means of evading the press were legion. The simplest was to hide while a hot press was on, or escape into the country.

The Cornish miners preferred Lundy Island, the men of Weymouth the Portland quarries, those of Dartmouth, Dartmoor. Others feigned illness, induced fits, rubbed oil of vitriol into old sores, or even cut off a finger. Bribery was common, though the standard of honesty on the part of regulating officers in the later part of the century was high. According to the ballad *The Seaman's Adieu to his Dear* (c.1700), captains were immune to heartrending appeals:

> I'll go to thy captain and fall on my knee;
> Perhaps he'll take pity on me;
> If five or ten pounds will buy thy discharge
> He shall have it to set my love free.

To which the captain replies

> Not ten pounds not twenty will buy his discharge,
> Fair maid, you must patiently bear . . .

The improper use of protections was, of course, common, especially after the United States became independent. Any protected man who stretched his protection too far, like the Greenland harpooner found on his way to Ostend, was in for trouble. At Sunderland forged protections were sold for 8/6 each, but "one Broucher living in St. Michael's Lane, London," charged £3. A New York lawyer called Riley created dozens of American citizens at a dollar a head in 1800.[18] There were also shyster lawyers in England prepared to exploit the fear of the press and its consequences. What was to be done, asked the Admiralty, about William le Cocq, who had been circulating a card offering his services to those who regarded themselves as illegally pressed? The Law Officers replied that the Inn to which the man belonged would prosecute him for improper advertisement.

There were fraudulent warrants as well as fraudulent protections. At the beginning of a war the Admiralty sent a number of blank warrants to magistrates and these sometimes got into the wrong hands. In 1755 a certain Nicholas Cooke got hold of one signed by Anson, inserted his own name and called himself a lieutenant. With some friends to act as a gang, he hired a vessel to cruise off the Irish coast, where he took seventy-three men, whom he transported back to Liverpool. Unfortunately for him, his vessel ran aground in the Mersey and the men were taken off by Captain Darby. But when Darby also found casks of brandy on board he notified the excise men, who boarded the vessel under the protection of Darby's men. Cooke was arrested and prosecuted.

Pressing in the British colonies in the West Indies and America presented special problems. "The pressing of seamen in the Plantations," wrote Corbett, "is often attended with ill consequences from the violent methods sometimes used on these occasions, not only to seafaring men, but sometimes the inhabitants themselves, or at least their servants, being compelled into the service, which makes many run away and heightens the price of provisions in the southern parts, by deterring ships to come from the northern, from whence they receive their supplies. And therefore it was declared in Council (1696) that when any captain of H.M. ships in the Plantations wanted seamen, they should apply to the Governor who, as Vice-Admiral, should have the sole power of pressing seamen and should furnish the ships with what they wanted."[19]

This did not satisfy the colonists, so by an act of 1708 pressing in the colonies was forbidden except for one important proviso: deserters from the Navy could be forcibly recovered. But the act did not specify how long it was to last. In 1744, when the Governor of Barbados refused to arrest members of a press gang on the demand of the inhabitants, the opinion of the Law Officers was sought. They considered that the act was still in force, certainly in America, if not the Sugar Islands. Whereupon the powerful West India interest in Parliament got an act passed in 1746 extending it to the island colonies provided that, in an emergency, if the Governor and the Admiral agreed, a gang might be landed. Further clauses gave the inhabitants of the West Indies more immunity than the Americans enjoyed. No seaman employed in a merchant vessel or a privateer could be pressed under a £50 penalty; on the other hand, if masters refused to provide muster lists on which the name of a deserter might appear, or if they refused to provide men in an emergency, they could be fined £50.[20]

Bearing in mind the appalling number of casualties from disease in those parts, as well as the fact that the enlistment of Negroes—"the woolly race," as one admiral called them—was not encouraged because they were either escaped slaves or had to be paid for, the problem of manning in the West Indies was formidable. Many Negroes certainly found their way on board, but there was only a small white population to be drawn upon and the wages offered by merchants and privateers were highly competitive. When Vernon found crimps selling deserters at £40 a head, he adopted a policy of pressing all idle seamen and hiring them out to merchants. Other admirals preferred the unscrupulous method of turning men over from ship to ship without payment of wages due in order to retain them. Even when a man had two or three years' wages due, he might willingly forfeit his "bank" in return for £10 in cash and ten gallons of rum offered by a crimp or a merchant skipper desperate for hands because his crew had been decimated by Yellow Jack. Nor could anyone prevent desertion from the primitive hospitals on shore.

The hostility to the press on the part of the colonists was chiefly due to their fear that it would deter merchants from the north trading at those islands where the fleet was stationed. This appears to have been the reason for the violent quarrel between the Governor of Jamaica and Admiral Vernon. After much negotiating, the merchants agreed to hand over a quota of men from homeward bound ships: if they refused, the Navy could not be blamed for failing to provide escorts for their convoys. At first the quota was one in five men, later one in seven, or a third of the crew of a slaving Guineaman.[21]

The numerous privateers offered greater problems because they could afford higher wages and many of them were American owned. Promises were made not to board them even when searching for deserters, but in 1743 Admiral Knowles failed to get the agreement of the Governor of Barbados over this, and at Antigua the admiral was actually arrested for pressing from privateers. At Boston, a famous privateering centre, Governor Shirley was forced to take refuge in his castle when an angry admiral threatened to bombard the town unless the men he wanted were handed over.

Since the Acts of 1708 and 1746 virtually immunised the white population of the colonies, the manning problem had to be solved by temporary agreements. It was hoped that the monthly packet boats from home could carry a sufficient number of supernumeraries to satisfy the demands of the fleet, but it was soon clear that this was impossible. It was agreed that all prisoners exchanged under a flag of truce should be put on board naval ships, but when it became a choice between a French prison and a British man-of-war attempts to desert became desperate. The only satisfactory long term solution was to replace ships stationed on the other side of the Atlantic with fresh ships from home at shorter intervals. This in turn meant a larger reserve force at home, but only in this way could the fever-ridden crews, turned over from ship to ship often without payment of their wages, hope to get home alive from an area which a naval officer like Nelson could call "the station of honour" but which seamen, ever since Penn's capture of Jamaica, regarded as worse than hanging.

When one considers the number of affrays which the turbulent methods of impressment inevitably gave rise to, it is difficult to know which side to sympathise with: the seaman desperately defending his liberty, or the pressing officer performing an unpopular duty, harassed not only by fear of legal penalties but by literally howling mobs of men determined to sell their liberty at such a high price that it might well include murder. The following selection of cases must necessarily be arbitrary, because of the great number which came before inferior courts from which no records have survived. At least they illustrate the legal problems which such a violent method of manning the navy produced.

In the year 1718 Captain Hildesley of H.M.S. *Flamborough*, having been ordered to press men in the river Thames, sent a lieutenant on board the *Philip and Mary*. The crew of the latter attacked the boarding party with handspikes, took the lieutenant prisoner and so severely wounded the coxswain that he later died. Hildesley therefore put out in another boat, having forced the merchantman to heave to by firing a shot across her bows. As soon as he came on deck he seized Haslam, the master, and White, the mate, striking them for using abusive language. According to Haslam, however, he was struck in the face because he was a Quaker and refused to remove his hat. White was struck with a cane, and a baboon which happened to be on board was loosed on him. Both were placed in the bilboes before being taken to prison, where they were charged with the murder of the coxswain. However, the Solicitor General advised against further proceedings; whereupon Hildesley himself was arrested for assault and fined £100. As the Admiralty complained, "If officers belonging to H.M. ships in the execution of their duty, as Captain Hildesley was, are treated in the manner he has been by the masters of merchant ships, and the people employed under them are assaulted and murdered when they are putting their orders into execution, and when controversies of this nature are brought before the Courts at Common Law, it will be next to an impossibility to man any considerable squadron of H.M. ships."[22]

The case of the *John and Elizabeth* pink of Sunderland in 1742 was similar. After three press boats had been repelled with shot, crowbars, capstan bars and boathooks, two midshipmen fired their pistols, "not knowing that there was any balls in the pistols," as they ingenuously pleaded. A man was killed and the two midshipmen imprisoned for manslaughter.[23]

Such was the usual verdict, though it might be murder. At Shields in 1779 Captain Dods pressed thirty-two men out of a Greenland ship, in the course of which three men were wounded and two died. He told the Secretary of the Admiralty: "I said everything I could think of to induce them to enter (the navy), or surrender themselves quietly, but their answer was that they were determined to die rather than be taken and that they would destroy every man that should attempt to come on board; the shores on both sides were lined with people who insulted me and all the officers with me in the grossest manner." His own men begged him to fire and he did so only when the vessel was escaping downstream. His life was in danger if he remained in the area. What was he to do?

The Admiralty lawyers said that since he was in danger of being prosecuted for murder, he should escape abroad and "a profound silence is to be kept as long as possible about your absence." Meanwhile, in court, his lieutenants said they did not know who gave the order to fire, so the verdict brought in was "feloniously killed by persons unknown." Dods, now at Ostend, was told that unless he could provide witnesses to prove it was manslaughter he had better "keep out of the way at present."

It is not clear why so little attempt was made to vindicate poor Dods, because the previous year in the case of *R. v. Philips* the officer who gave the order to fire when resistance was made was only convicted of manslaughter. As many officers, both then and since, have discovered to their cost, the use of undue force under extreme provocation is a very dangerous hazard. If an unofficial member of a gang killed a man not liable to impressment (a tobacconist, in the case of R. *v. Dixon* in 1756) he was guilty of murder, because the man's resistance was lawful.[24]

Naval officers were frequently sued for assault. A case in which this failed is vividly reported. On the night of 19 November, 1787, the City of Bristol tavern, which was a rendezvous, was entered by Lieutenants Allen and Hardy, who demanded to see the protection of one of the many drunks there. The landlord, Robert Seymour, more drunk than any, protested that they could not press inside a rendezvous. The onlookers started shouting "Damn their eyes, they would not be pressed by bougres." Allen was protesting against such insults when a troop of prostitutes entered shrieking "Damn my eyes, let us bundle them out." A scuffle followed, in which Seymour was wounded by Allen's broken cutlass. He sued Allen for assault, but a countercharge was brought against him, though it was admitted that he was right in maintaining that pressing could not be carried on at a rendezvous.

When armed attempts were made to rescue pressed men it was often possible to identify an assailant, who could then be indicted. Thus when in 1779 Midshipman Shepherd Goodeve was escorting four pressed men from Lymington to Southampton and was set upon by a party of men on horseback in the New Forest, he was able to identify one of them as a smuggler from Christchurch. He had to release his men when they threatenened to blow his brains out, but Morgan the smuggler was later caught and prosecuted.

Similarly the next year one Spence, from a Liverpool privateer, led an army of eighty men to break down the doors of the press room in the middle of the night, because in it were fifteen men pressed from a coach by Lt. Haygarth earlier that day. "Come, my lads, break away and stick together," he shouted as he hurried the men along to the privateer, which sailed before dawn. The Admiralty was advised to charge Spence, but whether he was ever caught is not known.

As we have seen, those employed in pressing were always advised to obtain the backing of the local magistrates, though this was not legally necessary. Too often, instead of assisting, as they were requested to do, the magistrates impeded the officers in the execution of their duty. In 1757 the Mayor of Gravesend refused to sign warrants because it made him unpopular in the town. It was held that he was legally entitled to do so, but that he must be held responsible for keeping the peace.

John Wilkes, well known for his interest in another kind of warrant, seems to have been responsible for the most serious attempt on the part of the civil power to question the legality of press warrants. In 1770 one Shine, a barber, was improperly pressed in the City of London and brought before Wilkes as one of the aldermen to be discharged. The Lord Mayor was persuaded to write a letter to the Admiralty protesting against the number of protections issued in the City, because if the men were not seamen such protections were unnecessary. The Admiralty replied that the employees had themselves requested the protections, but they were glad of the excuse not to issue any more. The Lord Mayor then moved on to more difficult ground by challenging the validity of the warrants themselves and asking if he was compelled to back them. The Lord Chief Justice replied that it was only advisable to do so, in order to ensure that they were not abused and the peace was not broken as a result. With that, the attempt to challenge the legality of pressing faded out.[25]

The assistance of the civil power remained in doubt and some magistrates even backed the mob against the press gang. One disgraceful case is of interest because it involved a man who later became a distinguished frigate captain and an admiral, but in 1791, as a lieutenant, was employed in the less pleasant duty of apprehending deserters at Rochester. Having chased a man he suspected of being a deserter into a house, Lieutenant Jahleel Brenton found the place surrounded by a mob which included the Mayor. The latter ordered him to be disarmed and taken in charge because his warrant had not been signed by him. Brenton complained that it was hard to be so treated when he was only doing his duty. The infuriated Mayor then shouted "I will show you my dignity as Mayor. I am not to be trifled with or insulted or dictated to." Brenton and his two midshipmen were dragged off to the worst cell in the local bridewell, having their hats knocked off and their shirts torn from their backs on the way. Next morning they were discharged by the Mayor with a warning that this would teach them how to behave towards magistrates in the future. The Mayor's conduct was found to be "extremely blameable" in the opinion of the Law Officers, but they doubted if a charge could be preferred. Nevertheless the man was prosecuted and fined £750.[26]

One authority whose "interference is the source of great annoyance and expense to the service" was the Lord Mayor of Dublin, who seems to have held the view that the pressing laws of England did not apply to Ireland and insisted on releasing men on his own account. The impress officer there in 1806, Archibald Hamilton, composed a learned treatise for his own use to disprove the Mayor's claim and urged the Admiralty to look into the city charters to see if there was anything bearing on the matter.[27] The facts seem to be that an act of 1707 empowered justices to imprison vagrants "and such as pretend to be Irish gentlemen" (i.e. those passing themselves off as dispossessed chieftains) before giving them the choice of being sent to the plantations or on board H. M. ships; but these powers were limited to the Dublin area by an act of 1735.

A sufficient number of instances have been adduced to illustrate the difficulties under which pressing officers laboured. The accepted view that the activities of the gangs were always wrong must be corrected. Usually they were on the right side of the law, however brutal their way of carrying it out, and their excuse for this is that so often they were doing their duty under extreme provocation. As to the fundamental question of the legality of impressment in principle, there can be no doubt about the answer. Even such a critic as Junius admitted in his fifty-ninth letter in 1771 that he was compelled

> to assent to one very unpopular opinion. I lament the unhappy necessity, whenever it arises, of providing for the safety of the state by a temporary invasion of the personal liberty of the subject. Would to God it were practicable to reconcile these important objects in every possible situation of public affairs. I regard the liberty of the meanest man in Britain as much as my own, and would defend it with the same zeal. I know that we must stand or fall together. But I can never doubt that the community has a right to command as well as purchase the services of its members. I see that right founded originally upon a necessity which supercedes all arguments. I see it established by usage immemorial and admitted by more than a tacit assent of the legislature. I conclude there is no remedy, in the nature of things, for the grievance complained of; for if there were, it must have long since been redressed. Though numberless opportunities have presented themselves highly favourable to public liberty, no successful attempt has yet been made for the relief of the subject of this article. Yet it has been felt and complained of ever since England had a Navy . . . Let bounties be increased as far as the public purse can support them. Still they have a limit, and when every reasonable expense is incurred, it will be found in fact that the spur of the press is wanted to give operation to the bounty.

IX

The Register of Seamen and Other Proposals

THE FIRST SUGGESTION for an alternative to impressment as a method of recruiting for the Navy came from an unusually intelligent sea officer, Captain George St. Lo. In 1693 he printed proposals on how to solve the problem in his *England's Safety*, which he repeated at greater length in his *England's Interest, or a Discipline for Seamen, wherein is proposed a new method for raising qualified seamen*, the next year. Underlining the obvious drawbacks of impressment, he pointed out the necessity of procuring "a competent number of able and rugged Sailers, instead of Shacomefilthies, Ragga-muffins and Scrovies to man the King's ships withal at a very short warning." The spelling "sailer" shows how the word was coming into general use; it is sad that the other expressive terms have become obsolete.

When a prisoner of war in France, St. Lo had been impressed with the recruiting system there. He therefore suggested appointing a naval officer at every port to register the names of seamen, shipwrights, caulkers and ropemakers, and to get the local authorities to keep lists of all those suitable for employment at sea or in the dockyards. Such lists should be posted on the doors of churches with the names of those required for service and the ships they should join when the Admiralty decided so. Men would only serve a year at sea, but those failing to register would be kept at sea for the duration of hostilities and would be debarred further employment in merchant vessels.

Other pamphleteers were soon making similar suggestions. John Perry, late captain of a fireship but now in prison for debt, declares in his *Regulation for Seamen* (1695) that he was ignorant of St. Lo's book when he wrote, but agrees with him that the only way of getting seamen out of their hiding places when the press was out in force was some sort of a register. George Everett, shipwright, that same year wanted something of the same sort "in order to prevent those many mischiefs and abuses daily committed by disorderly press-masters, both at sea and land, to the great prejudice of their Majesties and injury of the subject." He was somewhat optimistic in suggesting 28/- a month for the pay of a volunteer, compared with 24/- for the pressed man, but it was clear to him that a register, based on the muster books of merchant vessels, was the only solution which would be both equitable and practical.[1]

One other pamphleteer may be mentioned in this connection because he suggested that a hospital for seamen should be established, though Greenwich is not mentioned as the site, nor does he suggest linking it with a register. In his *England's Glory Revived . . . shewing an easie and speedy method for fully manning the Royal Navy with Saylers, without Charge or Obstruction to Trade* (1693), Robert Crosfield is more interested in attacking the press than in solving the manning problem. He suggested recruiting through customs officers rather than press-masters and the provision of a hospital for the maimed, for which every man should pay one shilling a voyage. Being a professional pamphleteer rather than a seaman, his ideas are not nearly so specific as those of St. Lo, nor had he the latter's experience.

Most of the reformers at this and at a later date had the French example in mind. It is significant that the idea of the *Inscription Maritime* or register, which developed into a mode of conscription, should have occurred to Colbert, France's greatest bureaucrat and the founder of her seventeenth century navy. In 1669 a maritime law laid down that a register should be compiled of all seamen and dockyard labourers who could be divided into four classes, one of which would be called up annually by posting lists on church doors. A retaining wage called the *demi-solde* was offered to all who enrolled and in 1673 a royal ordinance provided for the foundation of Les Invalides and other hospitals at Toulon and Rochefort. What the English admirers of the draft (as we would call it) did not mention was its extreme unpopularity, because the promised benefits never materialised, nor did a sufficient number of men ever answer the call of duty. If, as will be seen, the English system failed because it was voluntary, the French system failed because it was compulsory. In 1686 out of 46,950 men registered, only 14,462 served, so that in the later years of the war all classes had to be called out to reach the complement of 50,000. According to a French historian, the system was merely "a regularised press, made stricter by its legal character, unpopular with the people and disastrous to commerce." A detailed investigation of how it worked in southern France bears this out and describes how the *intendants* responsible for the call-up clashed with the local *parlements* in much the same way as the impress service in England had difficulties with the magistrates.[2]

With all its defects, the system did enable the French to mobilise quicker than her enemies and thus take the offensive. It continued in force until the Revolution, but it was never as efficient in practice as it looked on paper. In 1779, for instance, the number of ships in commission had to be seriously reduced because there were not enough men to man them, a thing which never happened in England. With the Revolution the system went to pieces, less than a quarter of the men enrolled in certain districts reporting for duty. Until Napoleon reimposed the register as a means of conscription, the balance of the crews had to be made up with soldiers and foreigners.

It is with this background in mind, together with the virtual destruction of the French fleet at the battle of La Hogue (the Trafalgar of the century, which deserved national commemoration) that we may turn to the two actions on the part of the government which linked the proposal of a monumental hospital for seamen with that of a register.

Plans for converting the old palace at Greenwich into such a hospital were discussed as early as 1690, but it was not until 25 October, 1695, that William and Mary issued a charter founding the Royal Hospital. Its intentions are set forth in the following clauses:[3]

1. The relief and support of seamen serving aboard the ships and vessels belonging to the Navy Royal of Us, our heirs and successors, or employed in our or their service at sea, who by reason of age, wounds or other disabilities shall be incapable of further service at sea, and unable to maintain themselves.
2. The sustentation of the widows of seamen happening to be slain or disabled in such sea service.
3. The maintenance and education of the children of seamen happening to be slain or disabled in such sea service.
4. The further relief and encouragement of seamen.
5. The improvement of navigation.

Plans for the building were discussed with Wren, the architect of the Chelsea Hospital for soldiers, which had just opened its doors to the first red-coated pensioners. Letters patent were issued in 1695, subscriptions invited and the King's determination to see the great project through as an act of piety was enforced by Mary's death soon after Wren's plans had been approved. The foundation stone was laid on 30 June, 1696, by Wren and Evelyn, until recently a Commissioner for Sick and Wounded Seamen, who became the first Treasurer.

Royal and public charity, a state lottery and a tax on coal

proved insufficient to finance this grandiose scheme. It was recalled that for a century past those serving in the Navy had contributed sixpence a month to the Chatham Chest. If the new Hospital was going to serve seamen of all sorts, those serving in the merchant marine should also contribute. This implied the necessity for a register of all those who "used the sea." Payments towards Chatham Chest ceased (in 1814 the funds of both charities were amalgamated) and all seamen were ordered to pay for the new Hospital which was intended for the benefit of all.

In the event, although every seaman paid his contribution to the Sixpenny Office, the clause of the Charter stating that the institution was for the benefit of those wounded in the naval service was used to exclude the rest. Unless a man could prove that his disability had been incurred while in the service of the Crown, he could not be admitted. No doubt it was unjust to mulct merchant seamen of their sixpences, but the vast majority of those injured had in fact at one time or another been in both services, and the number of pensioners accommodated rose so rapidly that there was no room for more. The first forty-two pensioners arrived in 1705; in 1763 there were 1,720; in 1805, 2,460; in 1814, 2,710. Thereafter the number fell off and the Hospital was finally closed in 1869, though the Charity and the Royal Hospital School continue to this day.

The Act for the Increase and Encouragement of Seamen of 1696 (7 and 8, W. III.c.21) instituted a Register of Seamen. It is thus contemporary with, and closely associated with the establishment of the Royal Hospital. It offers the benefits of the Hospital to all "such mariners, watermen, seamen, fishermen, lightermen, bargemen and keelmen as shall voluntarily come in and register themselves in and for His Majesty's sea service."

The suggestion for this act was made by Admiral Russell at the end of the previous year because he had suffered from a

shortage of men in the Mediterranean fleet.⁴ The preamble
repeats the intentions expressed in the Charter of the Hospital.
The act provides for a central registry near the Navy Office,
where the names of all those between the ages of eighteen and
fifty would be recorded from lists sent in by customs officials
at the ports. Those who enrolled were promised a bounty or
retaining wage of £2 a year, the enjoyment of the benefits of
the Hospital, and a double share of prize money. They alone
would be eligible for promotion to Warrant Officer, be free of
jury, parish or militia service, as well as having their widows
supported and their children educated at public expense in
the event of death. All such benefits would accrue provided
the number registering did not exceed 30,000.

These substantial attractions were to be paid for by a levy
of sixpence a month out of every man's wages, whether he
registered or not, to be collected at the ports. If registered
seamen failed to report for duty, or omitted to notify the
authorities of a change of address, all privileges were void.
On registration every man received a certificate which would
serve as a protection against the press. If landmen registered,
as they were encouraged to do, they also would be exempt
after two years in the sea service.

All this has a very twentieth century air about it. Unfortunately, it was quite premature for the seventeenth
century. Success depended on the response to the word
"voluntarily." So inadequate was this that in 1704 a suggestion was made for compulsory registration, but the government decided this was "not seasonable." In view of its continuing lack of success, the Register Act was removed from the
statute book in 1710. The one and only alternative to impressment had failed.

Responsibility for failure lay as much with the seamen as
with the government. Administrative machinery had been
promptly set up in 1696. An office was established on Tower
Hill. Four commissioners were appointed, two of them—

George Byng and Thomas Baker—being naval officers. Customs officers were instructed to receive the sixpences which masters stopped out of the wages of their crews before clearance was permitted. All masters and officers were asked to use their best endeavours to explain the advantages of the scheme to their men. The commissioners met weekly, kept minutes, hired a staff, wrote letters, and then found that neither masters nor seamen nor press gangs would do as asked. In 1699 the office was wound up and the business of receiving sixpences transferred to the Royal Hospital authorities, the Sixpenny Office continuing in existence until 1834.[5]

It had been hoped to register 30,000 men, which was regarded as sufficient for mobilisation purposes. Six months after the act was passed 4,656 names were enrolled, but by 1697 it was found that no watermen or fishermen had registered, nor, as the commissioners regretfully state, "a single seafaring man but as was at the time of his registering in actual service on board His Majesty's ships." In 1698 there were 13,000 names; in 1702, 17,600—just over half the anticipated number. Since the office was costing £37,000 a year, the whole organisation seemed futile. The Register Act was therefore repealed by another act in 1710 (9 Ann.c.21), the preamble of which admits that the scheme has "not had the good effects which were intended thereby for the service of the Crown, or for the encouragement of seamen, but on the contrary has occasioned much charge, vexation and trouble."

Why did the register fail? Chiefly because it was voluntary. The commissioners pointed out the necessity of sanctions against those who failed to enroll, but their advice was ignored. Unlike his modern counterpart, the seaman of those days was not acclimatised to bureaucracy, nor were the administrative habits of the time adequate for such an immense undertaking. There was to be no national census for a hundred years; was it likely that a register of such a shifting population as that of seamen could be compiled? Masters of coasting vessels refused to have anything to do with it; customs officers omitted to send in their receipts at the required times; press gangs refused to recognise the certificates as adequate proof of protection; forged certificates passed from hand to hand; one of the official receivers was suspended from duty for malversation of funds. Seamen, unless compelled to "volunteer" (as so often in the Navy), suspected a trap. As the years passed they found good reasons for doing so. Contemporaries agree that the two pound bounty was paid irregularly and that few widows ever received any benefits. Many landmen registered merely to get the bounty —"viz. cobblers, barbers, alehouse keepers and some grave seniors who could well digest the forty shillings per annum and to be exempt from all services and duties on shore. If they went to sea they lay like swabs in the scuppers and so many stumbling blocks in the way; for which reasons the common able seamen, who alone bear the burthen and undergo the whole fatigue, can hardly persuade themselves that they have had due or equal encouragement by the said act."[6]

All would be well, in the opinion of the pamphleteers, and men would be attracted both to the register and to the service, if they were paid more punctually. This alone would dispense with "the scandalous and oppressive way of pressing promiscuously seamen and landmen into the sea service, which is a grievance not to be heard of even under the arbitrary and despotic government of Louis XIV."

So the Register of Seamen died an unlamented death: only the collection of sixpences continued, for the revenue authorities (as is their wont) saw to it that this part of the act was not repealed; and the Royal Hospital expanded year by year to accommodate naval seamen fortunate enough to spend their last years "safe moored in Greenwich tier."

The idea of a register continued to be canvassed for the next hundred years, and indeed the Admiralty itself made half-hearted attempts to revive it, but every bill introduced was torpedoed by the shipping interest, who regarded it as an interference with the course of trade, or by hypocritical politicians, who thought that it infringed the liberties of the subject. It was not until well into the nineteenth century that the modern Register was introduced (see below, page 275).

In 1720 the matter was reconsidered in Parliament, but the proposed bill speedily dismissed. In 1727 a vicious attack on the legality of impressment appeared under the title of *The Sailor's Advocate*, probably written by Thomas Robe, who in the previous year printed a similar proposal in his *Ways and Means to Man the Navy*. Robe's second pamphlet was very popular, since he regarded pressing as no better than kidnapping. He scoffs at the argument that it was necessary as a mere excuse for not paying the men better. There was something in this, as well as in the foreign examples which he instanced. The French could raise 30,000 men by their method; the Dutch paid their men in advance; in Sweden they were provided with a uniform and married quarters and paraded monthly like a modern reserve. Some form of conscription was necessary in his opinion—an odd conclusion for an author who appealed to Magna Carta and the Petition of Right.

On the outbreak of the War of Jenkins's Ear, Admiral Sir John Norris revived the idea in another bill, which was introduced by Admiral Sir Charles Wager and had the backing of Walpole. The latter noted how deplorable it was that not another sailor was to be found until the press was lifted, whereupon "they burst out by thousands from their retreats." But when the bill was debated the mere mention of the French system, says Smollett, was "received with silent horror." The merchants denied that there was a manning crisis. The upholders of political liberty insisted that the bill denied the rights of free-born Englishmen. The country gentlemen displayed their usual jealousy of any extension of governmental power such as the register implied.[7]

No sooner had this bill been defeated than another was introduced. It met the same fate, though an emasculated version reached the statute book to limit the amount of wages merchants could offer in wartime and offered a bounty of £5 to volunteers. The element of compulsory registration in the original bill was variously compared to Ship Money, the Spanish Inquisition and the edicts of Genghis Khan.[8]

Needless to say, that inveterate pamphleteer, Admiral Vernon, participated in the debate as soon as (and even before) he resigned in the face of official disapproval. In his letter to the Board in 1744, printed without its approval, and in his *Infallible Project for the more effectual and speedy manning of the Navy of England*, published anonymously in 1745, he expressed the views of earlier writers that the Navy would be easily manned if the men were more punctually paid and their notorious hardships alleviated. Impressment was unfitting in the land of liberty: "Why should a brute, a mere Tar, a drunken Sailor, judge by the Force of his Cudgel who is, or is not fit for the publick Service at Sea?" A register along French lines was the answer. But he never mentioned how the original scheme had failed, nor how this talk about liberty could be squared with something very like conscription.

The same criticism applies to another publication, William Horsley's *Treatise on Maritime Affairs* (1744), which at least has the novelty of introducing the class issue. Why this discrimination between the duties of the upper and lower classes in service to their country, he asks? "Is there any certain law for this distinction? If not, on what principle of justice is it preserved?" Admiration for the French system went even farther in this pamphlet, which makes trenchant criticism not only of manning our ships but of our tactics in fighting them. Horsley fails to mention that the French were usually defeated.

After this spate of pamphlets and debates there is an interval of a generation before the matter was raised again and by that time all knowledge of the failure of the original plan had vanished. Other methods were indeed suggested, but of a register there is little mention before a Parliamentary Committee was set up in 1780 to consider more effectual methods of encouraging seamen. A series of measures was then debated, the idea of a register appearing in a new guise of a Fellowship of Seamen, for whose members certain privileges were suggested. The Fellowship was to be organised by a Marine Office, not by the Admiralty, financed by contributions of half a guinea per man per voyage and sixpence a ton on shipping, together with any unclaimed prize money (which had already been allocated to the Royal Hospital). Its members, conscripted by age classes as in France, would serve by rotation.

On 12 May, 1787, a bill along these lines reached a second reading but was once more defeated by the shipping interest, which regarded it as a mere tonnage tax. In a final effort to save the scheme a certain John Stevenson, once mate in an Indiaman, printed an Abstract of the Bill with his own comments. These are chiefly of interest for his analysis of the naval manpower at that time. He reckoned that there were in existence 14,000 naval officers, 36,000 Able Seamen, 36,000 Ordinary Seamen and 21,600 Marines, totalling 108,000 men, which was just about the total borne in 1783. He regarded the Fellowship as a more practical scheme than the defunct register, though it looked very much like the same thing. The bill was opposed by Pitt and defeated on the grounds of pressure of other business.

Pitt was later appealed to, with equal lack of success, by Lord Barham when First Lord. Six months before the battle of Trafalgar the latter wrote a memorandum on manning based on a plan he had read by Peter Holland of North Shields in 1804. This proposed a quota of men from the merchant service based on port registers to serve in the Navy. Barham added that the principle of impressment must be retained, because it "is now interwoven with the usage of the navy, and our seafaring men are habituated to the practice, founded upon this general maxim—that every person entering upon the profession of a seaman does virtually engage himself to be, at all times, liable to the call of his country in preference to all other service. This system must never be directly abandoned." It was not; nor was anything done to supplement it by other methods of recruitment.[9]

Proposals other than that of a register were made throughout the century. Some undoubtedly increased the size of the seafaring population; others improved the conditions afloat, though even in Nelson's day the average seaman preferred service in the merchant marine to that in the Navy; but no scheme provided an adequate substitute for impressment when the nation embarked on wars of ever increasing magnitude.

During the Seven Years War Admiral Boscawen wrote; "No scheme for manning the navy within my knowledge has ever had the success of the Marine Society." He was one of the original subscribers to this charity, along with Anson, Wilberforce and the King, who contributed a thousand guineas. The originator of this still flourishing Society was Jonas Hanway, a philanthropist liberally endowed with zeal and common sense, as might be expected of the populariser of the umbrella. He was a Governor of the Foundling Hospital and the founder of the Magdalen House for repentant prostitutes. He knew the needs of the Navy well, because his father was a commissioner of Portsmouth Dockyard, he himself became a commissioner of the Victualling Board, and his brother was a naval captain.

In 1756 he was inspired by the example of Lord Henry Paulet, captain of the *Barfleur*, who collected and clothed at his own expense a number of poor boys off the streets of London in order to fill the complement of his ship. Hanway, with his friend Sir John Fielding, the Bow Street magistrate who knew more about paupers, thieves and vagrants than any man in

England, realised that for once the needs of the Navy and those of the City coincided: the one wanted men, the other wished to get rid of its dregs. From a humanitarian point of view, Hanway saw that poor boys and vagrants could be channelled into the Navy, to their mutual advantage, provided they were clothed and cared for after demobilisation. Every captain was therefore asked to write a report on all those members of the Society employed in his ship and asked to see that they were returned to its care when the ship paid off. To prevent them returning to the streets at the end of a war, when the Admiralty with short-sighted economy paid off all those whom it had recruited with such difficulty, Hanway made arrangements with the masters of merchant vessels to sign on as many as possible.

In order to encourage "the industrious poor to send their children to sea," and to persuade parish officers to round up the destitute, both boys and adults, they were invited to send them to the New Prison, Clerkenwell (hardly an attractive address), or to the Society's offices at the Royal Exchange and at Prince's Street near the Bank of England. "The principle design of the Society with regard to boys is to contribute towards maintaining a nursery of seamen for the public service, and to lay the foundations of the good fortune of those who are willing to serve their country. Besides the wages given them, the boys are completely fitted out with clothing and bedding by the Society."[10]

Enphasis was placed on new clothes for a very good reason, which naval surgeons like Lind had already stressed, but about which naval authorities refused to concern themselves. Hanway writes:

The filthiness of landmen's garments had frequently occasioned distempers on our ships, which had proved fatal to thousands of men; and the filth and rags of boys could not be less pernicious. The good effects were apparent to our first officers in command, and no kind of encouragement to men or boys answered so effectually as this of clothing, for it operated like a charm in preserving the health of landmen; it facilitated their introduction into ships of war by destroying the distinction of land dress; and so far as clothing was given in place of entrance money, it prevented the debauchery of which money is so frequently the cause.

Wise words, which the naval authorities would have been well advised to heed. The ill consequences of bounties to volunteers were well known, since the money was usually squandered on drink before the men left the rendezvous. The way disease was spread by the failure to provide clean clothing for newly raised men will be described in another chapter. The realisation that young landmen (known as Long Toggies because of their clothes) were bullied by professional seamen, (who wore short round jackets), and that therefore they should be made as indistinguishable as possible, is an instance of Hanway's humanity and practical insight.

When the Society was founded it aimed at bringing 10,000 destitute men and boys into the service. By the end of the Seven Years War 10,625 had been entered, nearly all of whom continued their career as seamen in the merchant service. If masters accepted a quota of these trained men, a sizable naval reserve would have been built up, had the government agreed to Hanway's proposal that a retaining wage might be paid. Though this was not done, there is no doubt that the vast majority of the members of the Marine society re-enlisted later in their lives. The Admiralty co-operated to the extent that members were kept on board for a maximum period of three months after a ship had been paid off.

The clothing provided by the Society consisted of a brown pea jacket, waistcoat and breeches of white or blue kersey, a felt hat, two worsted caps, two pair of hose, three shirts, one pair of shoes with buckles, a knife, pillow and blanket, together with copies of religious tracts often written by Hanway himself. The cost of the outfit, together with lodging and transport to the fleet, amounted to £25 a head.

As the years went by, the Society increasingly aimed at providing for the children of what came to be called the deserving poor. This led to difficulties with Fielding, who was more interested in cleaning potential criminals off the streets. But the Society continued to flourish because of the practical way in which it benefited both its members and the country. In the generation after its founder's death, during the period 1793-1815, no less than 22,973 individuals entered the Navy under its auspices.

Hanway was also responsible for another naval scheme aimed at educating the more intelligent boys with a view to their becoming Warrant Officers. His was not the first of the naval academies, since Pepys had been interested in the navigation school at Christ's Hospital. There was now the large Royal Hospital School at Greenwich and other smaller mathematical schools to train boys for the sea, such as Neale's in Fleet Street, now St. Dunstan's. In 1729 the Admiralty itself had founded a Naval Academy at Portsmouth, now the Senior Officers Mess, which developed into the Royal Naval Colleges of today, but this was for the use of prospective officers.

Hanway's Maritime School in Paradise Row, Chelsea, was small and short lived. It only accommodated twenty-six boys from 1779 to 1783. None the less, Jonas Hanway must be credited with providing more men for the Navy than any other man in history. Not only did he enlist the support of public men in all walks of life, for a deserving charity, but he made a very substantial contribution to solving the problem of manning the Navy.

Boscawen's well-known interest in the welfare of his men, who delighted to serve under the man they called Old Dreadnought, was the reason why a certain James Moncrieff dedicated to him an anonymous pamphlet entitled *Three Dialogues on the Navy* in 1759. Compared with the spate of practical advice which flowed from Hanway's pen, this is a somewhat vague and pompous production, but it shows how the idea of a reserve was exercising the minds of the public. Moncrieff, like so many others, was appalled at the injustice of the press, which bore so hard on a particular section of the community: "I shall, without scruple, pronounce them (the seamen) to be the most injured race of men on earth." If 20,000 men were retained on half pay during peacetime, as were their officers, it would save all the expense and annoyance accompanying naval mobilisation. In such a way what Moncrieff calls a Maritime Army could be built up: "a small floating, and if I may make use of the word, an amphibious army, kept in a continual condition to strike a blow where and when it shall be least expected, would carry with it infinite terror and do more real execution than ten times the number differently situated." To pay a reserve of 30,000 men retaining wages of six shillings a week would cost £400,000 a year—a "paltry sum" if it avoided annihilating a trained force and then reforming it again a few years later on the outbreak of another war.

Nothing came of his proposals for a reserve until another century had passed. The same thing happened to his curious prophecy of the future of the Royal Hospital at Greenwich: "From the couch and sepulchre of age, I would change it into the cradle and, as it were, the forge of youthful merit." It was in 1873 that it became the Royal Naval College.

The best contribution to the subject in the latter part of the century is Lieutenant Robert Tomlinson's *Plan for a Practicable, Easy and Constitutional Method of Manning the Navy instead of the usual Mode of Impressing Seamen* (1774).[11] He had himself been engaged on the impress service and to a man of his serious, censorious character "the unspeakable distresses" which he witnessed compelled him to formulate a plan to avoid impressment. He tells how a congregation of a country church used to post a boy at the door to give warning of the approach of a gang, on which all seamen present escaped through the vestry, the women fainted and the preacher could not make himself heard above the hubbub. During a hot press in the winter of 1770, 33,000 men were raised: "To my certain knowledge, a very considerable number of these were the most miserable objects I ever saw in the Navy, or heard tell of." Coastal trade was brought to a halt. Thousands fled to Holland, where crimps called Silver Copens sold them to the Dutch East India Company. Disease spread so rapidly that the number of sick at Haslar hospital rose from 876 in January to 1,288 in February.

He estimated that 50,000 men were available for the naval service, of whom 12,000 were in the coal trade and 14,000 in the Newfoundland fishery. He aimed at persuading men to volunteer by limiting the term of their servitude to three years, since the chief deterrent to service in the Navy was in his opinion the undetermined length of service. Those serving more than five years should be exempt, but impressment must be retained as the ultimate sanction for those who refused to volunteer, or owned boats of under twenty tons which had obviously been purchased to avoid service in the navy. The men's pay should be raised to 30/- a month for an Able Seaman, and merchant's wages limited to 27/-. The nearest he got to a register was his suggestion that the names of all those serving in the fleet should be recorded in order that they might be entitled to the benefits of the Royal Hospital, but something of this sort was already done to check the credentials of pensioners.

The proposals were neither radical nor original. As Captain Lord Mulgrave said in criticising them in Parliament, they added nothing to twenty such proposals in the past. When a bill incorporating them was introduced by Tomlinson's friend Temple Luttrell in March 1777, the merchants and those members of the Board who were also M.P.s gave it short shrift. Mulgrave, a future member of the Board, defended impressment as not nearly as brutal as it was made out to be and quite economical in keeping the wage bill down. As far as he was concerned, the question before the House was "Whether we should adhere to a practice authorised by the constitution, and justified by the successful experience of all the wars of this country, or by adopting the motion endanger the existence of our commercial interest and naval power." More effective than such specious arguments was the intervention of the Attorney General, who pointed out that Luttrell had departed from the rules of procedure by failing to explain his bill before attacking the present system.

Poor Tomlinson, having seen his scheme mismanaged by his representative, had no alternative but to appeal to the public once more by reprinting these proceedings. But nothing more was heard of the bill, although some of his ideas continued to be canvassed in later years. The Parliamentary Committee of 1780 which discussed the Fellowship of Seamen entertained some of them, and William Pulteney in 1786 revived them in another abortive bill

The scheme for a Fellowship of Seamen and some sort of register found powerful support in an anonymous pamphlet printed on the eve of the war entitled *A View of the Naval Forces of Great Britain* (1791). The author was probably Sir John Borlase Warren, then a captain and later an admiral, whose early career is very mysterious. He appears to have been the only admiral who has been at one and the same time an undergraduate at Cambridge and an Able Seaman in the Navy. What is more, his name was marked Run, until the R was taken off by order of the Navy Board when, in 1772, he was rated midshipman. The names of the scions of the well-to-do often appear on ship's books without the presence of the boy on board, but in Warren's case it looks as if he actually served on board for a time.

Warren was a supporter of Pulteney's bill. After the usual

attacks on the press gangs, he gives for the first time in English a full account of how the *Inscription Maritime* worked, though he omits to mention its shortcomings in practice. His scheme for replacing pressing was to maintain a register based on Customs returns, where the names of seamen should be listed. The members of this reserve or Fellowship of volunteers would receive half pay as a retaining wage and be given priority in the appointment of such offices as harbour master when they retired from the sea. "By giving a small stipend and encouragement towards good behaviour and a fixed time of service, a registered seaman would not only consider himself as one of the first class amongst his brothers, but a privileged and protected man. The service would be rendered more respectable, and coveted, instead of being fled from and detested by all seafaring people."

Warren's book contains all the best ideas that had been put forward over the past century, but like its predecessors it foundered on the rock of finance. No one could persuade the government that a register or a reserve (as it ultimately became) was worth spending money on.

Yet it had support from the highest quarter. The only document on manning which Nelson wrote was a memorandum for his friend St. Vincent, when the latter was First Lord in 1803.[12] It is worth quoting at some length to conclude our survey of alternatives to impressment because it also throws light on the problem of desertion, which in the later years of the war exacerbated the manning crisis and brought this country into conflict with the United States.

At a time when I have been repeatedly told the Seamen, notwithstanding their good pay and abundance of the very best provisions, manifest a reluctance to enter into the Naval Service, it becomes, in my humble opinion, a duty for people conversant with the manners and disposition of Seamen to turn their thoughts on the mode of inducing the Seamen to be fond, and even desirous, of serving in the Navy, in preference to the

Merchant Service. Their pay and provisions cannot possibly be improved from what they are at present; but I think a plan could be brought forward to Register the Certificates given to Seamen; and a form of Certificate to be general, and filled according to regulations issued by the Admiralty under the authority of an Act of Parliament . . .

When we calculate by figures on the expense of raising Seamen, I think it is said £20 a man, that 42,000 Seamen deserted during the late War, the loss in money, in that point alone, amounts to £840,000; without taking into consideration the greater expense of raising more men—and certainly not so good as those who have been used to the King's Naval Service, I shall therefore propose that every seaman who has served faithfully five years in War, and by his Certificates never been concerned in mutinies, nor deserted, shall receive every New Year's Day, or on the King's birthday, the sum of two guineas; and if he serves eight years, shall have four guineas, exclusive of any pension for wounds . . . Prize money to be as regularly paid in London, Portsmouth, Plymouth etc. as Seamen's wages; this is so easy and simple that a very few days, in my opinion, would complete such a plan.

But the great thing necessary to guard against is desertion; for notwithstanding all I have proposed to induce Seamen to serve faithfully, yet a sum of money and liquor held out to a Seaman are too much for him; he allows himself to be seduced and hid, he first becomes fearful of apprehension, and then wishes and exerts himself to get out of the country in the Merchant's employ. It will be found, and I know it, that whenever a large Convoy is assembled at Portsmouth and our Fleet in Port, not less than 1000 men desert from the Navy; and I am sure one third of this number, from loss of clothes, drinking and other debaucheries, are lost by death to the Kingdom. I shall only relate one fact, of a thousand, which could be brought forward: a ship from London clears at Gravesend for her voyage to India. Amongst other papers, the names of her crew and number are necessary; the names, qualities etc. are properly filled up, the ship, to a common observer is fully manned; but the fact is this, the ship is navigated to Portsmouth by Ticket men (men who are protected from the impress for some cause or other). The Owner

or Captain send to Portsmouth (to crimps) I have been told in
one instance as far as fifty men—twenty-five Able Seamen,
fifty ordinary and ten landsmen, the bounty being, of course,
different according to their qualifications; the Ticket men leave
the ship, the deserters take up the names, and away they go.

Knowing the case, an Act of Parliament would, if not entirely,
very nearly prevent this infamous conduct; the regulation, I
think, would be very plain and easy. I am sensible that no plan
for these very important purposes can be matured by any one
head, much less than by mine; but as the ideas flow from a pure
source and a sincere desire to benefit our King and Country, I
submit them with deference to much wiser and abler men than
Nelson and Bronte.

X

The Age of Nelson

TO UNDERSTAND the extraordinary measures taken by the government to man the Navy during the twenty years war with Revolutionary and Napoleonic France it is necessary to bear in mind the violent fluctuations in effective strength to which attention has already been called. Moreover, competition for men fit to bear arms increased as commerce flourished after the first critical decade of the war, and in the post-Trafalgar period the Peninsular Army further sharpened the demand. Excluding marines, the peacetime strength of the Navy in 1792 amounted to 16,613 men borne for wages (see Table III on page 288). A year later, after the outbreak of war, there were 69,868. No wonder Collingwood complained that "the Navy cannot be manned, the difficulty every day increases." Yet by 1797 its strength stood at 118,788 men. This sudden expansion goes far to explain the outbreak of the great mutinies that year, since at least a quarter of that number were landmen brought into the service by devious means.

The manning crisis was repeated after the short-sighted rundown of the forces at the time of the Peace of Amiens. The small population of the British Isles was soon stretched to its utmost to provide men for both the Army and the Navy. The average strength of the latter during the last half of the war was 140,000 men, in spite of the high rate of desertion as an expanding merchant marine began to possess something like a monopoly of seaborne trade after the series of victories associated with the name of Nelson. An unsatisfactory expedient to solve the crisis, which brought Britain into collision with the United States, was an increasing employment of foreigners. A contemporary estimate is that one third of the personnel of the merchant service and one eighth of the naval were men of this description by the end of the war.[1]

Before discussing the methods of manning adopted to meet such unprecedented demands, it will be well to enumerate the various modes of seamen entry. Apart from Boys, there were adult Volunteers attracted by generous bounties. Occupying a position midway between them and the Pressed Men were the Quota Men, who also received a bounty but were conscripts rather than genuine volunteers. Most of "Billy Pitt's men," as they were called in the fleet, were not seamen at all, hence their rating as Landsmen and their unpopularity with regular seamen. The new rating of Landsman was instituted early in the war and the mutineers of 1797 objected to it as "totally new." Moreover, the old spelling of "landmen" began to give place to the modern "landsmen." Such men were paid less than seamen and formed an unsatisfactory element in the ship's company, partly because of their lack of experience and partly because of the diversity of their background, which entailed strict disciplinary measures. They might be tinkers or tailors, or they might be petty thieves. An unflattering description of them is provided by a professional seaman:[2]

Them were the chaps as played hell with the fleet! Every grass-combing beggar as chose to bear up for the bounty had nothing to do but dock the tails of his togs and take to the tender. They used to ship in shoals: they were drafted by forties and fifties to each ship in the fleet. They were hardly up the side, hardly mustered abaft before there was "Send for the barber", "shave their pates", and "send them forward to the head to be scrubbed and sluished from clue to earing", afore ye could venture to berth with them below. Then stand clear of their shore-going rigs! Every finger was fairly a fish-hook; neither chest nor bed nor blanket nor bag escaped their sleight-of-hand thievery. They pluck you—aye, as clean as a poulterer, and bone your very eyebrows whilst staring you full in the face.

As has been pointed out, the ratio between Volunteer and Pressed Men cannot be ascertained accurately. Professor Michael Lewis in his study of the navy during the Age of Nelson has estimated the following proportions of the above categories in 1812:

Volunteers (Boys)	8%
Volunteers (Men)	15%
Pressed Men	50%
Foreigners	15%
Quota Men	12%

The evidence of random samples of recruiting returns suggests that while this ratio of 25% Voluntary to 75% Compulsory may be true of the later war years, it should be revised to about 50%-50% for the earlier years. This was certainly the case at the beginning of the war, when regular seamen lay low in the expectation of higher wages being paid by shipowners. But the returns are so conflicting that no final estimate can be made; for example in 1805 at Yarmouth fifty-five men were pressed and 110 volunteered, whereas at Dartmouth 115 were pressed and fifty-four volunteered.[3] Nor can we say who really volunteered, because some captains marked pressed men as such in order to claim the head money.

By an Order in Council dated 16 April 1794, the Boy entry was reorganised.[4] The old style Captain's Servant was now called Volunteer First Class, to be carefully distinguished from Volunteers of the Second and Third classes because it only consisted of "young gentlemen intended for the sea service." In other words they were cadets on their way up to the quarter-deck. With them was a small category of Volunteers per Order or College Volunteers coming from the Royal

Naval College, Portsmouth. Boy Volunteers of the Second and Third classes were treated as part of the ship's company and seldom rose higher than Warrant Officer. They might be apprenticed to such officers, or they might serve as stewards to commissioned officers. Most of them came in under the auspices of the Marine Society. In 1794 there were 582 of them, in 1795 594. This was a valuable channel of entry which continued at a steady rate. The Society also sent large numbers of adult Volunteers—a total of 22,973 during the war.[5] Nearly all were landsmen, for whose unskilled labour there was plenty of use in the Afterguard or among the Waisters.

Other volunteers of a more seamanlike type were attracted by posters and proclamations offering prize money and bounties. A typically romantic appeal is Lord Cochrane's poster for the *Pallas* in which it is interesting to note how old stories about Spanish gold were still being exploited (see page 160). Other captains employed personal influence in districts where they were known, as Collingwood did at Newcastle. To judge from a complaint which he sent to the Secretary of the Admiralty, regulating captains might well send such volunteers to other ships. Having "exerted all my industry to raise men for her complement and being particularly connected at Newcastle, I engaged my friends there to use their influence with seamen, which they did so effectually that near fifty men were entered on the assurance given them by these gentlemen that they were to serve in the *Prince*," he wrote after only three had reached him. The rest had been diverted to other ships, as he was informed by one writing to him "by desire of the Rest of the Volunteers."[6]

The chief attraction for such men were the bounties offered by Royal Proclamation. That of November, 1805, extends the one issued in 1803 by offering 30/- to all able-bodied landsmen as well as seamen, and four guineas instead of three to anyone procuring one of the latter. This official bounty was supplemented, as in the past, by city bounties often amounting to ten guineas a man. There were cases of much higher bounties, but the recipients were not popular with those who had joined at a lower rate. The historian E. P. Brenton, brother of the lieutenant mentioned in the last chapter, tells an amusing story to illustrate his disapproval of this means of attracting the wrong sort of man.[7]

> The seamen who voluntarily enlisted in 1793, and fought some of the most glorious of our battles, received the comparatively small bounty of £5. These brave fellows saw men, totally ignorant of the profession, the very refuse and outcasts of society fleeing from justice and the vengeance of the Law, come on board with bounty to the amount of £70. One of these objects, on coming on board a ship of war with a £70 bounty, was seized by a boatswain's mate who, holding him up by the waistband of his trousers, humorously exclaimed, "here's a fellow that cost a guinea a pound!"

The measures responsible for so much trouble in the fleet were the two Quota Acts of March 1795, (35 Geo. III c.5 and c.9). The system therein adopted was an important innovation, not only because it brought in undesirable and inefficient men who gave the Navy an even worse name than before, but because it placed the responsibility of manning the Navy in the hands of the magistrates. By these acts they were ordered to produce a specified number of men within three weeks. Any parish failing to do so could be fined after the churchwardens had agreed among themselves the amount of bounty money to be offered. Justices of the Peace were empowered to override the decisions of the Regulating Captains whether a man was to be enlisted or not. The consequence was that the worst type of man in the parish was unloaded on the Navy.

By the first of these Quota Acts the number of men required was stated on an estimate of seamen available in each county, e.g.

Bedford	67	Devon	393
Kent	440	City of London	198
Oxfordshire	127	Middlesex	451

By the second act specified ports were ordered to produce their quotas before the embargo on shipping imposed the previous month would be lifted. In the following list it will be noticed how small was the quota for the traditional naval ports, because normal pressing methods prevented any surplus seafaring population there.

Bristol	666	Portsmouth	75
Chester	25	Rye	90
Dartmouth	394	Sandwich	74
Dover	241	Sunderland	669
Falmouth	21	Whitby	573
Hull	731	Whitehaven	700
London	5,704	Yarmouth	506
Liverpool	1,711	Clyde Ports	683
Newcastle	1,240		
Plymouth	96		

It is impossible to say how far these annual quotas were met. The only surviving detailed record of men raised under the scheme is the London list for 1795.[8] This shows that the required 5,704 men were raised, categorised as 1,371 seamen equal to 2,742 landsmen, 2,522 landsmen and 440 pressed men. The sum paid in bounties totalled £19,559, but £52,223 bounty money remained due. The average bounty for an Able Seaman was twenty-five guineas.

Quota Men were often referred to as Lord Mayor's Men. The usual definition of this title is "those who enter to relieve themselves of public disgrace, and who are sent on board by any of the City magistrates for a street frolic or night charge." But it came to mean any landsman distinguished by the clothes he wore. Thus a merchant seaman called Wilson on joining a new ship heard the sailors saying "Oh! here is another Lord Mayor's man (a name given by seamen to all who wear long coats and enter voluntarily); but I soon undeceived them by saying, 'No, shipmates, you are mistaken for once; I am caught like most of you in the same trap'."[9]

Professional seamen, particularly officers, were convinced that it was the Quota Men who were responsible for the mutinies at Spithead and the Nore in 1797. Collingwood told his sister:[10]

> The chief promoters and counsellors in all this business have been what they call Billy Pitt's men, the county volunteers, your ruined politicians, who having drank ale enough to drown a nation, and talked nonsense enough to mad it; your Constitution and Corresponding Society men, finding politics and faction too rare a diet to fat on, took the country bounty and embark'd with their budget of politics and the education of a Sunday's school into the ships, where they disseminated their nonsense and their mischief. Those are the fellows who have done the business, the seamen who suffer are only the cat's paws. Making seamen's letters free of postage has very much promoted the business; every lazy fellow finds an excuse from work by writing a letter, and what kind of correspondence were you to expect from the refuse of the gallows, and the purgings of a gaol, and such make the majority of most ships' companies in such a war as this? The respectable part, and comparatively harmless, the seamen, are but a small part.

Nothing is known of the leaders of the mutinies beyond their names, except in the case of Richard Parker, the so-called President of the Floating Republic at the Nore. Valentine Joyce, the leader at Spithead, was probably an Irishman and with Ireland in a state of rebellion at the time there were probably many members of the United Irishmen secret society serving in the fleet. His fellow delegate on board the flagship was called Evans, a lawyer and a quota man. It is likely that the original outbreak was promoted by a small body of such sea-lawyers, appalled by the prospects of a life at sea and not yet inured to its hardships. Such is the normal pattern of rebellion against authority. Some have imagined, as Collingwood evidently did, that the whole affair was engineered by the Corresponding Societies. Members of such Jacobinical societies, even readers of Tom Paine, were to be found on board and the usual accusations of French gold were levelled at the leaders, but no direct contact has ever been traced. The fact is that the mutineers had no political aspirations whatever: they were simply strikers protesting against intolerable conditions. Such being the case, their reasons for taking the law into their own hands are dealt with in our next chapter.

We can trace the previous career of Richard Parker in some detail because he had spent much of his life in the Navy. He is typical of the shiftless, unhappy individuals brought in by the Quota Acts. He had been pressed in 1782 and reached the rank of midshipman before being discharged sick two years later. Thereafter he served in various merchant and naval ships, even being offered the duty of a lieutenant on board one ship. Circumstances prevented him from accepting and in a fit of discontent on board another ship he told an officer "he would be damned" if he would do as ordered. He was court martialled and discharged sick a second time in 1794. He and his wife then moved from Exeter to Edinburgh, where there is a story that he taught in a school. What is certain is that he was imprisoned for debt, took the Quota bounty of £20 to clear himself and rejoined the Navy in 1797.

The next stage of his story has not been previously told. As soon as the Regulating Captain at Leith (Jahleel Brenton, father of the two Brentons previously mentioned) heard of the Nore mutiny, he informed the Admiralty that on March 22 Parker had been entered on his books as one of the Perth Quota Men.[11] He heard the news from his lieutenant, John Watson, who commanded the tender sent down to the Nore. Watson had an extraordinary story to tell. On arrival he found all the ships in the Thames flying the red flag. He had been boarded and dragged before the delegates on board the *Sandwich* like a culprit. There Parker recognised him as the officer who had only recently brought him down from Leith. He intervened in his favour and later came on board the tender to chat with his shipmates. Watson tried to influence him against the course he was taking, but whenever he raised the topic of mutiny Parker's "brain took fire, he seemed intoxicated with the idea of his own consequence and uttered nothing but incoherent nonsense." However, Watson succeeded in making him drunk, hoping that his fellow delegates with their strict discipline would deal with him. His recruits having been taken from him to swell the ranks of the mutineers, Watson was permitted to sail again on June 2 with the fidelity of his own crew unshaken.

It is sometimes said that the Impress Service was reorganised at the beginning of the war. It would be more true to say that it was extended and made respectable. More rendezvous were set up than in the previous war, and more officers were engaged, whose names had the honour of being printed for the first time in Steel's *Navy List* of 1793. In that year there were thirty-one captains and fifty-eight lieutenants listed. By 1797 there were thirty-six and ninety, with another thirty-one lieutenants in command of tenders. In 1805 there were twenty-seven and sixty-eight on the list, captains being paid one pound a day with five shillings subsistence, lieutenants five shillings and 3/6 subsistence a day. At first there were twenty-three rendezvous, but by 1805 another eleven had been added. Instructions to officers follow the same lines as before (see page 145): seamen between twenty and fifty years of age, landsmen between twenty and thirty-five were to be pressed; watermen employed by insurance companies, apprentices, foreigners, fishermen were exempt, provided officers were "very particular in the examination of such persons"; men should be invited to volunteer with a bounty before being pressed; merchant seamen were only to be taken out of homeward bound vessels.[12]

Captain Brenton's letters to the Admiralty when Regulating Captain at Glasgow at the beginning of the war show how the business was carried out in practice.[13] During the summer he received 2,190 volunteers from Dublin. Before being sent down to Plymouth in the *Polly* tender, they spent all their bounty money in drinking the King's health and surprisingly enough all returned to the rendezvous afterwards. At the same time Brenton sent to the city gaol for volunteers, but was reprimanded by the Admiralty for so doing. However, he accepted eight men sent in by the magistrates instead of having them sent to prison. Throughout the winter volunteers continued to come in at the rate of 160 a week, nor did press warrants reach the Glasgow magistrates until the next March. They took no notice, pointing out that since the city had raised £500 for extra bounty money men were still volunteering. In February there were 523 volunteer seamen, twenty-two pressed men, ten sent in by magistrates and 614 landsmen.

The sort of dialogue which was being carried on all over the kingdom is thus reported by a Captain of Marines who, writing in 1840, was convinced that impressment meant the ruin of the Navy because it made it so unpopular.[14] Richard Jennings is brought before the captain:

How long have you been at sea,
Four years, your honour.
Where have you served?
No where, your honour.
Come, sir, no slang or I'll marry you to the gunner's daughter. Send a boatswain's mate aft with a cat.
Beg pardon, your honour, I meant I had never served on board a man-of-war.
Time you should then, and learn manners. Will you enter and take the bounty?

Or James Baker:

What are you?
A tailor, your worship.
What brought you here?
That lieutenant and his gang took I just as I was going home last
night.
Well Mr. you are just going abroad instead. We want tailors on
board as well as on shore, so you'll drive your needle on board.
But, your worship, I'm no sailor.
I see that well enough, and so I rate you a landsman and make
you an idler (i.e. not standing watch).

On the renewal of war in 1803 volunteers were again
plentiful. Admiral Phillips, Inspector of Rendezvous, records
that in 1804, 5,128 men were pressed, 5,978 seamen volunteered and so did 3,211 landsmen. The boy entry numbered
1,285 and 559 adults were sent in by magistrates. The total
cost of the Impress Service that year was £47,869. A large
rendezvous like that at Yarmouth was staffed by a captain,
two lieutenants, four midshipmen and twenty gangers. A
small one at Dartmouth had one lieutenant, two midshipmen
and eight men.[15]

Ships from Cornwallis's fleet blockading Brest landed their
own gangs to stop the avenues inland. The admiral warned
them that since "very unpleasant and serious circumstances
having occurred at Portland, it is my direction that the service is performed with as much caution as possible, to
prevent bloodshed and violent measures." He was evidently
referring to Captain Wolfe's losses, when a party of fifty
seamen and marines was fired on by a mob of three hundred,
who fell back on the quarries after wounding sixteen men.
Four of the mob were killed, so that Wolfe and his officers
were indicted for murder at the assizes but were acquitted on
a plea of self defence.[16]

When a tender delivered 219 men to the fleet in Torbay, 132
of whom were landsmen, Cornwallis again tried to avoid
unnecessary distress: "I am sure I can, with great truth, say

I have no desire to enforce the law against the poor and innocent, where the interest of our country is not materially concerned." He told another admiral that the government was complaining that the Navy was ruining trade instead of protecting it by weakening the crews of so many merchant vessels.

These often resisted violently, especially if they were big East Indiamen. When in 1803 the boats of the *Amethyst* and *Lynx* tried to board one of such ships in the Thames they found the crew at quarters fully armed with cutlasses and pikes. The lieutenant in charge gave the order to fire and two men were killed. He was found guilty of wilful murder by a coroner's jury, but acquitted with difficulty at Maidstone assizes.[17]

Lieutenant Dillon (later Admiral Sir William Dillon) has left an entertaining account of his experiences as an impress officer at Hull that year. When he arrived he met an old shipmate, a sailmaker, who greeted him cheerfully, but as soon as he learned why he was there, "took to his heels and was out of sight in no time." Every sort of trick, bribe and threat was used by shipowners anxious to get him out of the way, including invitations to "a princely table with a vast quantity of wine," or to take charming partners to a Grand Ball. Dillon retaliated by combining business with pleasure. He attended

these pleasant dinners in uniform, my host placing me between two amiable young ladies, supposing their attractions would ensure my company for the remainder of the evening. However, on those occasions I directed the leading man of my gang to call at the house where I dined at eight o'clock, and to send a note up to me. He also brought with him a bag containing a change of dress. Then I hastened away, in spite of all the entreaties of the fair ones. Below, the contents of the bag were turned to account, and in the course of a couple of hours I had probably secured seven or eight fine seamen.[18]

The recruiting problem was exacerbated by the large

number of privateers licensed by the Admiralty after pressure
from the shipping industry and its influence in Parliament.
Such service, as always, was much more popular than the
dull routine of a blockading fleet, so that many prime seamen
were drawn to it. Between 1803 and 1806, 47,000 such
privateersmen were thus protected.[19]

Equally serious both for the Army and the Navy were the
absurd measures taken by the Addington government. By
the Militia and Volunteer Acts, a land force was raised by
ballot with the option of purchasing exemption or providing a
substitute. The Militia was the military equivalent of the Sea
Fencibles, established in 1798 for coast defence by manning
Martello towers and providing a last line of defence against
invasion, or supplementing the Revenue or Coastguard
services. The Sea Fencibles was disbanded at the peace, but
reformed in 1803 and soon grew to such an extent that few
would volunteer for naval service. As Pitt pointed out, such
measures encouraged a rush to join anything but the regular
Army or Navy. At the end of the year Castlereagh stated that
the land forces consisted of a Regular Army of 96,000, a
Militia of 84,000, Volunteers 340,000, and Sea Fencibles
25,000. No wonder St. Vincent complained that the object
of the whole scheme was "of no other use than to calm the
fears of the old ladies."[20]

As the fear of invasion increased, so did the number of these
equivalents of the Home Guard of 1940. By 1805, when
Admiral George Berkeley was Inspector of Sea Fencibles,
there were ninety captains involved. His invaluable report on
the state of defences reinforced the complaints of Lord Keith,
Commander-in-Chief in the Downs and so primarily responsible for the defence of the homeland against the
Boulogne flotilla, that the corps was far too numerous, that it
interfered with or duplicated the Impress Service, that it was
altogether "useless and expensive."[21] In May no less than
6,401 men enrolled in southern England. No doubt this was

at the height of the invasion scare, but the fact remained that most of the Fencibles could not be called on for service at sea. Out of 250 in the Southampton area, only thirty-four were liable to impressment. On the Isle of Wight, only 131 out of 608. In Berkeley's opinion amalgamation between the Impress Service and the Sea Fencibles would halve expenses, as well as preventing manifold abuses over protections.

As he went along the coast that summer he found the story repeated: men were either unjustifiably protected, or they escaped the press gangs. At Bristol 473 men were raised at a cost of £2,020, but only seventy-eight were pressed, because crews from returning merchantmen landed at the mouth of the River Avon and made their way up to the Forest of Dean. At Swanage 125 Fencibles were protected and crews returning from the Newfoundland fishery escaped to Lulworth or the Isle of Purbeck, "where they are defended by armed men who at a given signal have actually turned out against the Impress Gang." Out of 161 men raised, only twenty-five were pressed. The cost varied enormously. At Southampton it was £80 a man, at Exeter £28, at Dartmouth eight guineas.

This recommendation to amalgamate the two services was accepted in November, each area being put under one captain and their staffs similarly pruned. Nevertheless, the Fencibles, if not their officers, continued to increase long after the danger of invasion was past, so that in 1810 the peak number of 23,455 men was reached. Of course not all these men were lost to the naval service. Many were useful pilots or fishermen, many were too old for active service, but the establishment continued to drain the country's manpower, as did the Volunteer movement that of the Army. Neither Nelson nor Wellington had much use for either.

It might seem that there were no seamen left for the press gangs to seize, but if we turn to the sailor's point of view and look at the evidence of the few lower-deck autobiographies which have survived we can appreciate how and why the fear of being pressed continued to haunt every man who used the sea as a profession.

The experience of C. R. Pemberton who ran away to sea at the age of seventeen is typical.[22] He and another boy found themselves wandering about the streets of Liverpool in 1807.

I had observed, without discovering that it meant anything, for the last half hour or longer, two well-dressed sailors, that is to say, two clean white-trousered, neat blue abundant-button jacketed, glazed-hatted, long pigtailed, mahogany-waistcoated, quid-cheeked men, were our constant attendants; walking where we walked, and stopping as we stopped; admiring this fine ship, and that fine ship, as we admired them. But their admiration was conditional, a comparative and exceptive admiration, and mingled in it something which was like information intended for us; though not immediately addressed to us, it was talking at us, with some allusions to ships much larger and finer and more beautiful than any there. Really I thought them very obliging. Go where we would the pigtails swung attendance on us. At length one said, "Are you looking for a ship, boys?" Well, thought I, this is a very civil, kind-hearted fellow, spite of his mahogany face. This put an end to all our trouble. "I thank you, yes: I should like to go on board of a ship". "Well, come along with us," said first pigtail's duplicate, "our ship is a gallows deal finer than any you've seen yet, with a jolly good Captain too: he splices the main brace every week, and every time of close-reef topsails." "Aye", said pigtail the first, "and he'll order the pusser's steward to blow your kite out with lobscous and choke your luff with figgy-dowdy." What splicing the main brace, and choking my luff, and lobscous, and figgy-dowdy meant, I could not guess for the life of me; but as they were illustrations of the "jolly captain's" good qualities, there was a spell in the unintelligible jargon; (many with wiser heads than mine have been humbugged by such process); and with our guides who, seeing, we were strangers, kindly kept close to our elbows, we stepped lightly along, and entered a narrow street parallel with St. George's dock; several persons, as we passed, stood to look at us; and I noticed a shaking of heads, as if they meant "Ah! something is wrong;" there seemed to be compassion in it. "Look there," said one of

The Press Gang on Tower Hill in 1780. From a cartoon by Collins

The Liberty of the Subject: cartoon by Gillray in 1779

The Boatswain of the *Gloucester* in 1812. From a sketch by the ship's Chaplain, Rev. E. Mangin

Sailors carousing by J. C. Ibbetson

the sailors. I did look there, as he pointed, and saw an immense white flag, with a large red cross in its corner, sweeping and swinging magnificently from a second-floor window, down almost to the pavement. Into the door of the house we passed; ascended a flight of stairs, our bodyguard regularly placed, one leading, the other bringing up the rear . . .

The door opened and my eye glanced on ranges of pistols and cutlasses suspended and cutting Euclidisms and trigonometrics on the walls: this looked awful! A very handsome man, with an epaulette on each shoulder, an armless sleeve hanging from one, walked forward and seated himself in a leather chair. He smiled as he surveyed us both with a look which indicated anything but unkindness; and the bland manner in which he addressed us, captivated me . . .

At this stage of the business another personage entered and took the vacant chair, riveting his two great green glassy eyes on us; his whole face besides was a blank, but how those eyes seemed to grin! A tiger at his studies; and his light sandy hair stood bushily out like a wig of hemp, every thread of which had a quarrel with its neighbour. Between the captain and this queer-looking animal, a half-muttered, half-hissed conversation ensued; the tiger was proposing something to which he of the epaulettes objected, and I gathered the words "tender, the hold, pair of scamps, riff-raff", to which the gentleman shook his head and said "No, no". I learned the meaning of all this soon and Captain Mends, after twenty-five years, accept my thanks for your "No, no". A shilling was put into my hand, which I gave to one of the pigtails. My friend George received one also, and stood staring at it as it lay in his palm. We had sold our bodies to the king, and to all others, to that tiger-gentleman inclusive.

Taken down to Plymouth in the tender, Pemberton had his first sight of hell on boarding the receiving ship *Salvador del mundo*, which had been captured at the battle of St. Vincent. "I looked through a heavy wooden grating, across which was a strong iron bar, with a huge padlock attached to it; and I saw that which threw me back almost fainting with horror . . . In that hole, which could not be thirty feet in length, one hundred and eighty human beings were crammed to eat, drink and sleep."

A less melodramatic account of the same ship at the same date occurs in the memoirs of Robert Hay.[23] What impressed this boy was the bustle on board what appeared to be a floating multiple store peopled by strangers of every trade and tongue. Even spirits were for sale. On the day he joined, the ship's corporal noticed the swollen calves of a sailor's wife bidding farewell to her husband. "I am afraid, my good woman," said he, "that your legs are somewhat dropsical; will you allow me the honour of performing a cure?" On which he pricked her legs with his knife and down trickled "no other than a drop of sterling stingo."

Both boys recovered their spirits when they were drafted on board ships on active service, and both record their admiration of good captains in contrast to the tyrants they later encountered. In Hay's case it was Collingwood—"A better friend to seamen never trod the quarter-deck. Collingwood took especial care of the boys. Blow high or blow low, he had us arranged in line on the poop every morning, and he himself inspected us to see that we were all clean and our habilments in good trim . . . No swearing, no threatening or bullying, no starting* was to be heard or seen. Boatswain's mates or ship's corporals dared not to be seen with a rattan or rope's end in hand; nor do I recollect of a single instance of a man being flogged while he remained on board. Was discipline neglected then? By no means. There was not a better disciplined crew in the fleet."

None the less Hay deserted from his next ship, hid among the bales of sugar in the hold of a West Indiaman to escape the searching gangers, disguised himself as a landsman in

---

* Starting was an unofficial punishment by boatswains or their mates with a cane rattan or rope's end. It could not be easily supervised and was particularly dangerous when a man was struck on the base of the neck.

order to reach London, and was there caught in precisely the same way as Roderick Random had been seventy years earlier. In the end he managed to escape from his last ship at the Nore by attaching bladders to his body to keep himself afloat as he swam ashore.

Such young men were fair game for the gangs, but when a respectable shipowner was seized the result was serious. Thomas Urquhart, who printed some *Letters on the Evils of Impressment* in 1816, recalls how he and his wife were set upon while walking in east London: "the ruffians struck me on the head, tore my coat from my back and afterwards dragged me by the neck until life was nearly exhausted." He was rescued by a friendly crowd and, being a member of Lloyd's, was able to get the Lord Mayor to protest to the Admiralty, receiving £50 damages for assault.

The most extraordinary case of unjustified pressing, so extraordinary that a Parliamentary Committee was set up to look into it, is that of David Bartholomew.[24] He joined the Navy from the Greenland fishery in 1795, rose rapidly to master's mate and passed the lieutenant's examination. Unfortunately, the Peace of Amiens prevented him from obtaining his commission. On the resumption of war he petitioned the First Lord, St. Vincent, for his commission. Having received no reply to his eight letters, he threatened to publish the correspondence. Whereupon that stern old disciplinarian ordered the Regulating Captain at Tower Hill to press him, the order being endorsed "Send him to the Nore as soon as you can catch him."

It was the way in which he was caught which created the scandal. The midshipman of the gang tracked him to his house and tricked him into appearing at the Admiralty with the promise of his commission. As soon as he entered the building, he was seized and put on board the *Enterprise* tender. This is the only instance of a man being pressed inside the Admiralty building and at the instance of a First Lord himself. Admiral Berkeley (who disliked St. Vincent) called it a violent and arbitrary act. Admiral Markham (who admired him) said it was justified by the man's situation in life. While the Committee was concluding that it was not warranted by the usages of the Navy, poor Bartholomew was on board the receiving ship at the Nore. But influence, or "interest" as it was called, being the overwhelming factor in those days, his ability as a seaman attracted the attention of Commodore Sir Home Popham, who made him an acting lieutenant and he at last received his commission on the latter's expedition to capture the Cape of Good Hope. Bartholomew ended his career as a post-captain and a Commander of the Bath, one of the few success stories among ordinary seamen at that date.

Because of the threat of legal proceedings, a well conducted gang honoured genuine protections or tickets of leave even at the height of the war. Jack Nasty-face (whose real name was William Robinson) loathed the Navy and all its officers save Nelson, but having been given a ticket of leave after fighting at Trafalgar, he found to his delight that he could lead the gangs a dance all the way up to London and back. He was stopped repeatedly, but none dared seize him. However, a protection had to be genuine. William Richardson, having been left in charge of a small coaster when the captain went on leave, was pressed after an enemy had informed the gang that he was not exempt, as mates usually were, because he was only acting mate.

The relevant part of a fisherman's protection of this date directs "all commanders of H.M. ships, press-masters and others whom it doth concern not to impress the said James Payer into H.M. service provided his age and a description of his person is inserted in the margin hereof (James Payer, aged 28 years, 5′ 5″ high, complexion brown, has scar on right side of his head, marked with smallpox, and wears his own hair)."[26]

The chief difficulty was over the protections of foreigners, who were so largely employed in the last years of the war. In the *Victory* there were forty-nine of them in 1805. In the *Implacable* in 1808 there were eighty. In the *Warspite* in 1812 there were eighty-three, or 17% of the ship's company. Of the latter, ten were Americans. Samuel Leech, an Ordinary Seaman on board the *Macedonian* that year remarks[27]

> They were taken without respect to their protections, which were often taken from them and destroyed. Some were released through the influence of the American consul; others, less fortunate, were carried to sea to their no small chagrin. To prevent recovery of these men by their consul, the press gang usually went ashore in the night previous to our going to sea, so that, before they were missed, they were beyond his protection.

Before considering the War of 1812-14, which was chiefly caused by such grievances, one must remember that admirals had long been bombarded with requests from American consuls forwarded to the Admiralty by the Foreign Office, and how frequently these were complied with. The papers of Lord Keith contain numerous instances. An application for the discharge of five Americans in May 1803 was accepted, but the previous January he refused to discharge a man called Higgins because "he has no documents of citizenship to produce." In the case of a man calling himself George English in one document and George Ireland in another, "I apprehend some imposition has been attempted."[28]

Impositions there certainly were. One which succeeded is described by the man concerned, Samuel Stokes, whose memoirs are the most recent which have come to light.[29] He had deserted from ship after ship, both merchant and naval, until he thought himself safe in the Revenue Service, whose protections were much prized. Once again he deserted and then shipped as an American. Unfortunately the officer of the next press gang to come on board thought that he recognised him. He asked his name, "but he was not satisfied with my answers and especially when I told him I was born an American, for he said he was sure I was an Englishman, 'and there stands a gentleman that has sailed with you in the *Richmond* gun brig.' I told him I never had my foot on board a British man-of-war before, and I hoped the American consul would soon get a discharge for me," as indeed he did as soon as the ship reached Plymouth. But having read a proclamation pardoning deserters, Stokes gave himself up and ceased his pretences. Another example of a man trying to pass himself off as an American is quoted below, page 220.

The war between Britain and the United States in 1812-14 occupies a position of much greater importance in the history of the latter country than the former. At textbook level the issue has been inflamed by nationalistic prejudices, nor have the American records been sufficiently searched to ascertain the type of man shipped in her famous frigates. Involved in a life and death struggle with Napoleonic Europe, and ruling the seas with vast fleets, Britain did not take seriously the American complaints about her insistence on the Right of Search when they came from the other side of the Atlantic. When hostilities broke out, she learned to her cost that she had underrated the strength of the small U.S. Navy. It was not until she brought her preponderantly larger fleets to blockade the American coastline and her well-seasoned troops to burn even Washington that the issue was decided.

The impressment issue was far more complex than appeared at first sight. At the crisis of the European war it is not surprising that Britain refused to compromise over the exercise of belligerent rights to search neutral shipping for contraband and for any deserters who had made their way on board. For years past Madison had refused to admit the legality of this Right of Search, and for years to come it remained a contentious issue in international law, because the conflict of 1812-14 settled nothing. Between the American doctrine of the Freedom of the Seas, that jurisdiction over ships on the high seas was as absolute as jurisdiction over state territory, so that the flag covered the ships and the men on board, and the historic British claim expressed by Lord Stowell, the leading authority on maritime law, "that ships upon the high seas compose no part of the territory of the state, the surrender of which principle would be a vital surrender of the belligerent rights of this country," there could be no compromise. The only area for negotiation was the British admission that search could not take place in territorial waters, that American citizens should not be pressed, and that only deserters could be taken off merchant vessels, not warships.

But who was an American? In view of the manifest frauds perpetrated, citizenship papers were viewed with justifiable suspicion by British officers. At New York they were sold for two dollars and some 12,000 were issued annually. Moreover, as late as 1870 the British government insisted on the principle of Indefeasible Nationality or Indelible Alliance, in other words once a British subject, always a British subject. The United States insisted on only two years' residence or two years' service in an American vessel as a prerequisite for American citizenship. The British attitude was inconsistent, in view of the act passed in the previous reign, under which foreigners serving two years in a British warship could claim British citizenship. Now, since desertion to American ships was taking place on an enormous scale, the act was conveniently forgotten and the official position was defined by the Advocate General on 3 November 1803:

> His Majesty has a right to require the service of all his seafaring subjects against the enemy, and to seize them by force wherever they can be found. The right is limited by the territorial sovereignty of other nations, and therefore His Majesty cannot seize his subjects because he cannot exercise any act of force within the territory of other states. But the high seas are extra-territorial, and merchant vessels navigating them are not admitted to possess a territorial jurisdiction so as to protect British subjects from the exercise of His Majesty's prerogative

over them. This right l apprehend has from time immemorial been asserted in practice and acquiesced in by foreign nations.

This was embodied in a proclamation issued on 16 October recalling British subjects home; if they did not return, they would be seized if found on board foreign vessels. The position is finally restated in a Declaration of 9 January 1813: "His Royal Highness can never admit that in the exercise of the undoubted and hitherto undisputed right of searching vessels in time of war, the impressment of British seamen when found therein, can be deemed any violation of the neutral flag."[30]

There was, of course, no issue about the illegality of pressing genuine American seamen. British naval officers, desperate for want of men on the other side of the Atlantic, may on occasion have acted in a high-handed way, but they were invariably reprimanded for so doing. Certainly there were vexatious delays in discharging American citizens from British ships, because of the time required to scrutinise applications. But there is no ground for the view that the British were deliberately trying to weaken a rival merchant marine by kidnapping its sailors. Because they spoke the same language, the number of British seamen who deserted to American ships was probably far higher than the number of American citizens pressed, or (as so many did) who volunteered in the Royal Navy.

The exact numbers in either case will never be known. Between 1792 and 1802 we know that 2,410 genuine Americans were discharged from the Royal Navy. Between March and November 1803 there were 605 such applications, but only 140 were granted, the others being refused on the grounds that the applicant either failed to produce the necessary documents or, since he had accepted the bounty, must be regarded as a British subject. Between 1803 and 1812 there were 6,057 similar cases of discharge, but in all probability twice that number were never discharged for one reason or another.

A reasonable estimate would be that in any given year between one and three thousand Americans might be found on board British warships, and many more in British merchant ships. Because of the penalties attached to desertion and the anxiety of a man to cover his tracks by using another name, the number of British deserters can never be known.

Omitting any account of the ceaseless and fruitless negotiations which went on for twenty years, we will confine ourselves to particular incidents which illustrate the issue at stake. In 1804 a British captain took fourteen men, two of them Americans, off a British privateer named the *Pitt* in New York harbour. He was reprimanded for infringing territorial waters and strict orders were issued to prevent another such episode. On the high seas, however, such search for contraband and for deserters continued, because it was essential for Britain's reply to Napoleon's Continental System.

Matters came to a head on 7 June 1807, when Admiral Berkeley, Commander-in-Chief of the North American station at Halifax, having heard that there were four deserters on board the U.S. frigate *Chesapeake*, ordered Captain Humphreys of the *Leopard* line-of-battle ship to recover them "without the limits of the United States." The British government subsequently disclaimed this "unauthorised act of force," but the proclamation mentioned above, which was issued in October, makes it clear that this was only as regards warships, not merchant ships. Humphreys stopped the *Chesapeake* ten miles off Cape Henry. He politely asked Captain Baron if there were any deserters on board and was told that there were none. He remonstrated, then fired a broadside and after a sharp action in which three Americans were killed, he boarded the frigate and took off his four men—one, Jenkin Retford, a deserter from the *Halifax* sloop, now passing under the name of Wilson, and three others from H.M.S. *Melampus*, one of whom was a Negro. Retford was hanged as a British subject. Since there was some doubt about the others, they were im-

prisoned until the matter was cleared up. The British government later offered to release them and pay compensation, but
this was refused because it would mean conceding the Right
of Search.

This action between two warships, which under international law were regarded as extensions of national territory
as merchant ships were not, brought the two nations to the
brink of war. Jefferson stopped short of hostilities and even
when Madison succeeded him with his famous embargo on
American shipping he only aroused the hostility of New
England shipowners and imposed a choice on American sailors
either to starve on shore or ship themselves in British vessels.
Madison's continued rejection of the Right of Search in any
form made conflict inevitable. On 4 June 1812 he once more
rehearsed the American grievances in his message to Congress.
On 18 June he declared war, though on 23 June the obnoxious
Orders in Council relating to contraband were revoked.
Replying to Madison's charge that the British had "wantonly
spilt American blood" by extending "British jurisdiction to
neutral vessels," the Prince Regent on 9 January repeated the
government's insistence on the Right of Search to recover
deserters and accused the U.S. government of enticing and
harbouring traitors by unlawful transfers of allegiance.

A detailed examination of Madison's list of Americans who
were supposed to have been pressed was made in 1814.
Among the first names it was found that one produced papers
dated New Bedford when he was actually in Plymouth harbour; another was a Negro described as having a brown complexion, a point overlooked by the illiterate owner; another
was in the name of Oliver Cromwell, dated New York 29 May
1806, but since he was in London on 6 June and the age of
jet propulsion had not yet arrived, the forgery could not be
hidden.[31]

When peace negotiations opened at Ghent, no mention was
made on either side of the *casus belli*, so that the Right of

Search remained for another forty years a bone of contention between the two nations which almost, in the matter of searching American shipping for slaves, brought about another war.

In spite of his obvious anti-American bias, William James's *Full and Correct Account of the Chief Naval Occurrences of the Late War*, published in 1817, contains some remarkable instances of the extent of British desertion. We may discount his insistence that the valour and experience of such deserters, in addition to the size of the American frigates, was responsible for the defeats in the first year of the war, but when he says that in the action between the *Macedonian* and the *United States*, many Macedonians recognised old shipmates on board the latter and found that some of her guns were named after British ships and victories, he is supported by other evidence. One man found his brother on board and when the latter tried to persuade him to enlist in the U.S. Navy, where his experience would make him a Petty Officer in no time, he replied "If you are a damned rascal, that's no reason why I should be one."

Samuel Leech, then a surgeon's boy on board the British frigate, declares that since so many of the Macedonians were Americans and "some were pressed men; others were much dissatisfied with the severity, not to say cruelty, of our discipline; so that a multitude of the crew were ready to give 'leg bail,' as they termed it, could they have planted their feet on American soil. Hence our liberty was restrained"—when visiting Hampton Roads before hostilities broke out. But in the action with the *United States* they all "fought like tigers" until the *Macedonian* was dismasted and they were taken prisoner. Whereupon, "all idea that we had been trying to shoot each other's brains out so shortly before seemed forgotten. We ate together, drank together, joked, laughed, told yarns; in short, a perfect union of ideas, feelings and purposes seemed to exist among all hands." He was so taken with "the great principle for which the American so nobly contended" (he was writing for a Boston audience thirty years later) that he enlisted on the U.S. brig *Syren*, only to be recaptured by H.M.S. *Medway* in 1814. The end of the war saved him from hanging as a traitor and he betook himself to the United States for the rest of his life.[32]

We may now sketch, however briefly, the careers of some of those individuals already quoted who have left memoirs of their time on the lower deck. Some of the common features of such reminiscences are worth bearing in mind when they are considered as historical evidence. They were mostly written during the eighteen-thirties and forties when their authors were getting old, by which time manners in general (even in the Navy) had changed, so that memories of brutality and discomfort remained all the more vivid by contrast. Many of the writers became very religious, usually of the Evangelical or Methodist persuasions, and wrote their memoirs not just for family consumption but either for 'the object of improving conditions in a service they had long since left, or to pay off old scores. On some topics—flogging, tyrannical officers, lack of shore leave, or the unpopularity of the naval service among merchant seamen—all are agreed. On others —food, pay, living conditions—they differ. A difficulty which is apparent to all social historians using such evidence is the variation between happy ships and hells afloat, invariably depending on the type of officer in command. In every case the point of view of the author, whether he be a man with a grievance like Jack Nasty-face, or a contented pensioner like George Watson, has to be borne in mind.*

One conclusion which may be drawn from these rare and badly printed little books is the extraordinary success of rigid discipline, combined with good leadership, in welding the

---

* A selection from the few surviving letters from such seamen is printed below, Appendix page 294.

most effective instrument of war ever seen in the age of sail out of men of such diverse and unsuitable backgrounds. The same men who were so badly paid, fed and treated, who complained so bitterly of intolerable conditions, fought magnificently in battle. Every vice seems to have flourished in the ships of the old navy except that of cowardice. The attitude in action common to every writer is that expressed by John Nicol, a pressed man writing of the battle of St. Vincent:

> "The hotter the war the sooner peace," was a saying with us. When everything was cleared, the ports open, the matches lighted, the guns run out, then we gave three such cheers as are only to be heard in a British man-of-war. This intimidates the enemy more than a broadside, as they have often declared to me. It shows them the men in the true spirit, baying to be at them.

The Life and Adventures of John Nicol, Mariner was compiled in 1822 by a bookseller named John Howell, who met Nicol wandering penniless in the streets of Edinburgh and took down the old man's reminiscences verbatim.[33] "My life, for a period of twenty-five years, was a continued success of change. Twice I circumnavigated the globe; three times I was in China; twice in Egypt; and more than once sailed along the whole landboard of America from Nootka Sound to Cape Horn; twice I doubled it. Old as I am, my heart is still unchanged and were I young and stout again I would sail upon discovery; but, weak and stiff, I can only send my prayers with the tight ship and her merry hearts."

He was born at Edinburgh in 1755, volunteered in 1776, served throughout the American War and then went round the world with Captain Portlock. He served in convict ships and East Indiamen until he was pressed at the outbreak of the war with France. He fought at St. Vincent and the Nile, failed to obtain a pension and died in poverty at an unknown date: "I can look to my deathbed with resignation," he concludes, "but to the poor's house I cannot look with composure. I have been a wanderer and the child of chance all my days; and now look only for the time when I shall enter my last ship, and be anchored with a green turf upon my breast; and I care not how soon the command is given."

The longest of these autobiographies is by William Richardson, published under the title of *A Mariner of England* in 1908. It covers thirteen years in the merchant service and twenty-four in the Navy, from 1793 to 1817, during most of which time Richardson was a gunner. He lived to the age of ninety-seven, twice the normal life of a sailor in those days, and it is said that after his wife died he dismantled the bedstead and slung a hammock for the rest of his life. He gives the sober, detailed account of his services which one would expect from so reasonable a man. He seldom generalises about conditions at sea, because he was no propagandist and realised the difference between one ship and another. Having overcome the initial prejudice of the merchant seamen against the Navy, he found life quite congenial. Only once does he speak out with real emotion and that is after describing a flogging round the fleet for desertion:

> Horrid work! Could anyone bear to see a beast treated so, let alone a fellow creature? People may talk of negro slavery and the whip, but let them look nearer home and see a poor sailor arrived from a long voyage, exulting in the pleasure of soon being among his dearest friends and relations. Behold him just entering the door when a press gang seizes him like a felon, drags him away and puts him in the tender's hold, and from thence he is sent on board a man-of-war perhaps ready to sail to some foreign station, without either seeing his wife, friends or relations; and if he complains, he is likely to be seized up and flogged with a cat, and if he deserts he is flogged round the fleet nearly to death. Surely they had better shoot a man at once: it would be greater lenity.

Richardson experienced every stage in a sailor's career. Apprenticed to a tough skipper in the coal trade (his fellow apprentice, named Samuel Jackson, rose to the rank of rear-admiral in 1845), he knew the Baltic and the East Indies, as well as serving on board a slaver, of which he gives an unusually frank account. He was first pressed in 1791, but as his ship was soon paid off he sailed in an East Indiaman to Calcutta, where he was pressed again. He joined a fine frigate as a topman, but because he was a valuable seaman he was turned over to another ship as soon as he returned home. His new captain, Leveson-Gower, had more liberal ideas, declaring that he did not wish his ship to be regarded as a prison. Although his officers warned him that liberty men seldom returned on board, every one of them did, "for we thought it would be ungrateful now to desert, when we had got a captain who would give us liberty." Soon afterwards he was promoted to gunner, serving in that capacity for the rest of the war. He was granted a pension in 1817 and died at Plymouth.

The Adventures of a Greenwich Pensioner by George Watson, printed at Newcastle in 1827, is the rarest of these books. Like Richardson's, it is a contented record. Like him, he was a North Country sailor who, after six years in the coal trade, volunteered in 1808 at the age of sixteen because a friend of his found the life more pleasant than he had expected. So did Watson, who liked all his captains, even the one who after thrashing him with a stick ordered him a dozen lashes at the gangway. He enjoyed the rough life until he was crippled in an action in the Adriatic in 1812. After two years in hospital (where he "had a great deal to do to repulse the temptations I met with from these syrens"—the nurses) he was given a pension at Greenwich, where he wrote his book many years later.

Reference has already been made to Samuel Leech's *Thirty years From Home, or a Voice from the Main Deck*, published at Boston in 1843 and in London in 1845. It is full of complaints and propaganda, but it gives a vivid picture of life between decks when Leech joined the *Macedonian* frigate in 1810. The poor boy was disappointed in his prospects from the start, when his mother saw him off to sea at Gravesend with the gift of a Bible. He found life as a Volunteer, Second Class, bounded by the boatswain's pipe and the rope's end. After his frigate had been captured, he enlisted in the U.S. Navy but found discipline on board just as strict (a fact brought out in Herman Melville's *White Jacket*), so that he "felt as unhappy as when in the *Macedonian*." He found a job at Boston, turned Methodist, and took the opportunity in his book to preach temperance, sabbatarianism and the degeneracy of the British.

Another book, which, as might be expected from the title, leaves an unpleasant impression, is *Nautical Economy, or Forecastle Recollections of Events during the last War, dedicated to the Brave Tars of Old England, by a Sailor politely called by the Officers of the Navy, Jack Nasty-face. Published by William Robinson, Cheapside*, in 1836. Nasty-face was indeed the William Robinson who volunteered as a landsman, fought at Trafalgar, of which in the course of an excellent account he gives an idea of how Nelson affected all those who served under him: "he was adored, and in fighting under him, every man thought himself sure of success." But of his own captain, the Hon. Sir Charles Paget, and all other officers he has no good word to say: "this worthy, whose name was a terror to every ship's company, and was cursed from stem to stern in the British navy, now shines forth as an M.P." In spite of his appalling description of punishments (all of which, save flogging, had been abolished when he wrote, though he does not say so), he can still say of the service: "there is no profession that can vie with it; and a British seaman has a right to be proud, for he is incomparable when placed alongside those of any other nation." Nevertheless, this purser's steward deserted in 1811 and nothing further is known of him.[34]

Both Robinson, writing in 1836, and Charles Reece Pemberton, who began his memoirs under the pseudonym of Pel Verjuice in 1833, were anxious to combat the breezy picture of naval novelists like Marryat and Chamier, whose books were just coming into fashion: "They were officers that spoke

A Flogging at the Gangway. Illustration by G. Cruikshank to a story entitled 'The Point of Honour' in Barker's *Greenwich Hospital,* 1826. The offender is stripping off his shirt as he explains that the man seized up at the gratings is innocent. Note the Marines on the quarterdeck, the officers in the foreground, the boatswain and surgeon behind the grating, and the ship's company to the right

Greenwich Pensioners by I. Cruikshank

and wrote, and it is not unlikely, nor is it ungenerous to say so, that an interfering *esprit de corps* allured them away from statements which might have enabled the readers, and through them society at large, to arrive at a just conclusion on these matters." Pemberton claims to look with a really thinking eye on the condition of "England's Jolly Tars." His strikingly colourful style, rivalling that of De Quincey, leads him into rhetoric and exaggeration and ruins the architecture of his book, but it is starred with magnificent descriptive passages. The Celtic excess of his imagery is indicative of the fact that this Welshman was in later life a notable actor.[35]

As we have seen, he volunteered at Liverpool and was sent on board the *Alceste*, Captain Murray Maxwell. He gives a wonderful description of his pride in his ship. Of Maxwell he writes:

> Whenever Captain M– manoeuvred his ships the whole of the vast machine moved like clockwork, without jar or impediment. With him she was a feather in a cup of oil, floating and bounding so easily and smoothly. Why was this? True, he was one of the most skilful and cool-headed seamen that ever commanded a ship, as the thousands who knew him will allow . . . (His men) were willing, because they found he wished to be, would be, just; they put forth their strength, skill and cheerful alacrity because he was merciful and considerate in his discipline; he never irritated them by caprice; there was no *vexatious niggling* in anything he ordered to be done. Half the ships in the fleet during the last war contained crews that required only a spark to start them into open mutiny; the combustion was daily accumulated under their toil from the caprice of officers and their *vexatious niggling discipline*.

Pemberton followed Maxwell as a clerk in the *Daedalus* out to Ceylon, where she was wrecked in 1813. Nothing is known about him for the next fifteen years, after which he reappears in the guise of a radical lecturer and actor during the days of the Chartists.

A much more pedestrian but exactly contemporaneous

account of frigate service is that by Robert Mercer Wilson, who served in the same ship as Pemberton in the Adriatic in 1809.[36] Like him, his prejudice against the Navy when he was pressed in 1805 was dissipated at sea under a good captain, in this case Patrick Campbell of the *Unité*. There was no starting on board, so the crew did their duty cheerfully; but Wilson well knew the generality of boatswain's mates "who the moment they issue an order, follow it with a stripe," when he joined a less happy ship in 1811, from which he deserted.

Another recent publication is *The Adventures of John Wetherell*, edited by C. S. Forester in 1954 from a longer manuscript written about 1834. It is a very different book to the Hornblower series of novels and curiously enough less accurate. Though cast in the form of a diary, it is obviously written up much later and interspersed with newspaper accounts. Most of the published portion deals with Wetherell's eleven years in a French prison. The earlier part is unpleasant reading because of his fanatical hatred for his captain, Philip Wilkinson. It may well have been deserved, because when the latter's tyrannical treatment of the crew of the *Hermione* was followed by that of the sadistic Captain Hugh Pigot, who delighted in flogging the last man down from the yard arm, one of the bloodiest mutinies in naval history occurred.[37] According to Wetherell, the same thing might have happened in the *Hussar*, into which he was pressed as a Whitby collier's lad in 1803, had not the ship been wrecked off Brest the next year, so that he spent the rest of the war in prison. Like others, he attacks the petty tyranny of junior officers as much as that of his captain, but he points out that Admiral Cornwallis speedily reprimanded them when their behaviour was brought to his notice by petitions from the crew. Let one entry suffice:

> Lord George Gordon was Midshipman of the Main Top and as I spoke he kicked me in the breast with his foot and ordered me to leave the duty to him. I answered that it was too bad to be

kicked like a dog when in the act of doing what I thought was right, and made my way out on the yard arm. "Walk down Sir in a Moment, you damn'd mutinous rascal, and you shall have your desert," says my Lord, and down he goes to the lieutenant on the quarter deck and made his story right on his side. Down goes I to the tribunal of justice. First salute I met was a blow on my head with a speaking trumpet, then called the master-at-arms, and ordered him to put that damn'd young rascal in irons. This was readily complied with, so poor Jack was clap't in the Brig as we term it . . . Next day exercised guns fireing at a Barrel with a flag on it. Two or three got each 4 dozen thro' this day's amusement as Wilkinson calls it.

After the war Wetherell emigrated to the United States, where he wrote his memoirs at New York about 1834.

The much more attractive memoirs of Robert Hay were published in 1953 under the title of *Landsman Hay*. He ran away to sea in 1803 at the age of fourteen and his career ends when he deserted for the second time in 1811. He speedily regretted volunteering, but when drafted to the *Culloden* under Collingwood, he enjoyed himself, so that it is not easy to say why he deserted so often. In the end he settled down as a clerk in a Scottish canal company and would have got his son into Greenwich Hospital School, had not it been found that an R still stood against his name in the Admiralty records.

A final specimen of a lower deck autobiography is of a slightly later date. This is *Thirty-Six years of a Seafaring Life*, *by an Old Quarter Master*, whose name was John Béchervaise, published at Portsea in 1839. The author was a Channel Islander, the son of a master mariner, so that when seized by the press gang in 1803 he was discharged as an apprentice. He spent the whole of the war in the merchant service, but at the end found himself in prison for debt. In 1820, still penniless, he volunteered for the Navy: "Of all the places then dreaded by seamen in the merchant service, a ship of war was the most." But in view of his previous experience as a mate he soon became a Petty Officer and enjoyed naval life:

"sobriety and a desire to fulfil the duties imposed upon me carried me through with comfort, and I look back with a degree of pleasure to the day on which I first stood on a ship of war's books . . . Not a day passes but I hear seamen deplore their having run away from a ship of war; when, had they not done so, they might now, instead of poverty and rags, have enjoyed a good pension, in respectability and comfort."

It may sound like a recruiting pamphlet, but Béchervaise's book illustrates the better side of the Navy, the traditions of which were not entirely (as Churchill once said) those of rum, sodomy and the lash.

XI

Life at Sea

I. THE SHIP'S COMPANY

"No man will be a sailor who has contrivance enough to get himself into a jail; for being in a ship is being in a jail, with the chance of being drowned. A man in a jail has more room, better food and commonly better company." Dr. Johnson repeated the remark on more than one occasion. It may have been inspired by the fact that his Negro servant was pressed until, through the good offices of Wilkes, an application was made for his discharge; or by his one visit to a warship (unrecorded by Boswell) when, in 1770, he went on board the *Ramillies*, his parting remark being "Have the goodness to tell the First Lieutenant that I beg he will leave off the practice of swearing." When he was once reminded that some people were fond of being sailors, all that he could reply was "I cannot account for that, any more than I can account for other strange perversions of the imagination."[1]

The officer-man relationship is the key to any study of what life was like at sea in the Georgian navy. Never was the art of leadership of greater importance than in making a happy and efficient ship out of the heterogeneous material provided by the press gangs. After paying tribute to the "daringness of spirit in a British mariner, as is that of our mastiffs, a kind of natural haughtiness which eminently distinguishes him from the rest of man," an early writer who called himself Barnaby Slush, in his *The Navy Royal, or a Sea Cook turned Projector* (1709), wisely adds "Good mariners grow not up like mush-looms, without care or culture. It is morally impossible, nay, it is naturally impossible, to have a brave, active, skilful, resolute body of sailors without just and generous as well as understanding officers."

The social historian is confronted with the conflicting nature of the evidence about conditions at sea. The problem of making any valid generalisation is created by the wide powers conferred on a captain of a ship, particularly on a foreign station, which made each ship virtually a kingdom on its own, with its own mode of life and its own state of morale. Naval pay, food, even routine might be standardised, but the infliction of punishment, the standard of hygiene and clothing, above all the spirit of the ship varied enormously. If one was to accept the Articles of War and the Admiralty Regulations at their face value, the task of describing life at sea would be easy. But everyone knows how easily such rules were circum-vented at that time, how powerful interests prevailed, how corrupt was a system based on fees and perquisites. The Admiralty might attempt to impose some sort of uniformity on the conduct of naval officers, but while a Rodney could make his son a captain at the age of sixteen, or a Cochrane could be entered on the books of four frigates at the same time while he was still a boy, as well as being an officer in the Guards, it is obvious that the caprice of a captain remained largely unaffected. It was laid down that no women were to be carried to sea, and that no captain might inflict more than a dozen lashes as a summary punishment. In fact, women did go to sea, and five or six dozen lashes were often administered without any form of trial. Some ships were lax in their discipline, others taut, some officers were humane and con-siderate, others were sadists and capricious tyrants. The only means of complaint open to a ship's company was a petition or round-robin to the admiral commanding the station, and that was a dangerous and difficult proceeding.

Moreover, it must always be borne in mind that this was a crude and brutal age. When women were whipped at the cart's tail, when men were executed as a public spectacle, when flogging was far more severe in the Army (and when Cobbett protested he was imprisoned for seditious libel), naval punishments, however savage, assume their proper proportions. Customs in the armed services have always lagged behind the manners of polite society, but they have not proved immutable. Slowly, and by gradual degrees, the barbaric behaviour on board the ships of Queen Anne's reign, the illiteracy of the officers, the absence of hygiene, the savage relics of a penal system surviving from earlier times, such as keel-hauling, gave place to those of an age in which the officer was also a gentleman, who did not regard his men as inarticulate brutes. The great mutinies of 1797 may not have caused higher standards to prevail immediately, except in the matter of pay, but in the last decade of the Napoleonic war there was a notable humanising of life on board, and in the years which succeeded it was possible to make many overdue reforms in a smaller and less active service.

The most beneficent influence was undoubtedly that of the Evangelicals in the fleet and the spread of Methodist attitudes. Earlier adherents like Lord Barham or Lord Gambier were often figures of fun to officers of the old school. But Admiral Sir Charles Penrose, who was one of this persuasion, noted in 1824 the marked diminution of swearing and flogging during his career largely due to their influence, and Captain Marryat, before he became the naval novelist of the war, wrote at about the same date:[2]

Whoever has been fifteen years in the Navy, and will compare what took place at the period of his entrance with the present usages in the service, must acknowledge that swearing and abusive language, the oppression of the midshipmen's berth, the custom of starting and severe punishments at the gangway, have been discountenanced and checked. A quarterly return of all punishments inflicted is sent up to the Admiralty. Preserved meats, soups etc. for the convalescent are supplied to every ship in the Navy; and great improvements have taken place in the ventilating and lighting of ships throughout. The distribution of prize money had also been newly arranged, and the captains have had their shares considerably reduced, in augmentation of those of the best seamen.

When a ship was commissioned the men joining her were divided into two (occasionally three) watches, the starboard and the larboard (the word "port" not officially replacing it until 1844). The "people," as they were called, were then rated according to their ability, whether Able Seaman, Ordinary Seaman, or Landsman. They were quartered to each gun and allowed to subdivide themselves into messes of four or six, the mess tables being hung on hooks above each gun. A man might be given hammock No. 7 on the orlop deck below the waterline; he might be part of the crew of No. 8 gun on the middle deck, and be quartered at the fore stay on the upper deck when furling or reefing sail. In big ships about two-thirds of the ship's company might be thus "watched," the remainder being called Idlers because they did not stand a watch. This class comprised the Warrant Officers and Petty Officers, such as the boatswain, gunner, master-at-arms, sailmaker, ropemaker, armourer, cook, cooper, barber, tailor, writers, servants, stewards, and all their mates. There were some odd and inferior types, such as the Captain of the Head, responsible for keeping the "heads" or toilets clean, Loblolly Boys to assist the surgeon, the Lady of the Gunroom responsible for the behaviour of the midshipmen, or the Jack of the Dust (Jack Dusty), the purser's steward in the breadroom.

Those who were watched were divided into three classes: the Able Seamen, called Forecastle or Topmen; the Ordinary

Seamen and Landsmen composing the Afterguard; and the Waisters, who were older or less skilful men, seldom going aloft, but used for pulling and hauling. A watch bill for a first-rate of 100-guns with a complement of 839 shows how the crew was divided:[3]

Forecastle-men	60
Fore-top-men	63
Main-top-men	69
Mizen-top-men	27
Afterguard	94
Waisters	171
Quarter-masters	13
Quarter-gunners	30
Carpenter's crew	13
Boatswain's mates	8
Total No. watched	548

No. of Officers, Servants, Idlers, Widow's Men—291.

The new entry was soon made to realise that there was an elaborate hierarchy on board, quite apart from the commissioned officers, or those civilian officers who achieved quarter-deck rank in 1806—the purser, surgeon and chaplain. The seaman's immediate superiors, to whose rank he might attain in time, were the Warrant Officers or Standing Officers of old, who were virtually part of the ship, and their mates. Presiding was the Boatswain with his rattan of three canes bound together, or more simply a rope's end, with which the men were "started" at the least opportunity. He and his mates officiated at the formal floggings at the gangway, but more commonly, says one who suffered under them, "the moment they issue an order they follow it with a stripe . . . When Mr. Stokes joined us and was heard blustering and swearing boatswain-like, 'Ah,' says one of our officers, 'that's him will make our lads move'." Gentleman Chucks in Marryat's *Peter Simple* is the classical comic example of such a man who might, in real life, instil a reign of terror unless he was kept in check by the captain.

The Warrant Officer primarily responsible for good order was the Master-at-Arms with his Ship's Corporals, Claggart in Melville's *Billy Budd* being the most sinister example. He posted the sentries, saw that all lights were extinguished, counted the lashes at a flogging, put prisoners in irons. Truly, as young Wilson wrote, "he has great power and is what is called a great man among the little ones."

The Gunner, by the nature of his duties, did not inspire such awe. He was probably a more intelligent man and he was responsible for the welfare of the Captain's Servants in the Gunroom before they were old enough to join the "young gentlemen" in the Midshipmen's Berth in the cockpit on the orlop deck.

In the early Georgian navy the fact that six or seven hundred men were merely divided into two watches meant an indiscriminate mass of humanity, individually indistinguishable to the average lieutenant. This failure to supervise the men was undoubtedly responsible for most of the dirt and misery which prevailed on board. A great improvement came about after the introduction of the Divisional System. Charles Middleton, later Lord Barham, must be given the credit for introducing this on board the *Ardent* in 1775, though there are a few earlier examples. He owed much to the encouragement of Kempenfelt. There were usually four divisions, each under a senior lieutenant, who was responsible for seeing that the men in his division were clean, healthy and fit for duty, and who could order summary punishments ranging from extra scrubbing duty to a dozen lashes. In Kempenfelt's opinion this was the only way to prevent the people from deteriorating into a disorderly mob: "At present, their appearance in general is a disgrace to the service, very shabby and dirty . . . With order and discipline you increase your force; cleanliness and sobriety would keep your men healthy;

and punishments would be seldom, as crime would be rare."[4]

Much would have been done to improve their appearance as well as their morale had the Admiralty agreed to give the men a uniform. Officers were given one in 1748, but since the men were paid off with the ship, it was not thought worth-while to spend money on uniforms, apart from that of the Marines. Naval surgeons were always pressing for this, because they realised how easily typhus could be introduced via the receiving ships. "If the seamen of H.M. service were put into an uniform sea-habit," wrote Dr. Lind in 1757, "with some little moveable badges or variations by which it might be known to what ships they belong, each man would at first go cleanly and neatly on board H.M. ships." But all the Admiralty would agree to was some sort of hospital uniform to prevent men deserting. Blane and Trotter returned to the attack twenty years later, the latter suggesting the issue of "blue jackets, white waistcoats, white trousers and a small round hat with a narrow belt on which should be printed the name of the ship." Such advice continued to be ignored until, exactly a hundred years after Lind had written, a naval uni-form was granted. All that even the influential Sir Gilbert Blane could obtain was an issue of soap in 1796.[5]

Men rounded up by the press gangs were often so ragged and filthy, and the hard work at sea so soon ruined even ade-quate clothing, that the purser was authorised to sell slops, taking a shilling in the pound discount for his pains. The slop list for Anne's navy included grey kersey jackets lined with red cotton and ornamented with brass buttons, red kersey breeches with leather pockets, red waistcoats of Welsh flannel, grey stockings, linen shirts and drawers, leather or red woollen caps and buckled shoes.[6] The working rig amounted to little more than a canvas frock (which later, tucked in, developed into a blouse) and baggy breeches, for few seamen wore shoes on board. As time went on the cap gave way to the round, tarred hat or, after 1803, the straw hat, under which the pigtail continued to be worn until the end of the war. By that date the kerchief was standardised as black, jackets were blue and trousers bell-bottomed and white. Captains often dressed their own barge crews in a uniform of their own choice, that of the *Harlequin* favouring a theatrical costume. "Ocean swells" on shore leave were very particular about their appearance, especially the silver buckles on their shoes. But of uniform there was none: everything had to be bought from the slop chest, or made out of rough materials on make-and-mend afternoons and in the dog watches.

The normal routine seldom varied. At four or five in the morning the boatswain's pipes and a stentorian voice echoed through each deck—" 'Whe-e-ugh, all hands on deck, a ho-o-o-y. Do you hear the news there below? Come, jump up, every man and mother's son of you.' Still all was quiet. Boatswain's mates are, in general, no way remarkable for their store of patience, and finding no one stirring at the second call one of them springs down each hatchway, a lantern in one hand, a swinging rattan in the other, and cut away right and left is the order of the day. Those whose beds are on the decks are seen at once, and having no shelter fly towards the hatchways like so many rats with a brace of terriers in pursuit. The clearing of the hammocks is not so easy, but it must be done. They press their shoulders against every one of them, roaring out with a voice of thunder, 'A sharp knife, a clear conscience, and out or down is the word'." [7]

The decks are scrubbed with holystones shaped like bibles, or scrapers called hand-organs. The paintwork is washed down, the guns cleaned, and at seven bells the hammocks are piped up to be stored for airing in the nettings on the quarter-deck or waist. Five minutes was all that was allowed in a smart ship to lash up. Every hammock is numbered and has its allotted place. At eight breakfast is piped, after which "Clear Lower Deck" is the order and all hands go to quarters.

At ten on a Sunday it is "Clear For Divisions" and the captain inspects the ship's company before Divine Service is held under an awning rigged by the carpenter. After this, spirits are got up and the grog served out from a scuttled butt with an officer standing by. At noon hands are piped to dinner. At five they are piped to supper, and at eight piped down to their hammocks, after which nothing is heard or seen through the night, save the half hourly visits of the master-at-arms and the regular "All's Well" of the sentinel as he walks his lonely post. There they hung like bats from the roof of a cave, their hammocks crowded alongside each other at the regulation interval of fourteen inches a man, until the boatswain's pipe roused them to duty once more.

In a well regulated ship the whole routine worked so smoothly that every hour and every day was marked off for some duty. On Monday it was exercise at the great and small guns, cutlass and musket drill. On Tuesday it was boat work. On Wednesday exercise in reefing, furling and shifting the whole suit of sails. Thursday in peacetime was usually a make-and-mend. On Friday there was exercise at general quarters, manning all the guns and target practice. On Saturday the whole ship was cleaned.

Sunday service could be as unpleasant a duty as any. According to Captain Thompson (often called 'Poet' Thompson for his predilection for verse) in 1767 "the congregation is generally drove together by the boatswain (like sheep by a shepherd), who neither spares oaths nor blows." A sensitive Bath clergyman named Edward Mangin was ill-advised enough to become a naval chaplain for a few weeks in 1812. It was soon obvious to him that he was not suited to such a life:

> To leave the men unreproved and vicious, was possible; and I dare say it was equally possible to have transformed them all into Methodists, or madmen or hypocrites of some other kind; but to convert a man-o'-war's crew into Christians would be a task to which the courage of Loyola, the philanthropy of Howard, and

the eloquence of St. Paul united, would prove inadequate . . .
So I bid adieu to the sameness and (to me) insupportable vexations
of a naval life; to the necessity of dwelling in a prison; within
whose limits were to be found Constraint, Disease, Ignorance,
Insensibility, Tyranny, Sameness, Dirt and Foul Air; and, in
addition, the dangers of Ocean, Fire, Mutiny, Pestilence, Battle
and Exile.[8]

Orders shouted through a speaking trumpet were kept to a
minimum in a good ship. They were obeyed in silence. "So
confident was the First Lieutenant of every man's abilities
and exertions that instead of saying hoist away this, that or
the other sail, he had only to say two words—Make Sail—
and in a few minutes the ship, from the appearance of a naked
tree could be as a cloud, in so short a time that a landsman
would hardly credit his own sight, was he a spectator."[9]

The same was true of gun drill, when the ship's company
was summoned to Action Stations by drums beating the
rhythm of *Hearts of Oak*, Garrick's naval anthem composed
after the battle of Quiberon Bay. On the Middle-Deck, for
example, there would be some 180 men under two lieutenants
and five midshipmen. Each pair of 24-pounder guns had two
captains, one for starboard, one for larboard if the ship was
fighting both sides at once. Boarding parties stood ready with
cutlasses and pikes, lantern and firemen with buckets and
swabs, powder monkeys to fetch the powder and cartridges
from the magazines, gun crews ready to sponge, worm, load
and run out the heavy guns, each captain holding a smoulder-
ing match over the touch-hole. Every man and boy had his
duty allotted to him and stood ready for the supreme order
for which the whole floating machine was designed—Fire!

By Nelson's day all the details about running such a complicated thing as a ship were printed in useful little handbooks,
but from an early date admirals and captains had been in the
habit of issuing their own Standing Orders to supplement the
Admiralty Orders. Howe's, for example, cover such subjects

as how to form a ship's company into divisions, the duties of Marines and sentries, means for the preservation of health and cleanliness, rules for exercises in sail or gun drill. In a handbook published by an anonymous captain in 1804, which is practical, humane, and clearly expressed, the ideal captain is exhorted in these terms:[10]

> Let the health, ease, comfort and happiness of those under his command be his domestic charge, reserving their strength for opportunities which will compensate his attention. A system clear and methodical; the execution of it precise and regular. A friend to good and deserving men; a terror to bad ones; the protector of the weak, and an impartial administrator of the whole.

II. DISCIPLINE

Such unofficial guides were intended to supplement what was laid down in the Naval Discipline Act and the *Regulations and Instructions Relating to H.M. Service at Sea*. The act of 1749 (22 Geo. II. c.33) repealed all former measures and continued in force with few alterations until 1866, the end of the period covered in this book. It embodies thirty-six Articles of War to be read when a ship was commissioned and to be posted up in some convenient place. These formed the code which courts martial enforced. But they are an inadequate guide to what actually occurred on board. For example, the first lays down that Divine Service shall be held daily, though this was frequently omitted before the nineteenth century. Many carry the death penalty for Desertion, Mutiny, Sleeping on Watch, Correspondence with the Enemy, Cowardice, Failing to Pursue (No. 13, under which Admiral Byng was condemned) and Robbery. Theft was punished by flogging with a thieves' cat, in which there were more knots than usual. Capital punishment was, in fact, seldom imposed except for heinous crimes such as mutiny.

The Admiralty's Regulations were first printed in 1731 and went through thirteen editions almost unchanged until a new and expanded edition was completed in 1806. The chapter on Punishments had included the order that "No commander shall inflict any punishment upon a seaman beyond 12 lashes upon his bare back with a cat-o'-nine-tails, according to the ancient practice of the sea." No commissioned or warrant officer could be so treated. If the fault deserved severer punishment, the offender must be confined until a court martial was called. By 1806 no one seems to have paid much attention to this, to judge from the punishments entered in the logs. So in the new edition the captain is instructed in general terms "not to suffer the inferior Officers and Men to be treated with cruelty or oppression by their superiors. He alone is to order punishment to be inflicted, which he is never to do without sufficient cause, nor ever with greater severity than the offence shall really deserve."

It is frequently forgotten that naval punishments must be seen in the context of the age. They were not so severe as those inflicted in the Army, but they were terrible enough. Apart from hanging from the yard arm, the worst was a flogging round the fleet. The first instance of this seems to have been in 1698, when two petty officers found guilty of concealing a plot to mutiny were sentenced "to forfeit all pay due to them and to receive 6 lashes alongside every ship between Rochester and Gillingham."[11] During the nine years of the War of the Austrian Succession there were twenty such floggings of more than one hundred lashes. The appalling spectacle of a flogging round the fleet is described by many lower deck writers. The rigging of every ship was manned to witness punishment as the boat on which the sufferer was tied to a scaffold came alongside, the drums beating the Rogue's March, and a fresh boatswain's mate went down the side to take over his share of inflicting the punishment, which usually maimed a man for life.

Much more common was the order "All hands ahoy to witness punishment" for a flogging at the gangway or Jacob's Ladder leading up to the quarter-deck. The officers mustered on the spar deck, the people on the main deck and the Marines were drawn up on the quarter-deck. The cat used was an inch thick, two feet long, fixed to a stock covered with red baize. "The prisoner is made to strip to his waist; he is then seized by his wrists and knees to a grating or ladder; the boatswain's mate is then ordered to cut him with a cat-o'-nine-tails; and after six or twelve lashes are given, another boatswain's mate is called to continue the exercise; and so they go on until the captain gives word to stop. From one to five dozen lashes are given, according to the captain's whim, but the general number is three dozen; and this number the captain has power to give every day, if he has any bad feeling for an individual; and a tyrant of a captain will frequently tell the boatswain's mate to lay it on harder, or that he should be flogged himself. This punishment is also inflicted without trial by court martial, at the discretion of the captain."[12]

The worst unofficial punishments were Running the Gauntlet (or Gantlope) and Starting. For the former the entire ship's company were armed with "nettles" or cords knotted at intervals to strike the man who, bared to the waist, ran between the lines. It was abolished in 1806.[13]

Starting with a rattan was the most frequent punishment because it was quite arbitrary. Life could be made a hell by a tyrannical boatswain, or even by a midshipman who told the nearest mate to start a man—"those little minions of power drove me round like a dog," complained Leech. It was officially abolished in 1809, so that in Captain Price Cumby's journal of 1811 he says, "The highly improper practice of what is called starting the men is most peremptorily forbidden." But it continued in one form or another for a long time to come, even after its official abolition as a result of a court martial described below.

With the heterogeneous crews shipped on board as a result of impressment, discipline had to be strict, but the temptations for a sadist were very great. There cannot have been many such officers, and even the mutineers of 1797 did not officially complain of the punishments. Flag officers normally dealt swiftly with captains accused of brutality. Thus Captain Lord William Hervey was dismissed the service in 1742. Charnock, the naval biographer, dismisses him thus: "This gentleman, though so nobly descended and honourably educated, appears to have been very ill-qualified for a naval commander; austere in his disposition, even to a degree of cruelty, he became at once an object of both terror and hatred to his people."[14]

Captain Pigot met his deserts when he was murdered by the mutineers of the *Hermione*. There were others like him, if we may credit the petitions reaching the Admiralty before the outbreak at Spithead.[15]

In 1795 the ship's company of the *Bellerophon* wrote "We must be under the necessity of delivering up the *Bellerophon* without we find a great alteration in the conduct of Lord Cranston and the other officers." The men of four other ships make similar allegations: "We are put on board H.M. ships to fight and protect King and Country, but we are really used like dogs." The next year it was the turn of the *Shannon* —"our Captain is one of the most barbarous and inhuman of officers"—the *Brunswick*, *Eemrald*, and *Reunion*: "Captain Baynham has punished more men in the short time he has been with us than Captain Alms did in two years."

If the official grievances as presented by the Delegates of the Fleet to the Admiralty in the mutineers of 1797 were not concerned with discipline, there are many complaints in the petitions from particular ships. On 19 April the men of the *Glory* and *Duke* ask for the dismissal of officers by whom they have been "cruelly and unmercifully beaten." On 22 April the midshipmen of the *Ramillies* are described as "being of a most cruel and vindictive disposition," and the surgeon guilty of "extreme inhumanity and inattention to the sick." On 30 May the men of the *Prospero* complain of "the severest punishment for the smallest offences by three or four dozen lashes without any court of enquiry." Such complaints are supported by a letter to the First Lord written by Lieutenant James Burney (brother of Fanny Burney and a shipmate of Cook) to the effect that "the misapplication of the Articles of War and the power of punishment vested in individual hands is too well known to require proof. I served in a ship where every one of the maintopmen were stripped and flogged at the gangway for no other cause than that another ship in company got her topgallant yards up first, and not for any wilful negligence on the part of our men."

Let us take a later example to show that, although many of the lessons taught in 1797 were heeded, a captain on detached service abroad could still drive his men to mutiny. The court martial which resulted is important, because it occasioned the official order that starting must be discontinued as "extremely disgusting to the feelings of British seamen."[16]

Towards the end of 1808 the Commander-in-Chief of the East Indies station received a petition from the crew of H.M.S. *Nereide* at Bombay complaining that they "never before experienced such oppressive usage as we now labour under, under the command of Captain Robert Corbet, whose capricious temper on the least occasion will cause us to be beaten with large sticks." Twenty-three men had already deserted before the men mutinied off Madagascar. The rising was suppressed and a court martial was held in January, 1809, at which two men were found guilty but only one hanged in view of the circumstances revealed by the evidence.

These were described in more detail at the court martial of Corbet himself on 6 February. According to the prosecution, "he punished men with such cats as is customary in other ships in H.M. service to punish a thief, and when the skin was broke has put salt pickle on their backs; it is common to seize men up to the Jacob's ladder on the quarter-deck and beat them with sticks which we trust on your inspection you will allow to be such sticks and cats as are not customary in the service." One witness stated that he could not stand after being beaten with a broomstick. Another testified: "I was started to that degree I could not lift my right arm to my head," and for several months passed blood after "the flogging I got on my loins."

Corbet's defence was that this was the first occasion in twenty years' service, eight in command of a ship, on which his conduct had been arraigned. He protested that he "used no new method of punishment, no instruments unheard of or forbidden by law." He took over a ship's company which had served under a discipline "very contrary to what my ideas have pointed out to be as most beneficial to H.M. service." His threat to intertwine wire in the thongs of the cat was merely *in terrorem*. "An idea has crept in and is gaining head that the punishment they call starting is not legal. I combat this opinion strongly; it has been one of the customs used at sea since I have known it."

The court found the charges of cruelty partly proved and recommended a reprimand. The Admiralty put the question beyond doubt by prohibiting starting. Corbet himself was transferred to the *Africaine*, on board which he was killed in action with two French frigates the next year. The contemporary historian James rejects the rumour that he was shot by his own men, but adds a very unusual comment on his career: "He was an exceptionally severe officer. We trace him in his career of cruelty from the *Seahorse* to the *Nereide*, from the *Nereide* to the *Bourbonnaise* and from her to the

Africaine." What is so shocking about the case is that such a
man should so long have been in command of a ship.

Happily, far more numerous are the requests of men to be
turned over with a captain when he was appointed to another
ship. Nelson received many such testimonials to his popularity. An earlier example is Boscawen, whose men "beg and
desire the favour of your Honour to let us have the opportunity of entering on board H.M. ships under your command."
But neither he nor Nelson obeyed the regulations regarding
summary punishments, to judge from their logs. When in the
Namur Boscawen had to refuse shore leave, his men rioted
with cutlasses shouting "Liberty, liberty, it was liberty we
fought for and liberty we will have!" Next morning all reported for duty. After the riot fifty-seven men were charged,
three hanged, four sentenced to 500 lashes, two to 400, three
to 300, two to 200 and one to one hundred: the rest were
acquitted.

Lack of shore leave was a grievance which finds pride of
place in the 1797 petitions. But it could seldom be granted in
home ports because of the danger of desertion. Unless there
was an unusual degree of trust between the captain and the
crew, the temptation was too great. Admiral Penrose recalls
with pride that his ship was at Spithead in 1797 and because
he allowed each division in turn to go ashore he only lost
two men, whereas the ship alongside which had boats rowing
round it to prevent desertion lost far more. Captain Griffiths
in 1811 allowed it, "and I can never forget when hands were
turned up and the announcement made, the gleam of joy
which lighted up every countenance." He lost eleven men
out of three hundred.[18]

Because of this lack of shore leave, boat loads of prostitutes
met every ship when she arrived in harbour. No women were
supposed to be taken to sea, though officers frequently received permission to do so. Sailor's wives were occasionally
allowed to travel short distances as passengers. In Queen

Anne's day they served on board hospital ships, but their predilection for drink led to their replacement by male nurses for the next two hundred years.[19] Nevertheless some women found their way on board, where they were expected to live off their husband's rations. A baby born on board the *Tremendous* at the Glorious First of June was christened Daniel Tremendous Mackenzie. Another was born at the battle of the Nile where, according to John Nicol, his news of what was going on on deck was got from boys and women carrying up powder, "the women behaved as well as the men." One of them later petitioned Nelson for a pension on the grounds that she had assisted the surgeon for eleven weeks afterwards. When the strait-laced Gambier took over the *Defence* he insisted that all women must show their marriage lines: "Those that had any produced them: those that had not contrived to manufacture a few. This measure created an unpleasant feeling among the tars," writes Lieutenant Dillon.[20]

A pamphlet published anonymously in 1822, entitled *Statement of Certain Immoral Practices in H.M. Ships*, lifts the lid off the scene on board the lower deck of most ships in harbour. Its author was Admiral Hawkins, who seems to have been one of the Evangelical officers whose efforts did so much to improve the tone of the Navy after the war was over. His picture may be somewhat overcoloured, but there can be no doubt that what he describes was a common sight at places like Portsmouth.

It is well known that immediately on the arrival of a ship of war in port, crowds of boats flock off with cargoes of prostitutes. Having no money to pay for their conveyance, the waterman takes as many as his boat will hold, upon speculation, and hovers round the ship until she is secured at her anchors and the necessary work done, when he, with others, is permitted to come alongside. The men then go into the boats and pick out each a woman (as one would choose cattle), paying a shilling or two to the boatman for her passage off. These women are examined at the gangway for liquor which they are constantly in the habit of smuggling on board. They then descend to the lower deck with their husbands, as they call them. Hundreds come off to a large ship. The whole of the shocking, disgraceful transactions of the lower deck it is impossible to describe—the dirt, filth, and stench; the disgusting conversation; the indecent, beastly conduct and horrible scenes; the blasphemy and swearing; the riots, quarrels, and fighting, which often takes place, where hundreds of men and women are huddled together in one room, as it were, and where, in bed (each man being allowed only fourteen inches breadth for his hammock), they are squeezed between the next hammocks and must be witnesses of each other's actions; can only be imagined by those who have seen all this. A ship in this state is often, and justly, called by the more decent seamen "a hell afloat". Let those who have never seen a ship of war picture to themselves a very large low room (hardly capable of holding the men) with 500 men and probably 300 or 400 women of the vilest description shut up in it, and giving way to every excess of debauchery that the grossest passions of human nature can lead them to; and they see the deck of a 74-gun ship the night of her arrival in port.

The most important document representing the grievances of seamen at the end of the eighteenth century is the final petition of the mutineers at Spithead in 1797. This was composed with that sense of responsibility which characterised the first outbreak, the second at the Nore being a far more dangerous and unnecessary demonstration. We limit our complaints, the Delegates of the seamen declare, "in order to convince the nation at large that we know when to cease to ask, as well as to begin, and that we ask nothing but what is moderate, and may be granted without detriment to the nation."[21]

In the first place they complain that their wages are so low they cannot support their families. Next, they object to the purser's commission of two ounces in the pound, and the lack of fresh vegetables and meat when in harbour. Thirdly, they ask that the sick be better attended to. Finally, "that we may be looked upon as a number of men standing in the defence of our country; and that we may in somewise have grant and opportunity to taste the sweets of liberty on shore, when in any harbour, and when we have completed the duty of our ship, after our return from sea."

Most of these requests were granted by Act of Parliament or Admiralty Order, but not the last. On the other hand, it cannot be pretended that everyday life on board was materially altered until the decade after Trafalgar. Overcrowding, with all its attendant evils, and the severity of punishments, continued until national security was attained and the size of the Navy reduced. The chief reward gained by the succession of great naval victories was a rise in the status and popularity of the British seaman. No longer despised as a social outcast, or pitied as the victim of an unjust system, he became admired as the chief defender of the country at a period when the Army played a small and inglorious part in its defence. Nothing manifests this change of attitude better than the number of popular products dating from this time, which range from Staffordshire and Sunderland pottery to ballads, songs and innumerable cartoons of which the British tar is represented in the image of the national hero.

III. PAY AND PROMOTION

The scale of seamen's wages did not alter between 1653 and 1797, when the First Lord of the Admiralty was still objecting (as had all his predecessors) that a rise would make "an enormous increase to our disbursements already sufficiently burthensome."

The Able Seaman was paid 24/- a month, the Ordinary

Seaman 19/- and when the rating of Landsmen was introduced he received 18/-. Out of this, sixpence had to be contributed to the Royal Hospital, a groat of fourpence to the chaplain (who only received 19/- a month officially) and twopence to the surgeon (who got £5), together with a fine if a man was suffering from venereal disease. Volunteers received, in addition, their bounties, and Warrant Officers were reasonably paid at a rate of £4 a month.

The wage bill at the beginning of the century was in a parlous state owing to the abuses of the ticket system, or payment on tick short for ticket. In 1710, 4,503 men were claiming for unpaid tickets, and "there is hardly a man now in the fleet who has not wages due to him in one or more ships and though standing Discharged on those ships, would if they had liberty to come ashore, apply for their wages and make great clamour if not immediately paid." There were 83,225 men unpaid on the books of the previous reign, 54,747 on those of the present, all of whom were entitled to "recalls" i.e. being given back pay. The Navy Board adds that 28,000 tickets had never been claimed. By 1711 the wage debt amounted to £2 million. The reasons for this were supposed to be dishonest captains who forged tickets and pocketed the proceeds, and the system of turning men over from one ship to another without payment of wages due. In 1728 desperate measures were taken to clear the wage debt. A grant in aid of £500,000 was made for the purpose and stringent regulations were laid down to prevent the debt increasing again.[22]

The next year an act to encourage seamen promised volunteers two months' payment in advance, and that all ships would be paid off at the end of twelve months. It was a breach of the cynical old maxim, "Keep the pay, keep the man," and in Vernon's opinion it was the best thing possible to reconcile seamen to the service of the Crown. Administrative difficulties, however, made it impossible to implement the act on all occasions, so that further measures had to be passed in 1758 and 1759 at the beginning of the next war.

What annoyed both officers and seamen was that their counterparts in the Army were better off. The common soldier, for example, received 30/- a month. Naval surgeons and chaplains only had their pay brought up to Army levels after repeated petitions. The only thing the men could do was to strike, that is, mutiny. Faced by the unyielding Delegates at Spithead, Parliament and Admiralty gave way and on 9 May, 1797, £373,000 was voted to raise the wages of Petty Officers and Able Seamen by 5/6 a month, that of Ordinary Seamen by 4/6, that of Landsmen by 3/6. In 1806 a further increase of 4/- and 2/- was made.[23] This brought the total monthly pay of an Able Seaman to 33/6, that of an Ordinary Seaman to 25/6, that of a Landsman to 22/6.

Low wages might have been supportable, since men received food and shelter, had they been punctually paid. The record of the Navy Board in this respect was far better than in the previous century, but for one reason or another there continued to be scandalous examples of failure to pay wages every eighteen months, according to the Regulations. Part of the trouble was that before the age of paper money, a ship could only be paid off in hard cash at a recognised port after all her pay books, muster books and a multitude of forms had been passed. Hence a ship on a foreign station could only be paid off on her return home. As late as 1811 Lord Cochrane quoted examples of one ship that had been eleven years out East, another fourteen, another fifteen, and none of the men had been paid at all. Penrose recalls how "I was once paid off in a 74-gun ship at Plymouth and many of her men had never set foot on land for six or seven years, except in the dockyard at Jamaica. Entirely exclusive of commissioned and warrant officers, the payment exceeded £22,000, and in a few hours some, and in a day or two many, of these valuable men were as penniless as if they had shared between them so many shillings."24

The delights of pay day are vividly described by Jack Nasty-face:25

> In the early part of the day the commissioners came on board, bringing the money which is paid the ship's crew, with the exception of six months pay, which it is the rule of the government to hold back from each man. The mode of paying is, as the names are, by rotation on the books: every man, when called is asked for his hat, which is returned to him with his wages in it, and the amount chalked on the rim. There is not perhaps one in twenty who actually knows what he is going to receive, nor does the particular amount seem to matter of much consequence; for, when paid, they hurry down to their respective berths, redeem their honour with their several ladies and bombboat (*sic*) men, and then they turn their thoughts to the Jew pedlars, who are ranged around the decks and on the hatchway gratings, in fact, the ship is crowded with them. They are furnished with every article that will rig out a sailor, never omitting a fine large watch and appendages, all warranted, and with which many an honest tar has been taken in: they can supply them likewise with fashionable rings and trinkets for their ladies, of *pure gold*, oh, nothing can be purer!

No man was going to be defrauded of the pleasures which a few days ashore could buy. There are many such letters as this from the *Portland* to the Port Admiral: "Sir, We have spoke to Capt. Bretan and he can give us no satisfactory answer; we hope you'll acquaint their Lordships to dispatch this ship into the harbour, as we have a right to be paid as well as other ships. If your Honour sends us word in answer to this, it will give us great satisfaction, as we immagen its within your power to order us in. Otherwise you may expect to see the ship either on shore or in the harbour with the first fair wind that occurs. We remain your Honour's humble servants, Ship's Company."26

Two supplementary bonuses may be mentioned before

we deal with other rewards. One was the ancient practice of carrying fictitious names on the ship's books to be borne for wages, not victuals. The act of 1733 allows two such Widow's Men per one hundred complement, stipulating that the pay standing in their names shall be distributed to the widows of men killed in action. Widow's Men ceased to exist in 1829. Similarly, dead men's clothes were auctioned on board, always fetching a high figure from the natural generosity of seamen.

This money was supplemented by the charitable energy of John Julius Angerstein, Chairman of Lloyd's in the Nelsonian era, who organised Lloyd's Patriotic Fund for the benefit of the wounded and widows. Originally this was a public subscription to celebrate a particular victory—£21,281 for the First of June, £15,587 for Copenhagen—and a total of £193,331 was raised in this way between 1793 and 1801. In 1803 Angerstein put the Fund on a permanent basis, asking every captain for a list of his casualties, for which Nelson often expressed his gratitude. Great numbers benefited in this way, for example Lt. Pasco, the man who hoisted Nelson's famous signal, got £100 for the loss of his arm at Trafalgar. The list of subscribers ranges from Lloyd's and the Bank of England down to three watermen of Shadwell Dock Stairs.[27]

The chief supplement to a man's pay continued to be Prize Money. The distribution of shares was so often changed that it would be tedious to enumerate the various Prize Acts. The important thing is that from the passing of the Prize act of 1708 the whole value of a prize went to its captors and the admiral commanding the station, the Crown waiving its share. Each man's share was detailed in various schedules depending on the number of men engaged. Frigates which were employed on commerce destruction were therefore popular ships, quite apart from the varied nature of the life, whereas big ships engaged in blockading duties seldom had a chance to reap much reward unless they fought in a successful battle. Commanders-in-Chief did not suffer in this way, because they continued to take their sixths of everything captured on their stations. For the seamen all depended whether he was serving on an amphibious expedition, such as that which captured Havana in 1762, when the Admiral's and General's share was £122,697 each, and every seaman received £3; or in the capture of the *Hermione* treasure ship that year by two frigates, whose captains got £65,000 each and every man £485.

The incentive which Prize Money offered may be judged by the concluding sentence of a letter written after Vernon's capture of Porto Bello: "Our dead admiral ordered every man some Spanish dollars to be immediately given, which is like a Man of Honour, and so is every man of us resolved either to lose our lifes or conker our enemys."[28] Such distribution on the spot at the capstan head was discouraged by the Vice-Admiralty Courts, where all prizes were condemned. The consequences were, as Cochrane once dramatically demonstrated at the Bar of the House of Commons, that prize lawyers held up distribution for years, charged extortionate fees, and often failed to pay out the rewards so hardly earned.

Prize shares, like wages, increased as a man moved up the naval hierarchy, but the chances of promotion from the lower-deck were minimal. Captain James Cook, who volunteered in 1755 and was rated a master's mate, is the classic example of how a man could rise if he had exceptional talent, opportunity and patronage. It was easier for a Master to be commissioned Lieutenant than it was for a Gunner, though the latter's examination for Warrant Officer ranks looks far more difficult than that for passing for Lieutenant. Professor Lewis, who has analysed the officer structure of the Nelsonian navy, estimates that the chance of a lower-deck man being commissioned a quarter-deck officer was one in 2,500. Seventy per cent of those who were successful never rose higher than Lieutenant; only $2\frac{1}{2}\%$ reached flag rank.[29]

To list a few notable examples. The First Lieutenant of the

Victory, John Quillian, and her Signal Lieutenant, John Pasco, reached flag rank from the lower deck. Jack Larmour never rose above Lieutenant. He was, says Cochrane, whose "sea daddy" he became, "one of the not very numerous class whom, for their superior seamanship, the Admiralty was glad to promote from the forecastle to the quarter-deck, in order that they might mould into shipshape the questionable materials supplied by Parliamentary influence, even then paramount in the Navy to a degree which might otherwise have led to disaster. Lucky was the commander who could secure such an officer for his quarter-deck." Such, too, was James Bowen, Master of the *Queen Charlotte* in Black Dick Howe's victory. Having warned the admiral that he would run foul of the enemy flagship if he held his course, and having received the reply "What's that to you, sir?" replied "Damn'd if I care, if you don't. I'll take you near enough to singe your black whiskers." Howe rewarded him with a lieutenant's commission and he reached the rank of rear-admiral in 1825.

IV. FOOD AND DRINK

The victualling scale of the Navy altered as slowly as the wage scale. For two hundred years the basic ship's provisions per man were 1 lb. salt pork or 2 lb. of beef on alternate days. There was a daily ration of 1 lb. biscuit and 1 gallon of beer, and a weekly issue of 2 pints of pease, 3 of oatmeal, 8 oz. butter and 1 lb. of cheese. On southern voyages a pint of wine or half pint of brandy was substituted for the beer, which never remained fresh for long at sea. Rice was issued instead of oatmeal, olive oil for butter. When in port fresh meat was usually obtainable, but fresh vegetables did not become the rule until the end of the century. The full measure of all articles was reduced by an eighth to compensate the purser for wastage or seepage.[30]

It was a substantial, if unbalanced, diet which compared favourably with what the average man would get on shore, where meat was very seldom eaten. The food was probably as good as that served in merchant ships, though it had serious dietetic deficiencies which led to frequent outbreaks of scurvy or dysentery. The two problems which the Victualling Board could never overcome were the difficulty of preserving food when salt was the only known preservative, and the dishonesty of contractors. The amount of food could not be criticised: it was the quality which was so often called in question. Since the purser himself was really a civilian contractor afloat, the temptation to make an excessive profit was very great.

There was a third problem which we are apt to forget—the conservative taste of seamen. Cook had to flog two men for refusing to eat fresh meat and Flinders had to do the same to those refusing soup. Almost at the end of Cook's journal there occurs this disillusioned comment—

> Every innovation whatever on board ship, though ever so much to the advantage of seamen, is sure to meet with their highest disapprobation. Both portable soup and sauerkraut were at first condemned as stuff unfit for human beings. Few commanders have introduced more novelties as useful varieties of food and drink than I have done. It has been in great measure owing to various little deviations from established practice that I have been able to preserve my people from that dreadful distemper, scurvy.

It would be easy to compile a Bad Food Guide from the comments of eighteenth-century pamphleteers. Every writer retails stories about buttons made from cheese as hard as horn, sour beer, stinking water, inedible meat, weevilly biscuit full of large black-headed maggots etc. To the modern palate the seamen's own popular messes would be just as nauseating—skillygolee, lobscouse, burgoo or Scotch coffee, mostly consisting of porridge with gobbets of meat floating in it, sometimes sweetened with a little sugar or made palatable with vinegar.

The one universally popular issue was grog, named after Vernon's grogram sea cloak on account of his order of 1740 that the half pint of rum be diluted by a quarter of a pint of water when issued twice a day at noon and at six o'clock in the evening. His object was to combat the eternal vice of seamen, drunkenness. A ballad commemorates the occasion:

> A mighty bowl on deck he drew
> And filled it to the brink;
> Such drank the *Burford's* gallant crew,
> And such the Gods shall drink;
> The sacred robe which Vernon wore
> Was drenched with the same;
> And hence its virtues guard our shore,
> And Grog derives its name.

The strength of grog was progressively reduced in response to complaints from captains and surgeons that it impaired the efficiency and the health of the men. Over half the punishments were occasioned by drunkenness. By Nelson's day the procedure was to issue the grog at noon to the tune of *Nancy Dawson*, when the cook from each mess collected a pint consisting of one gill of rum and three of water, to which might be added a little lemon juice and sugar. Some commanders grew so tired of flogging their men for drunkenness that they added a fourth gill of water, but this was a dangerous proceeding because grog was prized above all else. Even when this was done on board a happy ship, Robert Wilson reports that "two men were reported groggy in the afternoon," a remark which illustrates the origin of the adjective.

Manning the Chains, by Atkinson, c.1810

The Sailor's Return. From a painting by Wheatley, c.1800. The boy carries his wages as they have been paid him in his hat

The rum ration could not be touched officially as long as the war lasted, lest there should be a murmuring in the fleet, but the evening issue was abolished in 1824 and the ration reduced to one gill in 1850. Long before that, tea and cocoa had been introduced. The former came in 1790 and took some time to become popular. The credit for the latter goes to Captain James Ferguson in 1780. Surgeon Trotter urged that it be extended from the West Indies station (where it was cheap) to the Channel Fleet in words which generations of seamen have echoed: "In a cold country it could be singularly beneficial. What a comfortable meal would a cup of warm cocoa or chocolate be to a sailor in a winter cruise in the Channel or North Sea on coming from a wet deck in a rainy morning watch!"[31]

Nearly all the more palatable additions to the basic ship's provisions began as Surgeon's Necessaries, or special foods for the sick. It is to the representations of the surgeons that any slow improvements in diet occurred. Such were sugar, currants, rice, garlic and other spices, including the popular salop made from orchis roots and long thought to be a specific against scurvy. The most important innovation was Portable Soup, similar to broth made from cubes, of which one specimen from Cook's voyage has been preserved. It was the invention of Mrs. Dubois in 1756 and at first supplied by the well-known Plymouth apothecary, Cookworthy. There was also sauerkraut, or pickled cabbage, recommended by both Dr. Lind and George III, which was indeed a possible alternative to fresh vegetables.

The discovery which changed victualling completely in the long run was that of canned meat and vegetables, first tried out in the Channel Fleet in 1813. It became known as bully beef because it was adapted from the French recipe for *Boeuf Bouilli*. In 1866 the Victualling Office itself began to manufacture it. Unfortunately, the next year a notable prostitute named Fanny Adams was murdered and her body cut up into small pieces. The word, of course, went round that what the authorities were providing was Sweet Fanny Adams.

Had canned meat been invented a generation earlier, the lot of the blockading squadrons would have been immeasurably eased and the ships would have been able to keep the sea for longer periods. As it was, the chief reason for the greatly improved standard of health in Nelson's navy was better victualling, partly due to the insistence of the surgeons on the relationship between diet and disease, partly to the protests of the mutineers of 1797.

V. HEALTH

The number of seamen in time of war who died by ship-wreck, capture, famine, fire or sword are but inconsiderable in respect of such as are destroyed by the ship diseases and the usual maladies of intemperate climates," wrote Dr. James Lind at the beginning of the Seven Years War. The figures for that war bear him out: 133,708 men were lost by disease or desertion, compared with 1,512 killed in action.[32]

This degree of wastage made the manpower problem far more acute than it need have been. Towards the end of the century the health of the navy certainly improved, but at the same time the problem of desertion became more serious.

The wooden line-of-battle ship killed far more men by the nature of her construction than she ever did by her guns. We have seen how an unsatisfactory diet produced deficiency diseases. Equally harmful was the overcrowding of ships, the lack of adequate ventilation in bad weather when the ports were closed (in spite of the adoption of Dr. Hales's invention for Newgate prison, or Sutton's air pipes), the low standard of hygiene on board and the fetid atmosphere between decks— all provided a perfect breeding place for disease. Since a great deal of military activity took place in tropical areas such as the West Indies, huge numbers of soldiers and sailors died from Yellow Fever ("black vomit") or malaria ("ague"). Medical knowledge of such ailments was pathetically small, because it was based on the climatorial or miasmatic theory of pathology, according which all disease emanated from noxious exhalations. Even Lind shared this view; but as the author of the first book on tropical medicine, as well as on scurvy and hygiene, he and his disciples—Blane, Trotter and Robertson—achieved great improvements where improvement was possible before the days of antisepsis and bacteriology. Neither the construction of Plymouth and Portsmouth naval hospitals (Lind was the first superintendent of Haslar, the largest brick building in Europe), nor the innumerable noisome little hospitals around the coast and abroad, could solve any problem save that of accommodating the sick. In the eighteenth century a hospital was a place where one usually went to die, not to recover, and there is no greater error than to suppose that the great increase in population which occurred during the latter half of the century was related to improved medicine.

The wastage due to disease was already apparent in Anne's reign, when it was estimated that the number of sick in the navy averaged 9,000 out of the 50,000 men serving. On Anson's voyage round the world, the most infamously manned and equipped on record, 1,051 men died out of the 1,955 who embarked. After a six weeks' cruise of the Channel Fleet in the spring of 1780, 2,400 sufferers from scurvy were landed at Haslar.

The three killers in the Georgian navy were scurvy, typhus and yellow fever. Scurvy was specifically the scourge of the sea because it was a deficiency disease which disabled three times the number of men it killed. We know now that it is due to a lack of vitamin C, the vitamin found in fresh vegetables which were then so notably lacking. Its manifestations were so various that no two doctors could agree on a reason or a cure, until Lind, shocked by the record of Anson's voyage, carried out the first controlled dietary experiment on record on board H.M.S. *Salisbury* in 1747 and published the results in his *Treatise of the Scurvy* in 1753. He put twelve cases on the same basic diet of salt provisions and added, for every two men, either elixir of vitriol, vinegar, salt water, an electuary of garlic and mustard, or two oranges and one lemon daily. By the end of the week the last two were fit for duty: the rest died. It was a conclusive experiment. Yet it took the Admiralty forty years to order a regular issue of lemon juice after six weeks on salt provisions, one reason for the delay being that Cook advised against it as too expensive. Since his voyages were such a contrast to that of Anson, and since the Royal Society awarded him a medal for the preservation of the health of his ship's company, his judgement rather than that of Lind was accepted. The true reason for Cook's excellent standard of health was that he gave his men a great variety of food, fresh whenever possible, and that his ships were the best equipped in men and victuals that ever sailed from this country in that century.

It was far otherwise in the big ships of the blockading squadrons. After every cruise, hundreds of men in various stages of scurvy were landed until after the American War of Independence, when the influential Sir Gilbert Blane, Rodney's personal physician, who became a Commissioner for Sick and Wounded, took up the cudgels on Lind's behalf. As he wrote, "Fifty lemons might be considered as a hand to the fleet, inasmuch as the health and perhaps the life of a man would thereby be spared." Supporting him was Thomas Trotter, Physician of the Channel Fleet at the beginning of the Revolutionary war. Between them they persuaded the

Admiralty in 1795 to order an issue of lemon juice to the whole crew, not just to the sick. Ten years later this "certain specific," as a medical handbook of the time calls it, had almost abolished scurvy. When we find Nelson ordering 50,000 gallons of lemon juice from Sicily we can understand the high standard of health which his fleet enjoyed. Unfortunately in the middle of the next century, lime juice was substituted for lemon because it was cheaper, though we now know that it possesses only half the antiscorbutic properties. By the beginning of the twentieth century medical knowledge of the disease was as ill-informed as it was in the days before Lind. Only when vitamins were discovered was the real cause of the disease made apparent.

The pathology of fever was equally confused because one type could not be distinguished from another. For a long time it was thought that ship, gaol and camp fever were different diseases, until it was found that they were all types of typhus. A comparison between the incidence of typhus and scurvy from the numbers per thousand sick at Haslar is as follows:

Year	Scurvy	Typhus
1759	119	393
1782	329	257
1799	20	200

One example will show how easily typhus, of which the body louse infesting dirty clothing is the carrier, spread through a fleet. In 1770 the *Tartar* frigate took on board 200 men, described as the refuse of mankind, from the receiving ship at the Nore. By the time she reached Deal the surgeon diagnosed seventy cases of typhus. By the time she reached Spithead almost the entire crew had to be landed at Haslar. No wonder the surgeons protested that only a clean uniform issued to every recruit would keep the number on the sick list down.

Men fresh from England enjoyed no immunity from tropical diseases, of which malaria was the most common and yellow fever the most fatal. A form of malaria common at Sheerness was called ague, but the forms found abroad were far more fatal. In the end it was kept at bay by the issue of Peruvian or Jesuit's bark, replaced by quinine at the time of the Crimean War, as a prophylactic. No one realised until the end of the nineteenth century that both malaria and yellow fever was caused by infected mosquitoes. In spite of all the recommendations made by Lind to anchor well out to sea, to avoid boat work as much as possible, to fumigate the ship, Yellow Jack, as it was commonly called, otherwise Black Vomit, carried off hundreds of men in the Navy and thousands more in the Army, where there was no alternative to sleeping on shore.

Of the other diseases common on board mention must be made of dysentery ("the bloody flux") which killed thirty-one men on Cook's first voyage, on which none died of scurvy. With the type of women allowed on board, venereal disease ("the pox") was common and until 1795 a man suffering from it had to pay a fifteen shilling fine to the surgeon, with the consequence that many cases went unreported until too late for mercurial treatment. On the other hand, smallpox was conquered by Jenner's discovery of vaccination. Trotter enthusiastically supported this, so that by 1800 all men were invited to volunteer for vaccination, which did not become compulsory until 1864. Judging by the number of trusses issued, about one-seventh of the navy of Nelson's day suffered from hernias, due to all the pulling and hauling required. Tubercular consumption was on the increase, but it was difficult to diagnose and treatment was useless: the evidence suggests that it became more widespread after the introduction of iron ships, on account of the condensation they suffered.

The panacea for most surgeons continued to be blood-letting. The result was frequently fatal. But many of them must have been skilful operators. In the age before antisepsis and anæsthetics, everything depended on the speed of an operation. The danger came afterwards, on account of tetanus and gangrene developing in the unhygienic surroundings of the midshipmen's cockpit. In this badly lit and badly ventilated hole on the orlop deck below the water line was the table used for surgical operations, the patient being partly stupefied with rum and a leather gag put between his teeth.

Before 1780, when Blane and Robertson began to record their cases, medical statistics are unreliable and scarce. Evidence from the hospital records shows a great advance during the last quarter of the century. In 1779 the hospital sick rate was 1 in 2.45; in 1813 it was 1 in 10.75. The hospital mortality rate in 1780 was 1 in 8; in 1812 it was 1 in 30; in 1836, 1 in 72; in 1913, 1 in 309.

The following table gives a general view of the chief causes of death between 1792 and 1815:

Causes of Death	Totals	Percentages
Disease and Accident	84,440	81.5
Foundering, Wreck, Fire	12,680	12.2
Enemy Action	6,540	6.3
Total	103,660	100

The striking thing is the low casualty figure for those killed in action. In six battles analysed by Professor Lewis only 1,483 men were killed and 4,266 wounded. At Trafalgar 449 were killed and 1,241 wounded out of 18,725 men engaged.[33]

A table based on hospital records, because medical statistics from surgeon's logs were not collated until 1840, shows the extent of the wastage of manpower due to disease and to desertion, since hospitals were easier places to escape from than ships.

Year	No. Voted	Sick	Dead	Run from Hospital
1779	70,000	28,592	1,658	997
1782	100,000	31,617	2,222	993
1794	85,000	21,373	1,606	563
1813	140,000	13,071	977	13

Had not something like a revolution in hygiene and treatment, within the limits possible at that date, occurred during the decade prior to the Nelsonian epoch, had the mortality been equal to that of the preceding war, according to Blane, "the whole stock of seamen would have been exhausted . . . For there would have died annually 6,674 men, which, in twenty years, would have amounted to 133,480, a number which very nearly equals the whole number of seamen and marines employed in the last year of the war."

VI. DESERTION

The number of deserters from the navy can never be ascertained until all the names marked Run in all the muster books are counted up. Even then, many rejoined under another name, or were apprehended later. Desertion was an age-old problem which increased as the number of pressed men grew. It varied from station to station, being worst in the West Indies, where merchant skippers could offer as much as £45 to tempt a man to desert and make the return trip home. In 1742 Vernon informed the Admiralty of "the great reduction of our seamen by death and desertion, not less than 500 having deserted from the hospital in Port Royal since my being in command; which I believe to have all been seduced out and gone home with the homeward bound trade, through the temptations of high wages and 30 gallons of rum, and being generally conveyed drunk on board their ships from the punch houses where they are seduced." By the end of that war the alarming fact became apparent that the manpower of the fleet was actually decreasing in spite of wider impressment, on account of mass desertion.[34]

Measures taken to check desertion included stoppage of shore leave, keeping the sick on board, withholding pay as long as possible, and (oddly enough) issuing proclamations pardoning deserters if they rejoined the service. Each of these checks carried with it peculiar difficulties and even the threat of the death penalty or a flogging round the fleet failed as a deterrent. Clemency was the easier way out. In 1742 the Board assured deserters that they would be paid their wages if they rejoined their ships, and a proclamation of 1758 promises to take the "R" from their names if they do so. The previous year it was officially reckoned that 13,047 men had been lost by death or sickness and that 4,748 had deserted.[35]

Between 1774 and 1780 it was estimated that whereas 175,990 men had been raised, 1,243 had been killed, 18,541 had died of disease and 42,069 deserted.[36] The American War was undoubtedly the worst on record from the point of view of wastage, so that such figures go far to explain both the reasons for the British lack of success at sea and the arbitrary methods adopted on land to make good such loss of manpower.

During the ten years war against the French Revolution we have quoted Nelson's guess that 42,000 men deserted. In the succeeding ten years the frequency of desertion increased, the example of men like Robert Hay becoming common with many others. Admiral Philip Patton made the following estimate for the period 1803-1805:[37]

Invalided by surveys	3,017
Able Seamen deserted	5,662
Ordinary Seamen deserted	3,903
Landsmen deserted	2,737
Total lost	15,319

What is significant about this indictment of service conditions and recruiting methods is, firstly, that Able Seamen deserted at a proportionally higher rate because they found good berths in the merchant service more easily; secondly, that while the sick rate was decreasing, the desertion rate was increasing. It is thus not surprising that on board the French flagship at Trafalgar there were said to be sixteen British deserters, and that so many men preferred to ship on board an American vessel if they could escape from the Royal Navy. A contemporary suggests that some 16,000 adopted the latter course.

To complete this gloomy picture, let us take a ship with the time-honoured name of *Revenge*. In the seven years between 1805 and 1811 she took on board 2,100 men in order to maintain her complement of 640. Such is Jack Nasty-face's statement and a modern check proves that he was correct, if the supernumeraries borne for victuals are included.[38]

Only better conditions on board could prevent wastage on this scale. As early as 1745 Vernon pointed out: "To be sure, the most effectual method to prevent desertions would be procuring some more humane method of manning our ships and of having our men more regularly paid in the service."[39] But, for reasons which have already been explained, this was impossible to achieve. So the vicious circle continued unbroken, with impressment becoming more rigorous and the reputation of the service more distasteful, until the great wars were over.

XII

The End of Impressment

MANNING THE NAVY by means of impressment inevitably ceased between the end of the Napoleonic wars and the outbreak of the Crimean War on account of the small size of the defence forces it was necessary to maintain. Immediately after the peace, demobilisation was rapid and radical. Petitions for discharge were acceded to with unusual promptitude: masters asking for apprentices, wives for husbands. Members of Parliament begging favours, and consuls demanding the return of their nationals: even in August 1815, 238 Swedes, twenty-one Russians and ten Danes were sent down to the Nore. At no other date would the Secretary of the Admiralty be able to minute one such petition: "This seems a pitiable case. Does it admit of relief without prejudice to the service?"[1]

Anxiety on the part of petitioners was only equalled by the Admiralty's desire to get rid of the men as quickly as possible, in the interests of economy. In 1813 there were in service ninety-nine ships of the line and 495 cruisers, manned by 130,127 men. In 1817 there were only thirteen of the line, eighty-nine smaller vessels and 22,944 men. The following table illustrates the rundown and the comparatively small increase necessitated by the Crimean War. (See next page.)

While the number of men (though not boys) was thus drastically reduced and the navy settled down to an average strength of between thirty and forty thousand men, the officer

Number of Men Borne, 1813-65

1813—130,127	1847—44,969
1817— 22,944	1853—45,885
1827— 33,106	1855—67,791
1837— 31,289	1865—67,712

corps was left virtually untouched because of the social and political interests involved. The consequences were to prove a serious handicap to efficiency over the next twenty years. Since there was no distinction between an Active and Retired list until 1864, only that between Full Pay and Half Pay, for every ten ships in commission there might be a hundred officers chasing posts. Something like 90% of the officers on the list remained unemployed, so that a fantastic ratio of men to officers was reached: in 1813 there were 28.7 men to every officer, in 1817 only 3.2.[2]

This failure to demobilise a proportion of the officers, along with the rigid rule of promotion by seniority, resulted in the upper reaches of the Navy List becoming blocked with ageing captains and admirals, most of them well over sixty years old. Young lieutenants found little chance of advancement, and there were no more commissions for men of working-class origins. As the Radical Joseph Hume complained in one of his annual attacks on the Naval Estimates, "Promotion in the army and navy is reserved for the aristocracy."

More serious from a national point of view was the age of admirals who, by the seniority rule, had to be given command when occasion arose. At the outbreak of the Crimean War the Commander-in-Chief in the Baltic, Sir Charles Napier (who a few years previously had said that admirals would now require nurses if they put to sea) was sixty-eight, his colleague in the Black Sea sixty-nine. Cochrane, now Earl of Dundonald, felt affronted at being refused a command at the age of seventy-nine: he had a case, because the Commander-in-Chief at Portsmouth was eighty-one.

This increasing age of senior officers undoubtedly delayed reforms in the way a ship was run. Old men brought up in wartime routine were slow to adopt changes which a more liberal Admiralty was anxious to make. When Exmouth's son, Sir Fleetwood Pellew, was appointed Commander-in-Chief, East Indies, at the age of sixty-four, after being unemployed for thirty-one years, a mutiny occurred because he was unwilling to allow his men the shore leave which was now common. Whig and Radical critics were exasperated at the slow rate of change, thougn it is hardly to the credit of the former that after they came into power little more was done than a thorough overhaul of the administrative machinery of the navy and still further financial savings. Until the international scene began to change in the forties, until the French and Russian navies began to expand, Britannia ruled the waves without troubling to alter her habits, either in the structure of the navy or in the ships employed.

One precaution which the Admiralty did take was to prevent any mass discharge of boy seamen. Every year a satisfactory rate of entry continued from the old sources, the Marine Society and the Royal Hospital School, though it was noted that the boys from the Upper School preferred the merchant service, only the more illiterate boys from the Lower School joining the Royal Navy. As they grew up, such boys formed the nucleus of the lower-deck and, in a way, the earliest members of the continuous service scheme which was tò change the face of the navy. With them may be counted the Royal Marines, who formed the only available reserve until the middle of the century. They were a standing force: unfortunately, when a ship was commissioned in a hurry, they were incapable of fitting her out because they were not trained in seamanship.

Hostility between merchant seamen and the Royal Navy certainly diminished during thirty years of peace, largely because the two services were growing further apart, just as their ships were even more distinct. It was replaced by ignorance of what the Navy had to offer as a career. The latter was increasingly manned from the southern counties, the former from the north and Scotland. Since men were no longer pressed out of one service into the other, each went its own way and neither lacked recruits in the lean years after the peace, when men in industry and even more in agriculture were on a starvation level.

Even within the merchant service there were sharp distinctions—the tough Geordie colliers, the superior seamen of the Indiamen who sailed Blackwall fashion, the Packet Rats of Liverpool, who have been called "the hardest men in the world, the most reckless, the most lawless, and in some cases the most fearless."[3] During the Clipper Ship epoch, when sailorising reached its climax, the Royal Navy saw little of such men. Its standards of diet and accommodation were generally far higher than those under which merchant seamen sailed before the Merchant Shipping Act of 1854, an act largely due to Cardwell, President of the Board of Trade. For the first time there was effective supervision of the build, registration, and conditions on board merchant vessels, and even of the competence of those who commanded them.

During the long debates which ended with the abolition of the last vestiges of the Navigation Acts in 1849, the admirals viewed with dismay the prospect of an end to that pool of seamen on which the navy had drawn for so many centuries. Without a flourishing merchant marine, said Admiral Sir T. Byam Martin, the navy could not exist. He was, of course, correct, but not in the sense which he intended. Nor were those shipowners who prophesied the assassination of British shipping at the hands of foreign competition. In fact, with the coming of the iron ship, British tonnage nearly doubled in twenty years, and with it the number of sailors. In 1850 U.K.

tonnage amounted to about 3½ million; in 1864, it was over 7 million.

A long period of peace produced innumerable attacks on Impressment in pamphlets (many of them by naval officers) and on the floor of the House of Commons. The admirals fought a rearguard action to maintain it in principle, but even they recognised that it could no longer be enforced in practice. Even Hume the radical, while stressing the unpopularity of the navy on account of its discipline, admitted that "the men had less labour, better food, better regulations, and more advantages than in the merchant service."[4] The one thing they had not got was better pay, though this gradually improved.

Year	*Table of Monthly Pay, 1797-1862*		
	Able Seamen	*Ordinary Seamen*	*Landsmen*
1797	£1. 9. 6.	£1. 3. 6.	£1. 2. 6.
1806	1. 13. 6.	1. 5. 6.	1. 2. 6.
1844	1. 14. 0.	1. 6. 0.	1. 3. 0.
1852	2. 1. 4.	1. 13. 7.	1. 8. 5.
1862	2. 9. 1.	1. 18. 9.	(abolished)

Stokers, instituted in 1826, received £2. 6. 0. rising to £2. 14. 3, with a 50% increase in the tropics when steam was up.

In 1831 a pension scheme for those serving over twenty-one years was introduced. More classes of Petty Officer were created in 1839 and their pay increased. Ten years later the gold lace stripe denoting a good conduct badge was introduced for those serving over five years, but by a piece of official stupidity if such a man became a Petty Officer he forfeited his good conduct bonus: a few years later this was rectified and the grievance of the Warrant Officers that their widow's pensions had been abolished was remedied.

Let us take a look at conditions in the service in 1827, the year of Navarino, the last great battle under sail. There is a lively account of the battle from the pen of Charles McPherson, who printed an anonymous account of his two years' experiences in the Navy, which he entered at the age of seventeen.[5] He joined the *Genoa*, 74, Captain Bathurst, a 60-year old veteran of the French Wars, "greatly beloved of the whole crew." She was the first ship to have a Commander (called Under Captain) according to the new regulations. Her Mediterranean cruise was agreeable enough, especially on moonlight nights when the order was given to pipe all hands to dance. She played a notable part in Codrington's fleet at Navarino, where she lost twenty-six men including her captain, even though at one point she fired on one of the allied ships, instead of the enemy.

McPherson speaks of nine Petty Officers' wives on board, who acted as nurses. He adds this typical account of a burial at sea: "I was making my way down the after-ladder when I met two of the men bearing a purser's bread bag, which I knew would contain the body of one of my shipmates. I asked who it was. 'Why,' said one, 'it's your messmate Tom Morfet—dead at last.' At this I could not contain myself. 'Lay him down here,' I said, 'and I'll wrap him in his spare hammock, and bury him myself, for you know he was my companion.' 'You're welcome to the job,' they said, as they deposited the body between two guns and left me." He got a friend to read the Burial Service while he slung a 32-lb. shot to the feet and pushed the body out of a gunport. Supper that night was punctuated by the sound of Turkish ships blowing up, which elicited the casual remark "There's another of the B—s blown up!"

The new captain was "despotic to the last degree, and used the thieves cat for the most trifling offence. Many a poor fellow who had fought bravely at Navarino Bay had his back torn and lacerated by the cat, for faults which under the ancient regime would only have been punished by a stoppage of grog. The *Genoa* was no longer *The Happy Genoa*." There

British Plenty. From a painting by Singleton, c.1800, showing some of the inhabitants of Portsmouth Point

Sailors in 1854 by G. Thomas. From *The Illustrated London News*

was no more shore leave and flogging occurred daily. Is it surprising that a lively lad like McPherson should leave the service as soon as his ship paid off?

Flogging died a long slow death, chiefly because officers of the old school were unwilling to give it up, in spite of the Admiralty's efforts to minimise it. An order of 1830 urges "a safe forebearance" on the part of captains, making more than two dozen without a trial illegal. Quarterly returns of all punishments were now demanded and from 1853 these were submitted to Parliament. From these we know that 2,007 men were flogged in 1839, but only 860 in 1847. However, even in 1852 there were ships where it was a weekly, if no longer a daily occurrence. "The young and plucky used to consider it a feather in their caps to be able to undergo a flogging without uttering a cry, and advanced themselves considerably in the estimation of their shipmates if they took their 'four bag' like a man." Clearly, it was no longer a deterrent. It was never formally abolished: in 1871 it was "suspended in peacetime" and in 1879 "suspended in wartime."[6] In 1881 it was abolished in the Army.

Another reason why it continued so long was the sailor's addiction to drink. When shore leave became common, he drank himself insensible at every opportunity. He could do this less easily on board after the grog ration had been halved, and then halved again in 1850. Victualling improved in quality and quantity after the new scale of rations was issued in 1825, in which such things as vegetables, tea and cocoa figure more largely than before. Tinned food, of course, proved the solution, but the biscuit continued to be very hard tack because of the Board's reluctance to adopt the new self-raising flour.[7]

As might be expected, the standard of health also improved slowly at this period. The mortality rate in 1812 was thirty-three per thousand; in 1856 it was twenty-one, compared with the national average of 9.2. This modest decrease is solely attributable to the fact that life in a peacetime navy was more leisurely, the decks less crowded and the ship's company composed of men of cleaner habits. When cholera struck, as it did during the Crimean War, an epidemic was just as fatal as before. There was less scurvy, because ships were at sea for shorter times, not because of the Admiralty's mistaken idea that lime juice was a cheaper substitute for lemon juice. Since "spit and polish" was the rule in ships where there was nothing else to do, the passion for washing decks ran riot, but it had serious consequences in an increase in tuberculosis, especially as the ships in commission continued to be seriously overcrowded. The distinguished naval surgeon Spencer Wells complained in 1852 that at night there was between decks "less breathing space than is enjoyed by the inhabitants of the lowest lodging houses in the narrowest alleys of London." Even then, conditions were better than in merchant vessels, whose avaricious owners in the days of laisser-faire prevented adequate inspection and even adulterated the lime juice they were now forced to provide, fifty years after the Navy had adopted it.

Of the many reforms which mark the end of our period, the most obvious was the issue of a naval uniform to all ratings after a circular dated January 30, 1857. Surgeons had been asking for this for a hundred years. It is true that slops had been more uniform of late, but eccentric captains could still indulge their fancies. The captain of the *Caledonia* issued Scotch bonnets. One who had fought in the Greek War of Independence was so struck with the uniform of Greek soldiers that he issued "petticoat trousers" to his crew.[8]

In 1857 the following "uniform dress" was laid down: a blue cloth jacket and trousers (which might be white); a white drill frock with a blue collar on which were three rows of white tape (which had nothing to do with Nelson's victories, as has been supposed, because the original pattern had four); a blue serge frock tucked into the trousers, which became a blouse; a pea jacket; a black silk scarf (much older than Nelson's funeral); a black canvas hat with a crown round which was a ribbon with the ship's name in gold letters; a working cap such as officers wore, without a peak; alternatively, a wide straw hat.

In 1834 the Sixpenny Office for the receipt of contributions towards Greenwich Hospital was abolished. Sir James Graham, as First Lord, proposed to replace it by reviving the old scheme of a Register of Merchant Seamen.[9] While taking care to defend the principle of impressment out of the merchant service, he argued that a ballot based on such a register would answer the navy's purpose as far as manning was concerned, especially if a man failing to obtain a Register certificate remained liable to be pressed. He took pains to prepare the ground for his bill by sending a questionnaire to senior officers at the ports asking what merchant seamen felt about impressment. Needless to say, the reply was "A feeling of horror, it being considered as unlimited slavery." Were volunteers deterred by fear of naval discipline? Yes, because stories about the last war still circulated. Would a ballot from the Register be preferable? Yes, if the term of servitude was limited.

On 17 March 1835, he introduced a bill by which all masters were compelled to keep crew lists, which must be lodged with the Customs before they could sail. The term of naval service was limited to five years, volunteers receiving a £10 bounty and a pension. A ballot of registered men would be taken if more were needed. But in the act as finally passed there was no mention of a ballot or of impressment. This was due to the opposition of admirals like Byam Martin, who declared "If Parliament should ever be so mad in its legislation as to rely on a system of registry, my unfeigned hope is that it will go one step further and order the fleet to be burnt, for it will then be a useless encumbrance." The act did, however, establish the General Register Office of Merchant Seamen and made it compulsory for a number of apprentices proportionate to the tonnage of a vessel to be carried, thereby increasing the pool of seamen. Lieutenant J. H. Brown, the first Registrar General, reported that in the year the act was passed there were 138,265 seamen in the country. In 1838, 175,417 were registered and there were 21,845 apprentices, as compared with 5,421 before the act. A further act in 1844 made registration virtually compulsory by laying down that a man could not be employed without a certificate.[10]

Brown was always convinced that a Register provided the means of manning the navy without recourse to impressment, provided a reserve of 5,000 could be obtained at short notice. He felt that pressing was no longer feasible. It must be replaced by a voluntary service, better paid and if necessary drafted by ballot from the Register. Certainly, the latter provided for the first time an accurate census of the seafaring population, but whether it could be used for manning purposes was another question. At least we can say that the Register Act of 1835 made the final distinction between the Royal Navy and the Merchant Navy, thereby creating a landmark in the history of the British seaman.

Many of Brown's ideas about a naval reserve were to be adopted in time, but not the ballot scheme. All that he could provide were facts about available manpower. In 1852, 148,465 names were on his Register, of which 53,600 were exempt under the old protection system, leaving 94,856 liable for service. Of these, he reckoned that no more than 21,000 would be in the country at any one time.[11]

Evidence about the success of the Register was very conflicting when enquiries were made that year. Most admirals regarded it as useless for recruiting purposes, because the ballot could never be operated justly with such a shifting population as that of seamen. It was called an annoyance to the men and an incentive to emigration, thereby ignoring the appeal which the United States had for the working-class at that time and the lure of the Gold Rush. If the admirals regarded it, as one of them put it, as a "total failure," those connected with the merchant marine thought it of "essential importance in preserving discipline in the mercantile marine," because a man's certificate made it difficult for him to jump ship. It was a real check on desertion and bad behaviour, since it acted as a testimonial for a good man and the reverse for a bad one.

Both points of view were justified according to the way the Register was regarded. As a means of solving the manning problem, it was clearly useless because it did not operate like the French system. The *Inscription Maritime* in 1839 listed 45,000 men, of whom 18,000 were serving in the French navy. By 1844, 55,000 men had done so. Whereas of the English total of 148,000 only a minute percentage had ever seen the inside of a man-of-war. It seemed a grim prospect on the eve of the Crimea War, but it should be remembered that French ships reached the Baltic over a month after the English fleet. As always, the French system appeared more attractive on paper than it proved in practice.

The manning problem had not been acute for a generation, but in the eighteen-forties it loomed large again. The awakening came with simultaneous crises in China and Syria, so that the Mediterranean fleet could not be fully manned. With the abolition of the old Navigation Acts, the pool of seamen available for impressment had disappeared, nor did anyone regard pressing as possible any more. The advent of the age of steam, with recurrent panics that the French could cross the Channel before a fleet was ready, required a force capable of rapid mobilisation. Many agreed with Palmerston that the Channel could be bridged by steam and 30,000 invaders thrown across it in a night. His fears were exaggerated, because the age of steam was only dawning. What was also dawning was a revolution in gunnery which, for the first time, made the skills of the merchant seamen useless on board a man-of-war. A trained, standing, regular navy was the only answer to such developments.

How could such a navy be formed? In 1852 a Committee of four naval officers was appointed to consider the modes of entry into the service, to see how those serving "might be permanently retained by the crown, as in the case of the Royal Marines, instead of being, as at present, discharged from the Navy after very limited service when their ships are paid off."

Their report is therefore in the nature of an inquest on the traditional Hire and Discharge system. This they regarded as "highly detrimental to the interests and efficiency of the navy," which must be brought into line with the army by offering long-term careers, which they called Continuous Service. During the previous decade they noted that 1,150 men had annually quitted the navy after short periods of service, and that in 1848 no less than 6,000 had done so.[12]

To prevent such wastage of trained men, which was the fundamental defect of the old navy, they considered methods by which the navy could be manned without impressment. Firstly, there was the boy entry, which had been consistently cherished. The number was satisfactory, but all agreed on the need for better educational facilities in new training ships. Then there were the Seamen Gunners, the best men in the navy though far too few, only 2,713 having passed through H.M.S. *Excellent* gunnery school since its establishment thirty years ago. They regarded the Register of Merchant Seamen as irrelevant to the needs of a long service voluntary navy. They also examined two sources which might be available in a crisis, the Coastguards and the Fishermen. From the former some 5,000 might be raised; from the latter it was hoped to form a body similar to the old Sea Fencibles, to be called the R.N. Coast Volunteers, but fishermen were notorious for their lack of co-operation in any official plan. Neither of these recommendations was adopted, but both reappeared when the question of a reserve was examined again after the Crimean War.

The Order in Council of 1 April, 1853, and the Continuous Service Act that year, adopted the other recommendations of the Committee, the chief credit for whose work goes to an Admiralty clerk named C. H. Pennell.[13] The preamble of the Order echoes their opinion that the old "desultory mode of proceeding is a cause of great embarrassment and expense in conducting the ordinary duties of the naval service. It creates uncertainty as to the period when ships may be expected to be ready for sea; and the evil becomes one of great magnitude, and a serious danger, when political considerations suddenly demand the rapid equipment of Your Majesty's ships."

It was therefore laid down that all boys of the age of eighteen should enroll themselves for "continuous and general service" for a period of ten years, increased pay being offered to adults who volunteered to do the same, until this became compulsory in 1862. A new rating of Leading Seaman, and a new class of Petty Officer was introduced with increased pay to provide opportunity for advancement. Pay was, indeed, increased all round and a man was even allowed to choose the ship he wished to serve in, though this soon proved impractical. Pensions were provided for all those serving over twenty years. The total cost of these long overdue reforms was estimated at a mere £140,000.

For the first time in her history Britain now possessed a standing navy, consisting of trained men engaged for a long term of service. These measures therefore mark the end of impressment as a means of recruiting, though it was to re-appear under the guise of conscription at a later date.

It might even have been re-introduced in Victorian times, had the Crimean War been of a maritime nature. If France, not Russia, had been the enemy (as so often looked likely in mid-century), the manning problem could never have been solved by such limited measures. Moreover, it took many years for them to bear fruit. Hardly had they been adopted than the Crimean War broke out. The immediate increase it necessitated, though marginal by eighteenth century standards, was serious enough, and as usual Parliament underestimated naval requirements. In 1853, 33,000 men were voted, 45,885 borne; the next year 48,000 were voted, 61,457 borne. The eccentric Sir Charles Napier, who had got himself appointed Commander-in-Chief in the Baltic, found that Graham, now First Lord for the second time in his career, was putting an unjustifiable trust in the efficacy of these new measures. Graham refused to issue the customary proclamation offering bounties to volunteers, because he imagined that men would now flock down to Portsmouth of their own accord. Napier was therefore ordered to sea with a fleet as badly manned and equipped as the Army which was being sent to the Crimea. When he complained, he received a letter in which there occurs this remarkable sentence: "By proper and successful management, you may perhaps contrive to pick up some Norwegian sailors, but they dislike the Swedes and will not pull together in the same ship."[14] Foreigners of course had been employed in large numbers before, but never had a First Lord told a British admiral to make good his manning deficiencies by picking up odd sailors on the way to battle. Before the hostilities broke out the Second Sea Lord, who was responsible for manning, admitted that the Navy had come nearly to "a dead stand as to seamen." After it was over he added, "We had got to the length of our tether, and what we should have done if we had had a maritime war I really do not know."

The answer was of course the formation of a naval reserve. In 1846 an ineffective scheme had been launched to use Seamen Riggers in the dockyards (posts reserved for ex-naval ratings) and the younger member of Coastguard Service, formed in 1831 and by now half manned with men who had served with the fleet. But on account of the bad reputation which the Navy still enjoyed, under half of the 5,000 eligible were found willing to serve. Ten years later the Coastguard Service was transferred from the Board of Customs to that of the Admiralty, which tried to create within it a reserve of Fleet Men, but in 1858 only 6,577 of these were available.[15]

That year, therefore, a Royal Commission was set up to enquire into the best means of manning the navy, with specific instructions to consider methods of creating a reserve force. It was presided over by the Earl of Hardwicke and consisted of three naval officers and four civilians, of whom Edward Cardwell (later to reorganise the Army) and W. S. Lindsay, the historian of the Merchant Navy, were the most important. When their report was printed in 1859 the latter wrote a dissenting statement on the grounds that the Commission had not sufficiently regarded the needs of a steam navy, in which he considered that the list of superannuated officers should be drastically pruned. As a shipowner, he was displeased that the power to press men was still held in reserve, and that it was still possible for a discontented man to hoist his shirt in the rigging of a merchant vessel as a signal for a man-of-war's boat to come and take him off. But the Commission was not interested in the officer list, which was shortly to be divided into the Active and Retired Lists, and its recommendations to form the Royal Naval Reserve have stood the test of time chiefly because the reality of the distinction between the Royal and Merchant navies was accepted.

Attention was first turned to the Coastguards, now regarded as the core of a reserve because half manned with ex-naval ratings, but only 6,577 Fleet Men could be obtained from this source. Then there were the R.N. Coast Volunteers, of which there were 7,000, diminishing to 2,000 in 1871 and altogether disbanded in 1873, to be replaced by the R.N. Volunteer Reserve in 1903. Thirdly, there were the Short Service Pensioners, of whom it was hoped to obtain 5,000: only 175 enlisted. The Seamen Riggers were equally unsatisfactory,

only 300 being available. Finally there were the Royal
Marines, who were unsuitable for ship duties.[16]

The target for a Royal Naval Reserve aimed at by the Commission was 60,000 men. The average strength of the fleet
being 40,000, it was thus hoped to raise it to 100,000 in an
emergency. The following figures show how far short of that
target the actual entry fell:

From R.N.	*Estimated*	*Actual*	
(1) Reserve in Home Ports	4,000	4,000	
(2) Coastguards	12,000	7,000	
(3) Royal Marines	6,000	6,000	
(4) Short Service Pensioners	5,000	175	
(5) Seamen Pensioners	3,000	3,000	
From Merchant Marine			
(6) R.N. Reserve	20,000	12,000	(1862)
(7) R.N. Coast Volunteers	10,000	2,000	(1871)

Actual Reserve   1858—17,000
1866—34,000
1871—26,000

If the Commission's expectations proved to be far too
optimistic, many of its recommendations were nevertheless
of lasting value. More men became Seamen Gunners.
Barracks were built to replace the insanitary old hulks. Free
uniforms, bedding and mess kit, increased rations, better pay
and badge money—all marked the advent of the new standing
navy, providing a career for seamen as secure as that for naval
officers. The possibility of using impressment was once more
reviewed and unanimously rejected.

The formation of the Royal Navy Reserve came about as
the result of the Naval Reserve Acts of 1859 and 1863, implemented by the Order in Council on 1 March, 1864.[17] This was
based on the Commission's report, which approved Lt.
Brown's earlier scheme to induce rather than compel merch-

ant seamen to enlist in a crisis. By the 1859 act, masters were asked to select their best men to form a Royal Naval Volunteer Reserve, the title being changed in 1864 to Royal Naval Reserve. These men were to serve annually for twenty-eight days, for which they were paid £6 a year and given a pension if they continued on the reserve for fifteen years. There was a great deal of suspicion of the scheme at first, only 3,000 men entering. But after the Trent affair in the American Civil War had roused patriotic emotions, membership rose from 12,000 in 1862 to 17,000 in 1865.

As far as the Navy was concerned, the Age of Sail ended in the eighteen-fifties, the *Warrior*, the first ironclad, being launched in 1861. The amount of tonnage under sail in the merchant marine continued to predominate over steam until the eighteen-eighties, but the great Merchant Shipping Act of 1854 also marked a new era in the life of the merchant seaman. The almost contemporary launching of the Continuous Service scheme for naval seamen, and the establishment of a Naval Reserve eleven years later, ended the wasteful and frequently cruel methods of manning the navy which had continued for so many centuries. In the same way, the Naval Discipline Act of 1866 (29 Vict.c. 109) humanised the rules of the service which had continued almost unchanged since the act of 1749. It is true that of the forty-six Articles of War listed many nominally carried the death penalty, but while the disciplinary code remained formidable on paper, the reform of court martial procedure and the limitation of punishments (48 lashes were now the maximum for a flogging, the practice of which was very shortly to be suspended), led to less arbitrary tyranny on board.

It would hardly be an exaggeration to say that a new type of seaman, the Naval Rating who made the service his career and was encouraged to do so by the provision of better pay and conditions, made his appearance after the Crimean War. His status in society became more respectable as the popularity of the Navy became more widespread. The authorities could be more selective in the men they took and they could afford to be more humane in their methods of recruitment. Those who did not like the disciplined way of life essential to a man-of-war could find employment in an expanding merchant marine, in which the chances of promotion to posts of responsibility were better, even if conditions improved more slowly until public opinion, led by men like Samuel Plimsoll, compelled the government to intervene in order to protect the interests and often the lives of the seamen. It is to the epoch of the eighteen-sixties that the British people may therefore date the end of the old navy under sail and the beginning of the Royal Navy and the Merchant Navy as we know them today.

APPENDIX I

Table 1

TONNAGE OF ENGLISH-OWNED SHIPPING
(000 *tons*)

A	B
1686—340	
1702—323	1700—273
1753—468	1750—609
1774—588	1774—795
1786—752	1782—552

Sources—The figures in column A are from R. Davis, *The Rise of the English Shipping Industry* (1962); those in column B are from B.M. Add. MSS. 38,432 (Liverpool Papers).

Table 2

NUMBER OF SHIPS AND MEN IN THE MERCHANT NAVY
1792 and 1800

	Ships		Men	
ENGLAND AND WALES	*1792*	*1800*	*1792*	*1800*
Totals of all Ports	10,633	12,198	87,569	105,037
Selected Ports				
London	1,289	2,666	26,427	37,104
Coastal	—	3,773	—	4,356
Liverpool	584	796	8,076	12,609
Newcastle	551	632	6,123	7,054
Hull	467	611	3,645	4,223
Sunderland	393	506	3,020	3,400
Yarmouth	405	375	2,756	2,442
Plymouth	114	232	501	1,053
Whitby	262	227	2,825	2,014
Portsmouth	120	212	340	604
Dartmouth	284	209	1,929	1,048
Bristol	307	186	3,620	1,674

SCOTLAND	1792	1800	1792	1800
Totals of all Ports	2,143	2,155	13,491	13,883
Aberdeen	187	281	985	1,585
Greenock	343	377	2,744	3,804
Leith	168	134	1,172	899
IRELAND				
Totals of all Ports	1,193	1,003	6,730	5,057
ISLANDS				
Guernsey	97	77	513	781
Jersey	91	53	728	631
Man	177	238	866	1,285
WEST INDIES AND CANADA				
Totals of all Ports	1,745	2,161	8,389	12,047

Grand Total of Ships Registered in H.M. Dominions in 1792
- Ships — 16,079
- Tonnage— 1,540,145 (1800=1,855,879)
- Men — 118,286

Sources—The figures for 1792 are taken from B.M. Add. MSS. 38,432; those for 1800 are from D. Macpherson, *Annals of Commerce*, (1805) Vol. IV, p. 535

Table 3

SHIPS AND MEN IN THE ROYAL NAVY
1701-1855

Date	No. of Ships	No. Voted	No. Borne	No. Mustered
1701	150	30,000	20,916	19,632
1702	272	40,000	38,874	34,650
1703		40,000	43,397	38,871
1704		40,000	41,406	38,873
1705		40,000	45,807	41,734
1706	277	40,000	48,346	44,819
1707		40,000	44,508	40,121
1708	291	40,000	47,138	44,668
1709		40,000	48,344	41,885
1710	313	40,000	48,072	43,950

Date	No. of Ships	No. Voted	No. Borne	No. Mustered
1711-13	—	—	—	
1714	247	10,000	49,860	
1715		10,000	13,475	
1716		10,000	13,827	
1717		10,000	13,806	
1718		10,000	15,268	
1719		13,500	19,611	
1720		13,500	21,118	
1721	229	10,000	15,070	12,576
1722		7,000	10,122	9,582
1723		10,000	8,078	7,723
1724	67	10,000	7,037	6,637
1725		10,000	6,298	6,001
1726		10,000	16,872	15,408
1727	233	20,000	20,697	19,105
1728		15,000	14,917	13,682
1729		15,000	14,859	13,892
1730	238	10,000	9,686	9,187
1731		10,000	11,133	10,504
1732		8,000	8,360	7,887
1733		8,000	9,684	9,056
1734-37	—	—	—	—
1738		20,000	17,668	16,817
1739	228	12,000	23,604	21,516
1740		35,000	37,181	32,006
1741	228	40,000	43,329	39,013
1742		40,000	40,479	35,149
1743		40,000	44,342	38,908
1744	302	40,000	47,202	43,537
1745		40,000	46,766	42,723
1746		40,000	59,750	46,021
1747		40,000	51,191	48,200
1748	334	40,000	44,861	41,377
1749-53	—	—	—	—
1754	296	10,000	10,149	9,797
1755		12,000	33,612	29,268
1756	320	50,000	52,809	50,037

Date	No. of Ships	No. Voted	No. Borne	No. Mustered
1757		55,000	63,259	60,548
1758		60,000	70,518	70,014
1759		60,000	84,464	77,265
1760		70,000	85,658	
1761	412	70,000	80,675	
1762	432	70,000	84,797	81,929
1763		30,000	75,988	
1764		16,000	17,424	17,415
1765		16,000	15,863	
1766		16,000	15,863	
1767		16,000	13,513	
1768		16,000	13,424	
1769		16,000	13,738	
1770		16,000	14,744	
1771		40,000	26,416	25,836
1772		25,000	27,165	
1773		20,000	22,018	
1774		20,000	18,372	
1775	340	18,000	15,230	15,062
1776		28,000	23,914	
1777		45,000	46,231	
1778	450	60,000	62,719	
1779	490	70,000	80,275	74,479
1780		85,000	91,566	82,751
1781		90,000	98,269	
1782	600	100,000	93,168	95,095
1783	617	110,000	107,446	
1784		26,000	39,268	
1785		18,000	22,826	
1786		18,000	13,737	13,478
1787		18,000	14,514	
1788		18,000	15,964	15,946
1789		20,000	18,397	
1790		20,000	20,025	
1791		24,000	38,801	
1792		16,000	16,613	
1793	411	45,000	69,868	69,416

Date	No. of Ships	No. Voted	No. Borne	No. Mustered
1794	457	85,000	87,331	73,835
1795	510	100,000	96,001	
1796	592	110,000	114,365	106,708
1797	633	120,000	118,788	114,603
1798	696	120,000	122,687	114,617
1799	722	120,000	128,930	
1800	757	120,000	126,192	118,247
1801	771	120,000	125,061	117,202
1802	781	130,000	129,340	118,005
1803	663	50,000	49,430	
1804	703	100,000	84,431	
1805	807	120,000	109,205	
1806	920	120,000	111,237	119,627
1807	973	130,000	119,855	
1808	1,032	130,000	140,822	
1809	1,061	130,000	141,989	
1810	1,048	145,000	142,098	
1811	1,019	145,000	130,866	
1812	978	145,000	131,087	138,204
1813	1,009	145,000	130,127	
1814-25	—	—	—	—
1826	179	23,000	28,607	27,085
1835	172	22,000	21,141	23,830
1846	239	40,000	36,181	30,313
1851	199	38,500	32,914	28,741
1855	303	58,500	61,246	49,739

Sources
(1) Number of ships in Navy from C. Derrick, *Memoirs of the Rise and Progress of the Royal Navy*, 1806; W. James, *The Naval History of Great Britain* 6 Vols., 1902 ed; monthly lists of ships in commission, Adm. 8/. The numbers in commission 1754-1806 may be found more conveniently in Adm. 7/567.
(2) Number of men borne,
  1701-10 B.M. Add. MSS. 5439
  1715-47 B.M. Add. MSS. 33,046; 14,032
  1754-1806 P.R.O. Adm. 7/567; Parl. Papers 5 April 1804.

N.M.M. Adm./b/8. Feb. 1758 gives 63,259; discharged 13,047; run 4748. N.M.M. Adm./BP/1 gives 73,570 for 1779; discharged 4,544; marines 11,409; B.M. MSS. 33, 048.

1806-55 from monthly lists of ships in commission, P.R.O. Adm. 8/.

(3) Number of men voted, from Derrick and House of Commons Journals. The total voted included marines; e.g. 1794: 72,885 seamen, 12,115 marines; 1805: 105,000 seamen, 30,000 marines; 1813: 113,600 seamen, 31,400 marines.

(4) Number of shipwrights employed in royal dockyards rose from 1869 in 1702 to 3,193 in 1805 (Derrick).

(5) Numbers mustered 1796-1855 from MS. in Navy Dept. Lib. kindly contributed by Cdr. P. K. Kemp. Discrepancies often depend on the month the count was taken, or whether prisoners or supernumaries were included, the distinction being between Born for Pay and Mustered for Victuals.

APPENDIX II

OFFICERS AND MEN EMPLOYED ON SHORE
ON THE IMPRESS SERVICE AND THE
NUMBERS RAISED, WITH EXPENSES IN 1779
(N.M.M. Adm./BP/1. 10 April 1789—Navy Office)

Headquarters	Officers and Men	Number Raised
Gravesend	12	304
Faversham	20	236
Dover	70	1,337
Hastings	36	134
Chichester	32	117
Fareham	12	133
Southampton	24	327
Poole	12	238
Weymouth	14	99
Exeter	24	326
Okehampton	6	134
Dartmouth	16	136
Plymouth	12	45
Falmouth	34	335
Penzance	12	60
Barnstaple	12	120
Bridgewater	12	101
Bristol	24	664
Swansea	12	125
Haverfordwest	24	138
Carnarvon	12	18
Chester	12	72
Liverpool	16	735
Lancaster	6	24
Whitehaven	7	72
Greenock	24	384
Edinburgh	38	1,039
Berwick	11	72

Headquarters	Officers and Men	Number Raised
Newcastle	48	1,009
Stockton	36	140
Hull	48	554
Lynn	12	139
Yarmouth	24	194
Harwich	12	91
Colchester	12	123
Maidstone	10	23
Gloucester	12	79
Salisbury	9	50
Godalming	4	25
Norwich	12	122
Isle of Wight	20	419
Guernsey	—	16
Jersey	—	17
Dublin	24	1,591
Waterford	24	534
Cork	36	663
Belfast	12	436
Narrowater	12	194
London	106	6,514

Persons employed in procuring men and delivering them to the Regulating Captains raised 1,878 men in London. Constables brought in 889 straggling seamen.

TOTALS—1,019 officers and men employed; 21,367 men raised; expenses £106,591. 5. 1.

Officers and men employed in Tenders, 1779

Lieutenants	44	Expenses—	
Masters	61		
Mates	61	Freight	£39,380
Midshipmen	88	Wages	25,859
Surgeon's Mates	19	Victuals	18,136
Men	874		
Totals	1,147		£83,375

Pay and Allowances on Shore

Captain	£5 a week, plus 1/- mile travel.
Lieutenant	5/- a day in addition to half pay, plus 9d. a mile travel.
Rendezvous	£1. 11. 6. a week
Beat of Drum	10/- a week
Boat Hire	10/6 a week
Invitation Bills	£1. 10. 0. a month
Volunteers employed in Gangs	1/3 a day

APPENDIX III

The first three of the following letters from seamen are printed from those intercepted by the Post Office (Adm. 1/4073); for what reason they were intercepted it is hard to say. The fourth letter is printed in J. R. Thursfield's edition of "Five Naval Journals", Navy Records Society, 1955.

From Richard Hall, H.M.S. *Zealand*, at the Nore, June 19, 1800.
To Mrs. Hall, to be left at the George, Wanstead, Essex.

Dear Wife, I received your letter 14 instant. I sent a letter the second time. I have had no answer from that, which made me send directly. I should be glad to know how you live, where I am it is as a prison. If I had known it was so bad I would not have entered. I would give all I had if it was a hundred Guineas if I could get on Shore. I only lays on the Deck every night. I hope me wife is easy in her mind as well as she can. There is no hopes of my getting to you. (We) are looked upon as a dog and not so good. Dear mother make yourself as easy as you can. There is people in the ship would give all the world if they could get on Shore. We lay at the Noor yet there is so much Arbatory Power that a man must not say is Soul is is Own. It is worse than a prison. They flog them every day only if they get drunk. Only one shilling on Shore is better than a dozen on board of Ship. My Ankles of my Legs swell over my shoes. Dear wife, do the best you can for the children and God prosper you and them till I come back, which there is no fear of and send an answer as soon as possible. I think I could get off for a little money, if it is possible to get off I will. I have no more to say at present. Give my love to me brothers and sisters—your ever loving Husband, Richd. Hall.

From John Taylor, H.M.S. *Elephant*, June 20, 1800.
To Abraham Parsons, On Board H.M.S. *Royal William*, Spithead.

Worthy Friend, Your old shipmate Crawford begs to be excused for not answering your letter himself, but must plead Incapability owing to a very severe fit of Sickness which has almost deprived him of the use of his Limbs, but can venture to assure you he regrets your unfortunate Dilemma and hopes with the blessing of God that you'll surmount every obstacle that may arise between you and your Acquaintance from the unfortunate Affair you stand Indicted for. We have no particular News on Board here, no more than we have had several men Run from us, Amongst the rest Tom Bell and Benson, and James Burgess after being brought on Board and Punished made the third escape the last time we were in Torbay. All your old friends desire to be remembered to you, and if it is any service to offer up the prayers of a Sailor for your Deliverance believe me I think you would have little to fear, for you and your unfortunate Partner in Adversity have the prayers and hearty wishes of many cn Board here. We can't but admire the Prowess of Belton the tinker. I think he richly deserves to get clear after his noble Achievement. I conclude in wishing an Answer from you to know how you succeed. Believe me my worthy friend when I subscribe myself your sincere well wisher, John Taylor.

From Jacob Lindiman, H.M.S. *Princess*, March 16, 1806.
To Mrs. Ellen Vince, Salthouse Lane, Liverpool.

You will oblige me by coming on board as I wish to speak to you personally. Before you come on board speak to Mr. Lemon to know how much money the Consul wants for my Clearance or Discharge and beg you will tell Mr. Lemon to tell me the truth about this affair, as I have told you all I know. I remain your obliged servant, Jacob Lindiman.

P.S. If you get me clear I will behave better for the future.

Covering letter to the Secretary of the General Post Office—

The writer of the enclosed letter appears to be an English seaman, who having been impressed on board H.M.S. *Princess* is endeavouring to get released by passing himself off with the American Consul as a native of that Country. It may be worth the attention of the Government to make enquiry into this matter, particularly as the man writes to know what money the Consul wants for his clearance.

From J. Brown, H.M.S. *Victory*, Chatham, December 28, 1805.
To Mr. Thos. Windever, at the Sign of the Blue Bell, New Albs St.,
Liverpool.

Dear Sir, I received your very welcome letter and happy I am to hear
that your Family are in good Health and happiness. We sailed from
Spithead on the 10th with Lord Nelson on board as usual but when
we got abreast of Dover the wind came to the NE and blowing a
very heavy gale of wind was obliged to come to anchor in Dover
roads where we lay 5 days. When it came a little Moderate we beat
our poor crippled Ship up to the Downs whilst every Ship we past
cheered the Noble *Victory*. Now we have got all her guns out and
almost ready for docking. Whilst we expect to be drafted on board
the new *Ocean* as Lord Collingwood is going to have her, him that
was second in command in the Action. There has been great dis-
putes between admirals and captains wanting this Ships company
but government will let nobody but Lord Collingwood have them
as he was Commander in chief when Lord Nelson fell. There is three
hundred of us Pickt out to go to Lord Nelson Funral. We are to
wear blue Jackets white Trowsers and a black scarf round our arms
and hats, besides gold medal for the battle of Trafalgar Valued
£7–1 round our necks. That I shall take care of until I take it home
and Shew it to you. We scarce have room to move, the Ship is so
full of Nobility coming down from London to see the Ship looking
at shot holes.

Now Mr. Windever I am going to give you an account of the
action. On Monday the 21st at day light the French and Spanish
Fleets was like a great wood on our lee bow which cheered the hearts
of every British tar in the *Victory* like lions Anxious to be at it.
The signal was made Prepare for battle and that England expected
every man would do his duty. So we cleared away our guns whilst
Lord Nelson went round the decks and said my Noble lads this will
be a glorious day for England who ever lives to see it, I shant be
Satisfied with 12 Ships this day as I took at the Nile. So we piped
to dinner and ate a bit of raw pork and half a pint of Wine. When
coming close to the enemy, beat to quarters, got our guns double
shotted to give them a doce and all ready for action standing at our
quarters. When the four decker fired a broadside into us before we
could get a gun to bear on them they lay in a half moon and we
going in two divisions towards them, for we formed no line . . .

I hope youl have a full bottle in the bar for me and William Windever to have a toothful for you may depend that I will break the bell ropes I will pull so hearty for its a long time since I had a good toothful. So Farewell I will write to you as soon as I am drafted. Yrs. sincerely, J. Brown.

REFERENCES

NOTE: In the following References to note numbers marked in the text, all books are published in London unless otherwise stated. The following abbreviations have been used:

Adm.=Admiralty records in the Public Record Office.
B.M.=British Museum
C.S.P.=Calendar of State Papers
N.M.M.=National Maritime Museum
N.R.S.=Publications of the Navy Records Society
M.M.=*The Mariner's Mirror*, the journal of the Society for Nautical Research.

Chapter 1

THE MEDIEVAL MARINER

1. Sir Harris Nicolas, *History of the Royal Navy* (1847) I. 261; K. M. E. Murray *Constitutional History of the Cinque Ports* (Manchester 1935) 144; T. Rymer *Foedera* (1707) VII. 784

2. Nicolas I. 142; F. W. Brooks, *The English Naval Forces 1199-1272* (n.d.) 140, 155

3. *Black Book of the Admiralty* ed. Sir T. Twiss (1871) 350

4. Sir R. Hawkins, *Observations*, ed. J. A. Williamson (1933) 127

5. Nicolas I. 363; on the history of the naval profession see M. A. Lewis, *England's Sea Officers* (1939)

6. Nicolas II. 409; Rymer IX. 238

7. Nicolas II. 507; Rymer V. 815, VII. 195

8. Brooks 47

9. J. J. Keevil, *Medicine and the Navy* (1957) I. 8-11

10. Nicolas I. 295; II. 177; *Black Book* I. 13

11. Nicolas II. 191, 486

12. M. Oppenheim, *History of the Administration of the Royal Navy* (1896) 25, 34

13. 2. R. II. c. 4; *Black Book* 67

14. Nicolas I. 404, 466; II. 176

Chapter 2

THE TUDOR MARINER

1. Corbett MSS. in Navy Department Library 138; Oppenheim 74.

2. Oppenheim 74, 77

3. C. Derrick, *Memoirs of the Rise and Progress of the Royal Navy* (1806) 19-37

4. *Defeat of the Spanish Armada* ed. J. K. Laughton, 2 vols. N.R.S. (1895) I.xli, 252; M. A. Lewis, *The Spanish Armada* (1962) 81

5. Sir R. Hawkins, *Observations*, ed. J. A. Williamson (1933) 20

6. R. Davis, *Rise of the English Shipping Industry* (1962) 7, 10

7. Monson's *Naval Tracts* ed. Oppenheim, 4 vols. N.R.S. (1893) III. 188. Oppenheim's figures, op. cit. 176, differ slightly; he adds the figures for Northumberland

8. J. Webb in M.M. 1960

9. N. Boteler, *Dialogues*, ed. Perrin, N.R.S. (1929) 39

10. R. Hooker quot. K. R. Andrews, *Elizabethan Privateering* (1964) 4

11. Monson I. 292; II. 237; IV. 21

12. W. Raleigh, *History of the World* IV, ii, 4

13. C.S.P. Ven. 1592-1603, 505; C.S.P. Dom. 1547-80, 390, 677; 1591-94, 551; 1595-97, June 25, 1595, May 3, 1596

14. Calendar of State Papers Domestic July 8, 10, 1597

15. C.S.P.D. Aug. 8, 1598; Aug. 15, 1599; Jan. 16, 1600

16. Rymer XVI. 22

17. Quot. Lewis 89; cp. Laughton I. 62

18. Laughton passim; Keevil I. 72

19. Keevil I. 123

20. ibid. 61

21. ibid. 78, 80, 93

22. ibid. 101, 112; Hawkins 40

23. Monson II. 244

24 C.S.P.D. Oct. 5, 1595; 1591-6, p. 525

25. 43 Eliz. c.3

26. C.S.P.D. July 11, 1597; Oppenheim 82, 140

27. Oppenheim 134; Hist. MSS. Com. Coke XII. i. 13; B.M. Harl. MSS. 442, 173

28. Oppenheim 384

29. C.S.P. Ven. 1581-91, 648

Chapter 3

THE EARLY STUART MARINER

1. Davis, 10, 15

2. Derrick, 27, 37, 61, 94, 106

3. Oppenheim 244

4. *The Trade's Increase* quot. Davis 114

5. Quot. Davis 152

6. *Naval Songs and Ballads*, ed. Firth N.R.S. (1898) 45

7. N. Boteler, *Dialogues*, ed. Perrin N.R.S. (1929) 35, 57, 65

8. Quot. Oppenheim 235

9. H.M.C. Coke XII. i. 105

10. C.S.P.D. 27 Feb. 1623

11. ibid. 25 March, 9 April 1623

12. Quot. Oppenheim 188, 219, 237, 258

13. J. Hollond, *Discourses*, ed. Tanner, N.R.S. (1896) 372

14. Oppenheim 197

15. ibid. 236, 237

16. I. G. Powell in M.M., 1921; G. E. Manwaring in M.M., 1923; H. M. C. Coke XII, i. 357

17. C.S.P.D. 6 Dec. 1636

18. Oppenheim 223

19. H. M. C. Coke XII. i. 266

20. Oppenheim 231; Keevil I. 183

21. Keevil I. 187, 190, 209

22. ibid. 204, 220

23. Oppenheim 231

24. Monson III. 185; C.S.P.D. 9 Sept, 1626; 1652-53, p. 43; Acts of Privy Council 254, 397

25. Hollond xli

26. ibid. 131; C.S.P.D. 1655-56, p. 163; 1667-68, p. 426

27. C.S.P.D. 29 March, 1628; Oppenheim 233

28. H. M. C. Coke XII.i.274, 356; Oppenheim 228

29. Oppenheim 214

30. *Seaman's Grammar* 35

31. M.M. I. 313

Chapter 4
THE DUTCH WARS

1. Oppenheim 349

2. *Inquiry into the Cause of our Naval Miscarriages*, Anon. 1706

3. Oppenheim 306

4. *Catalogue of Pepysian MSS.*, ed. J. R. Tanner N.R.S. (1904) I. 110; *Pepys's Naval Minutes*, ed. Tanner N.R.S. (1926) 90, 273

5. *Catalogue* I. 306; A. Bryant, *Samuel Pepys: Saviour of the Navy* (1938)

6. B. M. Egerton MSS. 2522; *Catalogue* I. 240; cp. J. Ehrman, *The Navy in the War of William III* (1953) 109

7. Oppenheim 314, 319

8. C.S.P.D. April 5, 14, 15; May 22, 1651-52; May 14, 25, 1656-57.

9. *Catalogue* I. 129

10. Corbett MSS. I. 53

11. *Catalogue* I. 130; III. Nos. 3915, 3920

12. ibid. I. 131; II. 1156; III. 2320; IV. 6

13. C.S.P.D. 31 Dec. 1653

14. Quot. Oppenheim 318

15. C.S.P.D. 12 Dec. 1651

16. *Catalogue* I. 201

17. B.M. Harl. MSS. 6287

18. J. R. Powell, *Expedition of Blake and Mountagu in 1655* M.M. 1966

19. Oppenheim 309, 328

20. *Catalogue* I. 118, 119

21. C.S.P.D., 1667. p. XXXIII

22. *Minutes* 24, 274

23. Coventry Papers, May 15, 24, 1666

24. C.S.P.D. 31 Jan. 1660; Oppenheim 328

25. B.M. Add. MSS. 11,602

26. *Catalogue* I. 155; *Barlow's Journal*, ed. Lubbock (1934) I. 127

27. C.S.P.D. 1653-53, 413, 422; see G. E. Manwaring *Flower of England's Garland* (n.d.)

28. C.S.P.D. 30 Sept. 1665; Keevil op. cit. II. 85, 105

29. Barlow I. 213; Keevil II. 13

30. Quot. Keevil II. 83, 89

31. P.R.O. Adm. 2/1725; for a picture see M.M. IV. 54

32. B.M. Harl. MSS. 6287

Chapter 5
SOME STUART SEAMEN

1. *Diary of Henry Teonge* (1825); *Journal of James Yonge*, ed. F. N. I. Poynter (1963)

2. See *William Dampier* by C. Lloyd (1966); *A Cruising voyage round the World* by Woodes Rogers, ed. G. E. Manwaring (1929)

3. *Adventures by Sea* by Edward Coxere, ed. E. H. W. Meyerstein (1945)

4. Coxere 23, 76, 101, 118

5. *Barlow's Journal*, 2 Vols., ed. Basil Lubbock (1934) 60, 128

6. Barlow I. 51, 115, 146; II. 426

7. *Ramblin' Jack: the Journal of Captain John Cremer* ed. R. R. Bellamy (1936) 39, 45

Chapter 6
THE MANNING PROBLEM

1. G. Chalmers: *Estimate of the Comparative Strength of Great Britain*

... with *Gregory King's Celebrated State of England*, 1804 ed. Ehrman op. cit. p. 111 gives 50,000 seamen, but King thought that such was the number of families, not of men.

2. *Sergison Papers* 164; *Queen Anne's Navy* ed. Merriman N.R.S. (1950, 1961) 185; Ehrman 111; a copy of *An Expedient* is in the N.M.M.

3. Parl. Papers Census returns; the returns for the Channel Islands etc. are here omitted. It is difficult to see how Chalmers op. cit. p. 360. reckons "the fighting men" at 2,188,529 or a fifth of the population.

4. Ralph Davis, *Rise of the English Shipping Industry* (1962) 27, 395; B.M. Add. MSS. 38, 432

5. R. Davis, *Seamen's Sixpences; An Index of Commercial Activity* in *Economica*, 1956

6. Davis, *Shipping Industry*, 115, 327

7. B.M. Add. MSS. 5439; for other references see Table sources.

8. C.S.P.D. 16 Jan. 1703

9. M.M. 1926

10. P.R.O. Adm. 36/5747

11. Adm. 36/15900; *Keith Papers* ed. Lloyd, N.R.S. (1955) Vol. III. p. 321

Chapter 7
THE METHODS OF IMPRESSMENT

1. Ehrman op. cit. 449

2. Quot. A. Watteville, *The British Soldier* (1965) 80

3. D. Baugh, *British Naval Administration in the Age of Walpole*, Princeton (1965) 206

4. Adm. 1/3663

5. Adm. 1/1502

6. ibid.

7. Baugh 152

8. J. R. Hutchinson, *The Press Gang Afloat and Ashore* (1913) 65

9. ibid. 58; J. A. Gardner's *Recollections*, N.R.S. (1906) and *Above and Under Hatches*, ed. Lloyd (1955).

10. Proclamations in N.M.M.

11. Corbett MSS. X; 6 Ann c.65

12. *Annual Register* 1770, 162

13. Baugh 168

14. *Queen Anne's Navy* ed. R. D. Merriman, N.R.S. (1961) 201

15. B.M. Add. MSS. 19, 032

16. N.M.M. 13/196

17. N.M.M. A/2643

18. Adm. 1/3663

19. C.S.P.D. 1760 . . . Nos. 62; 1324

20. H.M.C. Various VIII. 75

21. C.S.P.D. 1760 . . . Nos. 272; 604

22. Quot. Baugh 162

23. Hutchinson 181

24. ibid. 253; Smollett, *Roderick Random* chap. 24

25. Baugh 156

26. ibid. 178; cp. Hutchinson 224

27. Quot. Davis op. cit. 322

28. Adm. 1/920

29. By courtesy of Cdr. P. K. Kemp; cp. *Keith Papers*, ed. Lloyd, N.R.S. (1955) Vol. II, 161

30. Adm. 1/1495

31. Baugh 224

32. *Vernon Papers*, ed. B. M. Ranft, N.R.S. (1958) 488, 547; *Seasonable Advice* 85

Chapter 8

THE LAW AND THE PRESS

1. Quot. C. Butler, *On the Legality of Impressing Seamen*, 1778

2. Parl. Hist. XI. 428

3. Adm. 7/299-301. Unless otherwise stated, all cases are taken from these, under date.

4. A. Hildesley, *The Press Gang* (1925)

5. Two copies exist, one in Corbett's Precedents in the Navy Department library, the other at the British Museum, Add. MSS. 32, 628

6. State Trials, Vol. 18

7. H. Cowper, *Cases of King's Bench*, 1800, II. 512

8. Adm. 1/161

9. Adm. 7/363-400

10. Goldswain's Case, 1778, in Blackstone's *Cases*, II, 1206

11. Baugh 187; 13 Geo. 11.c.3

12. Adm. 1/4278

13. H.M.C. Dartmouth, I. 200; Corbett X. 46; Adm. 1/2733, 7 March 1756; Hutchinson 162

14. Corbett X, 46; Baugh 172

15. Corbett XIII, 232; 14 Geo. III.c.21

16. Adm. 1/1448; 1/1494

17. Adm. 1/1507; Blackstone's *Cases* I, 251; East V, 477

18. Hutchinson 169-171

19. Corbett X, 90

20. R. Pares, *Manning in the West Indies*, 1702-63, Trans. Roy. Hist. Soc. 1937; Baugh 220; 19 Geo. II.c.30

21. *Vernon Papers* 260, 419

22. M.M. 1923, 1931

23. Adm. 1/1439

24. Cowper II, 830; East I, 313; cp. *Enquiry into the Practice and Legality of Pressing* (Anon.) 1772

25. *Ann. Reg.* 1770, 157

26. *Memoirs of Sir J. Brenton*, by his son (1858) 8

27. Hamilton MS. in possession of Cdr. P. K. Kemp; Acts of 6 Anne c. 11; 9 Geo. II. c. 6 (Ireland).

Chapter 9

THE REGISTER OF SEAMEN AND OTHER PROPOSALS

1. G. Everett, *An Encouragement for Seamen and Mariners* (1695) in Harl. Misc. IV. For a list of such publications see Ehrman, op. cit. 597

2. Eugene L. Asher, *Resistance to Maritime Classes*, University of California (1960); J. Tramond, *Manuel de l'Histoire Maritime de la France*,

Paris (1927) p. 195; N. Hampson, *La Marine de l'An II*, Paris (1959) p. 209

3. Quot. *Greenwich: Palace, Hospital, College*, by C. Lloyd (1961); cp. Ehrman 441

4. Ehrman 599

5. Journal of Commissioners Adm. 105/41; Letters of Register Office, 1696-1715, Adm. 1/3997; B.M.Add. MSS. 5439; Ehrman 601

6. J. Dennis, *Essay on the Navy* (1702) p. 38; cp. A. Justice, *Dominion of the Sea* (1705) p. 636

7. Parl. Hist. XI. 414; Baugh, op. cit. 235

8. Baugh 238; cp. J. Green, *Plan to form . . . the Fellowship of Seamen* (1780)

9. *Letters of Lord Barham* ed. Laughton, N.R.S. (1897) III. 59, 82

10. *A Letter from a Member of the Marine Society* (J. Hanway), 4th ed. 1757

11. Reprinted in *The Tomlinson Papers*, ed. Bullocke, N.R.S. (1935)

12. *Letters and Despatches*, V. 44; the original is in Adm. 1/580

Chapter 10

THE AGE OF NELSON

1. *Edinburgh Review* 1825, p. 161

2. Quot. C. N. Robinson, *The British Fleet* (1894) 438

3. Adm. 1/581; M. A. Lewis, *A Social History of the Navy, 1793-1815* (1960) 139

4. *Keith Papers*, III, 163; cp. Lewis op. cit.

5. N.M.M. MS. 57/031

6. *Correspondence of Lord Collingwood*, ed. Hughes, N.R.S. (1951) 37

7. E. P. Brenton, *Naval History of Great Britain* (1837); *Keith Papers* III, 182

8. Adm. 7/361

9. Wilson in *Five Naval Journals*, ed. Thursfield, N.R.S. (1951) 129; *Nautical Economy* (1836) 2

10. Collingwood 85

11. Adm. 1/1517; C. Gill, *The Naval Mutinies of 1797* (1913) 306; *Keith Papers*, III, 17; G. E. Manwaring and B. Dobree, *The Floating Republic* (1935) 269

12. *Keith Papers* III, 157

13. Adm. 1/1508

14. R. Steele, *The Marine Officer* (1840) I. 134

15. Adm. 1/581

16. *Blockade of Brest* ed. Leyland, N.R.S. (1899) I.1, 8, 10, 70, 122; Lewis op. cit. 111

17. A. Crawford, *Reminiscences of a Naval Officer* (1851) I. 108

18. Quot. Lewis 110

19. J. Barrow, *Life of Anson* (1839) 467

20. *Keith Papers* III, 133-4, 155, 168; for the Army cp. R. Glover, *Peninsular Preparation* (1963)

21. Adm. 1/581; Parl. Papers Vol. 39, 1857/8

22. C. R. Pemberton, *Pel Verjuice*, ed. Eric Partridge (1929) 93-97

23. *Landsman Hay* ed. M. D. Hay (1953) 42, 67, 77

24. J. Marshall, *Naval Biography*, XII, 444

25. *Nautical Economy* 38; W. Richardson, *A Mariner of England* (1908) 67

26. *Keith Papers* III, 173

27. S. Leech, *Voice from the Middle Deck* (1844) 28

28. *Keith Papers* III, 166

29. Kindly contributed by R. Baynham

30. Quot. J. F. Zimmerman, *Impressment of American Seamen* (New York 1925) 24. Many of the following details are taken from this thesis which should be supplemented by the article by A. Steel in *Cambridge Historical Journal*, 1949. Most of the correspondence will be found in P.R.O., F.O. 5/104

31. *The Right and Practice of Impressment as concerning Great Britain and America considered*, anon, 1814. The Cromwell case is also mentioned in F.O. 5/104

32. Leech 120; James 161 and appendix

33. Ed. G. Grant (1937)

34. *Nautical Economy* 21, 105. Cp. Pitcairn Jones in M.M. 1953

35. *The Autobiography of Pel Verjuice*, ed. Eric Partridge, (1929.) Cp. Pitcairn Jones in M.M. 1953

36. In *Five Naval Journals* op. cit.

37. See *The Black Ship*, by Dudley Pope, 1963

Chapter 11

LIFE AT SEA

1. Boswell's *Johnson* ed. Hill and Powell I. 348, II, 438, V, 514

2. Quot. C. Lloyd, *Captain Marryat* (1939) 186; for Penrose see note 18

3. *Observations and Instructions, by a Captain* (1804); cp. M. A. Lewis *Social History of the Navy, 1793-1815* (1960) 272; F. Marryat, *Suggestions for Abolition of Impressment* (1822) 31; R. Wilson in *Five Naval Journals*, N.R.S. 245ff.

4. *Letters of Lord Barham*, N.R.S., I. 39, 304-12

5. Quot. C. Lloyd and J. L. S. Coulter, *Medicine and the Navy*, (1961) III. 77ff.

6. *Queen Anne's Navy* N.R.S. 191

7. Hay 45; Wilson 254; Leech 14; Béchervaise 110

8. C. Thompson, *Sailor's Letters* (1757) I. 147; E. Mangin in *Five Naval Journals*, N.R.S.

9. Wilson 255

10. *Observations* op. cit.; Howe's orders in *Keith Papers*, I. 29 ff.

11. Adm. 1/5259

12. Leech 50; *Nautical Economy* 110, 115

13. *Keith Papers* III. 183

14. J. Charnock, *Biographia Navalis*, IV. 181

15. Adm. 1/5125; Burney quot. C. Lloyd, *St. Vincent and Camperdown* (1965) 101

16. Adm. 1/5391; 1/5392; 1/181; Raigersfeld, *Life of a Sea Officer* (1929) 17; James, V. 183

17. Adm. 1/1478

18. C. V. Penrose, *Observations on Corporal Punishment* (Bodmin, 1824) 47; A. J. Griffiths, *Impressment Fully Considered* (1826) 158

19. *Queen Anne's Navy* 213, 219, 235

20. *Narrative of my Professional Adventures* by Sir W. Dillon ed. Lewis, N.R.S. (1953) I. 96; cp. Lewis, *Social History* 280 ff.

21. Adm. 1/5125; reprinted in G. E. Manwaring and B. Dobrée, *The Floating Republic* (1935) 266; cp. Lloyd, *St. Vincent* op. cit.

22. B.M. Add. MSS. 22,617 and 5439; *Sergison Papers* 181; *Queen Anne's Navy* 44, 172; Baugh 199; Vernon Papers 447; acts of 1 Geo. II c.9; 2 Geo. II. c.33 and 36; 31 Geo. II. c.10

23. 37 Geo. III c.53

24. Dundonald, *Autobiography of a Seaman* (1859) II. 182; Penrose 42

25. *Nautical Economy* 63

26. Adm. 1/982

27. Warren Dawson, *Nelson Collection at Lloyd's* (1932); I. Schomberg, *Naval Chronology*, III. 620

28. *Gentleman's Magazine*, 1740, p. 183

29. Lewis 48; gunner's examination in B.M. Add. MSS. 19,033

30. Lloyd and Coulter op. cit. III. 81ff.; *Queen Anne's Navy* 248 ff.; Baugh 373 ff.

31. On cocoa, see Lloyd and Coulter III. 90; on tea see also G. Hamilton, *Voyage of H.M.S. Pandora* (1793)

32. For sources in this section, see Lloyd and Coulter op, cit.; also the medical treatises reprinted in *The Health of Seamen*, ed. Lloyd, N.R.S. (1965)

33. Lewis, quot. Lloyd and Coulter III. 183; cp. IV. 271; Barrow's *Life of Anson* 480; *Edinburgh Review*, 1825

34. *Vernon Papers* 324; Baugh 200, 208

35. N.M.M. Ad/B/8 Feb. 1758; Baugh 212

36. Laird Clowes, *History of the Royal Navy* III. 339

37. Quot. Lewis 134; *Edinburgh Review*, 1825

38. *Nautical Economy* 120; Pitcairn Jones in M.M. 1953

39. *Vernon Papers* 518

Chapter 12

THE END OF IMPRESSMENT

1. Adm. 1/3664

2. M. A. Lewis, *The Navy in Transition*, (1965) 66; Hansard, 4 March, 1836

3. Basil Lubbock in *Early Victorian England*, I. 389

4. Hansard 1827, p. 450

5. *Life on Board a Man-of-War*, by a British Seaman, Glasgow, 1829

6. Adm. 1/5554; Parl. Papers (1847) xxxvi, 121; Lewis 169; Laird Clowes, *History of the Royal Navy*, VI. 217

7. On Victualling and Health, see Lloyd and Coulter, op. cit. IV. 93, 103, 266

8. Laird Clowes VI. 213

9. Hansard, 4 March 1834; a memo sent to him in 1832 may have suggested it, see Adm. 7/713; or Napier's letter to Melville in 1816, reprinted in C. Napier, *The Navy Past and Present* (1851)

10. Hansard, 27 June 1834; 17 March 1835; 4 March 1836; 10 March 1837. Acts of 5 and 6 Will. IV. c.19 and c.24 (1835); 7 and 8 Vict. c.112 (1844); J. Gourly, *The Great Evils of Impressment* (1838); Barrow's *Life of Anson* 459; letters from Register Office, 1835-39, Adm. 1/3998

11. An anonymous pamphlet by Brown, *Some Observations of Manning the Fleet and the Operation of the Register Office*, appeared in 1847; cp. his remarks in Adm. 7/714; Parl. Papers (1853) LX, pp. 143, 157, 181 (Manning Committee)

12. Report of the Manning Committee op. cit.; R. Taylor, *Manning the Royal Navy; The Reform of the Recruiting System*, M.M. 1958, 1959

13. 16 and 17 Vict. c.69

14. H. Noel Williams, *Life of Napier* (1917) 265; C. J. Bartlett, *Great Britain and Sea Power, 1815-53* (1963) 310, 340

15. Bartlett 306; Lewis passim.

16. Report of the Manning Commission, Parl. Papers (1859); Taylor op. cit.

17. 22 and 23 Vict. c.40; 26 and 27 Vict. c.69; Manning Commission Report 353.

GENERAL INDEX

INDEX OF SHIPS

318

HOUSTON PUBLIC LIBRARY
CENTRAL LIBRARY

This book may be kept for FOURTEEN DAYS.
With due notice, it may be renewed once
for the same period. A charge is made for
overdue books.

5-2-70-30M-1